AUTHOR'S PREFACE - Murphy's

Just before you begin to read this b
The law was named for Edward A. Mur
development engineer working for a brier time on rocket
sled experiments done by the United States Air Force in
1949. I hope you enjoy his sentiments – I do!

MURPHY'S LAW - If anything can go wrong, it will.

1. MURPHY'S FIRST COROLLARY - Nothing is as easy
as it looks.

2. MURPHY'S SECOND COROLLARY - Everything takes
longer than you think.

3. MURPHY'S THIRD COROLLARY - If there is a
possibility of several things going wrong, the one that will
cause the most damage will be the one to go wrong.

4. MURPHY'S FOURTH COROLLARY – Whenever you
set out to do something, something else must be done
first.

5. MURPHY'S FIFTH COROLLARY - Every solution
breeds new problems.

6. MURPHY'S SIXTH COROLLARY - It is impossible to
make anything foolproof because fools are so ingenious.

7. MURPHY'S SEVENTH COROLLARY - Nature always
sides with the hidden flaw.

8. MURPHY'S EIGHTH COROLLARY - Left to
themselves, things tend to go from bad to worse.

9. MURPHY'S CONSTANT - Matter will be damaged in
direct proportion to its value.

10. O'TOOLE'S COMMENTARY - Murphy was an
optimist.

About the Author

- Over 34 years of international experience in various industries
- Helped major organisations to increase revenues or save over £150M (250M US dollars)
- Published more than 35 papers, won two awards, lecture world wide
- Business methodologies accredited by the Institute of Management Specialists (IMS)
- Certificate of Professional Status and Fellow of the IMS
- Member - IT Compliance Institute
- Member – Professional Risk Management International Association
- Member – American Society of Mechanical Engineers
- Licentiate Engineer and Fellow – Institute of Maintenance Engineering
- Certificates in Advanced Mechanical Engineering and in Commercial Engineering & Management (British Institute of Engineering Technology, and University of Bath)
- Post-graduate diploma in technology (Oxford Brooks University)
- Certificate in Advanced General Business Studies (ICS)
- Regression Therapist & Cognitive-Synergy™ Practitioner (British School of Yoga)
- Life Member – Associated Stress Consultants

Author's Feedback

"Abe
Thanks for your contribution to our project these last months. As a Compliance consultant, covering analytical areas and measures such as Sarbanes-Oxley, IFRS, Basel II, and others, in connection with IBM's Insurance Information Warehouse (IIW), Banking Data Warehouse (BDW) and related products, you have fulfilled your role in a highly professional manner and added value, contents and quality to our products. I would not hesitate to recommend you to other companies."
Regards, Marc Delbaere, Actuary
Insurance Application Architecture, IAA / IIW
Development Manager, IBM

"Abe Abrahami was engaged by Barclaycard UK with a brief to construct an end-to-end process model for project management within Change Delivery.
Abe's role as project manager required him to rationalise multiple complex processes, whilst retaining the support of a diverse group of stakeholders.
Despite very tight deadlines, Abe produced the required Roadmap and associated training, which was very well received by our teams, and continues to serve as a platform for our continuous improvement approach."
Dick Parkhouse
Change Delivery Director, Barclaycard UK

"Abe has helped us to successfully deliver a significant phase of a complex programme to migrate 5 separate business units into mainstream systems. Abe has adapted and employed his unique Programme Management Structure (PrMS) methodology and delivered the prescribed methodology with a great deal of enthusiasm and professionalism."
Martyn P Horton, CTP Programme Manager, LTF

"Dear Abe,
You have provided us with professional and personal consulting and technical support services in a number of diverse and complex areas associated with IT services and applications.
I very much hope to work with you again in the not too distant future, and have no hesitation in recommending your services to other companies, who I am sure will benefit from your considerable experience and diversified skills as we have done."
Eur Ing Glenn M Smith, C Eng, Project Director, Seabank Power

"Dear Sir,
I refer to Professor Abrahami's excellent article 'The evolving Computer Environment', in the June issue of Management Services Magazine.
His two paragraphs under 'Computer Usability' precisely outline one part of the problem - user friendliness.
The distinction between hardware and software used to be that software did not hurt you when you dropped it on your foot, but now any standard manual is likely to cause severe damage.
The suppliers usually provide the information, but where in that stack of manuals is the part the user needs? In my experience - and my work involves trying to bridge the gap between 'I know that I want' and 'How do I get it' - many users simply give up and use their software at a very basic level, if at all. A recent case was where a client had excellent accounting information and retyped all the names and addresses into a word processor for a mail shot! he had never heard about of transferring data electronically, or using macros, possibly because the manuals were too daunting to comprehend."
Yours faithfully,
A S Goodenough MMS ACIB
Chorleywood, Hertfordshire

"Dear Abe,
I read with great interest your excellent "Insuring for the Future" article in Computer Consultant. It clearly identifies that a holistic approach is needed to ensure the accurate specification, development, delivery and maintenance of any IT project. I thought that your final paragraph was particularly pertinent, where you observe that engineering and manufacturing have been successfully operating a total quality/value approach for many years, and that it is about time that IT adopted a similar approach. Your paper clearly identified the parameters, which need to be addressed to strive towards a similar degree of conformance to quality and specification in the IT industry."
David Hoare, Director, DJH Associates

"Hello Prof. Abrahami,
Greetings!
I have read your article title "SOA Compliance" which was published by IMS journal recently. Indeed it is a good article written by you. Also you have an impressive profile and achievement records. Congratulations to you."
Best regards, Roger Haw
NOTE:
Prof. Dr. Roger Haw is the Founder cum Chairman of the First kind of World Book of Records with a Focus on Corporate Social Responsibility aspects 'SRW RecordPedia' and Founded the Ansted Social Responsibility International Award (ASRIA) to recognize those Corporations, NGOs and individuals around the world. The publication, which has been distributed to over 80 countries, includes commendable messages from four Nobel Prize Laureates.

Endorsement

This is a most useful book, admirably suitable and recommended for managing directors, chief executives, financial, Compliance-audit, operation and IT officers and business managers.
The book is also highly recommended for business management, finance, accounting and IT students, both undergraduate and postgraduate, particularly MBA candidates.
It describes change management and business transformation, together with banking, financial, IT and business operations and Compliance mandates. For example, Sarbanes-Oxley Act, Basel II, Solvency II, and numerous other regulatory measures have been covered.

Sample checklist questionnaires are provided together with relevant information to help readers with their change programmes and Compliance projects.
The book contains notable contributions from leading consultants and vendors, including IBM, and others.

Relevant frameworks and methodologies, IT applications, risk and security measures are also described.
What makes this book unique, among other things, is not only the description and impact of relevant Compliance mandates and what they mean to businesses globally, but how and why a culture change and business turnaround play such a vital role.

The Author combined his 34-year experience and multi-faceted career in engineering, management, computing, counselling and coaching into a magnum opus. He combined 'hard issues' of business, together with 'soft issues' concerning the psychology of change.
His innovative psychology of change, Cognitive-Synergy™ (C-S), is simple, cutting-edge and effective.

C-S is a groundbreaking concept and practice used to successfully model and implement a culture change and related Compliance within the firm. This is an instrument to facilitate a successful turnaround of any enterprise from a struggling entity into a mature organisation in business-balanced scorecard terms.

The Author also 'borrowed' from the laws of physics, engineering-science and cybernetics to form a modulated approach to design and implement Compliance mandates together with business transformation successfully.

He explained the '80-20 rule' and Murphy's Law, and how to use them advantageously and wisely to steer around problems and resolve issues to improve profitability, Compliance and best-practice.
Professor Dr Abe Abrahami's unique methodologies, techniques and training courses are recognised and accredited by The Institute of Management Specialists in the UK.

Professor H J Manners
President & Founder
Group of International Professional Bodies

The Group of International Professional Bodies is a United Kingdom examining and professional association, the diplomas and membership diplomas of each body are qualifications in their own right and are recognised as professional British qualifications. Each individual body within the Group is listed in "British Qualifications" – the British Council's reference book, published by Kogan Page Ltd.

The Group comprises

- The Institute of Management Specialists (IMS) Founded in 1971

- Professional Management Specialists and Specialists involved in Modern Management, Computers, Technology and Systems
- The Institute of Manufacturing (IManf) Founded in 1978
- Professional Manufacturing, Modern Technology and Systems.
- Professional Business & Technical Management (PBTM) Founded in 1983
- Industrial, Commercial, Computing, Technological and Associated Management
- The Academy of Multi-Skills (AMS) Founded in 1995
- A Professional Body for all Multi-Skilled Personnel, Skilled Trades, Crafts and Professions
- The Academy of Executives & Administrators (AEA) Founded 2002
- Management, Business, Public Sector, Industry, Commerce, Manufacturing, Manufacturing Management, Computers, Technology and Systems

There are several levels and grades of membership available to cater for the varying experience, qualifications, positions and skills of professionals.

Head Office

Warwick Corner, 42 Warwick Road, Kenilworth, Warwickshire CV8 1HE United Kingdom
Tel: 01926 855498   Fax: 01926 513100
Website: www.group-ims.com
Email: info@group-ims.com

Professional Membership – Advance your Career

Author's Acknowledgement and Disclaimer

The Author is grateful to the individuals and companies who contributed essential information to this book, and each one is personally acknowledged and thanked in the relevant Chapters concerned.
The reader may find a mix of English-English and American-English styles, which reflect the contributors' input.
The Author hopes that editing has not changed the essence of the contributions, and although a great deal of effort was spent on reviewing and editing the final text, one cannot guarantee that errors may not appear, and if you spot any, please contact the Author directly, thanks.

Contact the Author

Please feel free to contact me with ideas, questions or in case you found errors, or if you wish to book lectures and training sessions via his web site: www.peachqc.com

Copyrights© and Trademarks™

This book is the Copyrights of Abe Abrahami.
Readers may quote verbatim up to one complete page of text and give full credit to the Author and source of information.
All trademarks of the entities mentioned in this book are acknowledged and attributed to their rightful owners.

Table of Contents

The Book a Filing Cabinet of Topics

A. Leading compliance mandates and tools

1. Compliance and Governance
2. Basel II Accord
3. Federal Deposit Insurance Corporation (FDIC)
4. Gramm Leach Bliley Act (GLBA)
5. Health Insurance Portability and Accountability Act (HIPAA)
6. Ecora's Practical Guide to Implementing HIPAA Security Standards
7. International Financial Reporting Standards (IFRS)
8. Markets in Financial Instrument Directive (MiFID)
9. Sarbanes-Oxley Act (SOA or SOX)
10. Ecora's Practical Guide to Sarbanes-Oxley IT Internal Controls
11. Solvency II
12. Redwood Blueprint for Sustainable Compliance Solutions
13. IBM's Insurance Information Warehouse Support for Regulatory Compliance

B. Leading compliance-change delivery methods

14. Business Change and Compliance
15. Business Performance and Change Management
16. Change Management and E-Learning
17. Changing the IT Dept. - A Case History
18. Successful Change Delivery with Programme / Project Management Structure (PrMS)
19. Risk Management and Costs
Appendix: Compliance Audit and Triggers
Peach Multi-Compliance and Change Delivery Course

1.   Compliance and Governance

Introduction

This Chapter describes some of the most important issues concerning corporate Compliance and summarises briefly governance in the context of information management within large and medium size entities. By definition, this Chapter cannot include all relevant points concerning Compliance laws and regulations.

Corporate Governance

The term "governance" is very versatile. It is used in connection with several contemporary social sciences, and corporate business.

It originates from the need of economics (concerning corporate governance) and political science (concerning State governance) for an all-embracing concept capable of conveying diverse meanings, not covered by the traditional term "government".

In connection with exercising power overall, the term "governance", in both corporate and State contexts, embraces action by executive bodies, assemblies (e.g. national parliaments) and judicial bodies (e.g. national courts and tribunals).
The term "governance" corresponds to the so-called, post-modern form of economic and political organisations.

Governance[1] is concerned with accountability and responsibilities; it describes how the organisation is directed and controlled, touching 3 major entities:

---

[1] According to International Journal of Business Governance and Ethics

- <u>Organisation</u> – the organisational units and structures, groupings, and co-ordinating mechanisms (such as steering groups) established within the organisation and in partnership with external bodies, for the management of change
- <u>Management</u> – the roles and responsibilities established to manage business change and operational services, and the scope of the power and authority which they exercise
- <u>Policies</u> – the frameworks and boundaries established for making decisions about investment in business change, and the context and constraints within which decisions are taken.

OMP – Organisation, Management, Policies – mentioned above, are not and cannot be isolated from Compliance, but embrace it.

Corporate Compliance

Meaning

"Compliance" means conformity - acting according to certain accepted or mandated standards and/or regulations; for example - "their financial statements are in conformity with generally accepted accounting practices". "Regulatory Compliance" refers to individuals, systems, entities and public agencies – players - acting to ensure that personnel, information and communication means are aware of, and act in adherence with relevant local and international laws and regulations.
Given today's business and legal environment, many companies are establishing Compliance activation and management programs to proactively manage their organizational risk.
Fuelled by the increasing jungle of regulatory, legislative and corporate requirements established each year, the

task of managing overall Compliance for an organization has become a challenging and a costly endeavour.

Challenges and Seven Truths

With the substantially increased costs of Compliance failure - including fines, litigation, and criminal penalties - companies are seeking solutions that provide them with a way to manage this challenge, while possibly exploiting this as an opportunity to do better.
This is an opportunity if not just an obligation to improve, re-engineer, re-structure, change-manage, optimise and right size the corporate financial controls, business processes, Information Technology (IT), data warehouse and information content management applications.

There are seven truths to bear in mind in connection with Compliance mandates.

The first truth is that there probably is no single entity in the world today that has rationalised and optimised side by side each and every Compliance measure, for overlap, contradiction and gaps.

The second truth is that some of these measures, such as Sarbanes-Oxley, Basel II, and others, are still a subject to debate and interpretation, and individuals do their best to thread carefully through their measures, to avoid penalties.

The third truth is that many firms are still poorly positioned to deal with the new challenges posed by Compliance measures. Instead of using this situation as an opportunity to put their house in order and capitalise on business-culture change, process re-engineering and added value, they are more worried about ticking the boxes on their Compliance checklists.

<u>The fourth truth</u> is that many companies do not slice the Compliance cake through its full depth, breath and length; so let me explain.

Imagine your Compliance cake consisting of 3 main interrelated layers, as a change in any of these layers causes a chain-reaction, affecting the others:

1. Financial controls, processes and procedures, including audit and accounting
2. Business processes and procedures, including risk management and security
3. IT processes and procedures, including risk management and security

It is the inter-play, cause and effect between these 3 major layers, which can be as complex as a multi-phase flow (to coin a phrase from fluid mechanics), and it is not a simple linear model.

Accordingly, a relatively small change in one area could create a substantial impact on another.

<u>The fifth truth</u> is that many companies do not have a full and updated list of all their business and IT assets, who are their responsible owners, and where the assets are located. This could be a breach of regulatory Compliance rules.

For example, a 10% discrepancy in IT assets such as computer servers or PCs[2] could be considered a material weakness under the Sarbanes-Oxley (SOX) Act. It could also impact financial reporting and transparency, including risk and security management, health and safety.

---

[2] http://www.husselbaugh.com TOTAL ASSET MANAGEMENT, Sarbanes-Oxley and the Autodiscovery "Watchdog" Process A MANAGEMENT WHITE PAPER BY: WILLIAM B. HUSSELBAUGH FRANK KASSEL, see Chapter on Sarbanes-Oxley

Therefore, the first step for these organisations is to list what they own, where it is, where/what is the documentation for the asset, who owns it etc.
And this is well before you even get to other, more complex Compliance issues...

The sixth truth is that many companies do not have a regularly updated Intranet portal with up to date organisation structures, roles & responsibilities to do with Compliance, business continuity, and disaster recovery. Such a system should include online documentation and hot links to business processes, and Compliance rules, relevant training materials and automatic trigger alerts to indicate that something has changed and a change request has been raised to verify if, when and how action is required, and by whom.

The seventh truth is that Compliance is a cyclic work, part of the job of every person in the organisation, and should be linked to job specification, performance and reward. This is not a one-off exercise or project, although the first step may be regarded as such, in the long journey of work until we retire – it's a lifetime endeavour.
The trick is to strike a balance between Compliance, good business practice and commonsense via buy-in incentives, education and continuous improvement.

Basic Questions

If you go back to basics and trace your organisation's business procedures and transactions, and how they would be done using pen and paper, you will realise that technology has not made these interactions much different or necessarily better in all cases.
Essentially, technology speeded up these processes very considerably, while making controls more complex, and at times perhaps less transparent (here is a paradox).

However, behind all the Compliance, accountancy, audit, legal and IT jargon, there are twenty basic questions, HOW WOULD YOU ANSWER THEM?

1. Who creates and changes a business procedure, transaction or document?
2. Who certifies that any of these records are current, correct, complete or incomplete?
3. What trigger the above actions, what is the audit trail, and who is responsible?
4. According to which Compliance rule[s] are processes and actions conducted?
5. Does the record amended or created agree or contradict another one?
6. If yes, why, and what action to be taken, if any, by whom, and is it clearly documented?
7. If yes, is the variance deliberate or due to incompetence, oversight or cheating?
8. What and where is the proof and consequence for doing things right?
9. What and where is the proof and consequence for doing things wrong?
10. How does your company train and test staff in Compliance and change management?
11. How quickly can you retrieve documents and records at TRANSACTION LEVEL?
12. Can you retrieve ALL key documents and related records, which are 5-25 years old?
13. Do you know the head of Compliance and change management in your company?
14. Are Compliance and change procedures clearly visible on your company's Intranet web site?
15. Is Compliance and change management linked directly and transparently to business continuity, disaster recovery, and security controls?
16. If yes, how, and if no, why, and what do you intend to do about it?

17. Do you know how your business-balance scorecard ties up with Compliance and change management? If yes, how, and if no, why, and do you intend to do about it?
18. How do governance and Compliance work together in your company and department?
19. Are you aware that if you do not know with certainty the answer to at least two of the above questions, you could bring down your organisation?
20. Are you aware that if you do not know with certainty the answer to at least two of the above questions you could be in breach of regulatory Compliance mandates, face penalties, or lose your job?

If your company's management has not kept governance and Compliance up to date and in sync, clearly visible, and linked to business continuity, disaster recovery, business processes, information management and security controls, your organisation could be in serious trouble.
Your CEO, CFO and CIO are particularly and personally vulnerable.
There is no place to hide any more!

Key Performance Indicators (KPIs) and Compliance

How an organization defines and measures progress toward its strategic goals and business objectives are measured by KPIs.
KPIs, which may be the same as Key Success Indicators (KSIs) or Key Goal Indicators (KGIs) or Key Business Indicators (KBIs), help an organization define and measure progress toward its aims.
Once an organization has analyzed its mission, identified all its stakeholders, and defined its goals, it needs a way to measure progress toward those goals.
Key Performance Indicators are those measurements.

Key Performance Indicators are quantifiable measurements, agreed to beforehand, that reflect the critical success factors of an organization. They differ depending on the company concerned.

KPIs should be linked to industry-related benchmarks and Business-balanced Scorecard (BBS) to provide an overall picture as to how the business is doing overall in meeting its objectives and strategic goals, and how KPIs are relatively balanced in the total score.

KPIs, BBS and industry benchmarks cover not only business, but also regulatory Compliance and related IT and security; for example:

- How do Compliance and change management score in relation to other KPI measures?
- How long does it take to retrieve a 10-year old record for inspection purposes?
- How long does it take to, and can you actually retrieve ALL related documents?
- What is the average cost of a record storage, maintenance and retrieval?
- What is the impact of a financial rule change on your business, security and IT?
- What is the impact of a Compliance rule change on your business, security and IT?
- How many errors or amendments has your company made with financial reporting?
- How many of its targets has the company met in the past quarter, half and full year?
- How much does the company spend on Compliance and what are the returns?
- How many in the firm see Compliance as an opportunity versus a costly challenge?

And there are many more – below are revenue and performance-related examples from insurance, banking and other financial services' KPIs:

- Billing and fee collection analysis:
    - Collected revenue
    - Collection cost per revenue
- Business activity performance analysis
    - Average number of policies per intermediary
    - Revenue growth rate
- Investment performance analysis
    - Investment income growth
    - Return on investment portfolio
- Market analysis
    - Evolution of market share
    - Market growth share
- Overall performance analysis
    - Capital deployed to cover underwriting risk
    - Value at risk per revenue

Compliance Mandates

There are numerous Compliance mandates, and listed below are some major ones, although the Table is obviously not exhaustive.

Table 1.1: Compliance mandates

Mandatory Compliance	Industries affected	Impact
Sarbanes-Oxley Act (USA / international)	Currently all US-SEC Listed Companies. The Act might be extended to private companies, see http://www.sarbanes-oxley-forum.com	The Act impacts the storage of the company's' electronic records together with the recording & reporting of its finances
Combined Code on Corporate Governance Higgs Report, Smith Report etc. (UK)	All UK Listed Companies, see http://www.accountancyage.com/	There are numerous different codes and guidance all contributing towards increased Corporate Governance
Turnbull Report Combined Code - Internal Controls (UK)	All UK Listed Companies, see http://www.icaew.co.uk/	Risk Management
Basel II (International)	All Financial Institutions - Banks, Building Societies, Insurance Companies etc. see http://www.bis.org/	Risk management and capital minimum requirement for financial institutions, encourages the banking industry to use more sophisticated risk management methodology and tools. Basel II will be the biggest driver of IT investment amongst the financial community since Y2K

IFRS / IAS Approx. 27 standards (EU / international)	All EU-listed companies initially - currently numbering 7,000 Furthermore, the DTI are considering extending to private companies, see http://www.iasb.org/	Not just an accounting issue, but impact on information systems
FSA Mortgage & Insurance Regulations (UK)	Mortgage Lenders & Brokers Insurance Suppliers & Brokers, see http://www.hm-treasury.gov.uk/	Internet quotations will increase over telephone quotations. Greater disclosure between all parties necessary
Data Protection Act (UK)	All industry sectors, see http://www.businessli nk.gov.uk/	All staff need to know & understand the rules & management need to update with development of new technologies - IM, WiFi etc.
Privacy & Electronic Communicatio ns Regulations (UK)	All organisations that utilise E-Marketing, see http://www.informatio ncommissioner.gov.u k/	Impacts what customer data can be stored, for how long, how it can be used etc.
Health Insurance Privacy & Accountability Act (USA)	USA Healthcare Service providers & insurers, see http://www.hipaa.org/	Increased IT spend within Healthcare sector
Freedom of Information Act (UK)	Central & Local Government - approx. 75,000 Departments ranging from councils, health authorities plus private firms under	Increased IT spend within Public Sector. Records management will be a big issue, together with security

	contract to Public Sector, see http://www.foi-uk.org/	
Graham-Leach-Bliley Act (GLBA) (USA)	All consumers, see http://banking.senate.gov/conf/	Security and confidentiality of customer records, requiring all financial institutions to disclose to consumers and customers their policies and practices for protecting the privacy of non-public personal information
Solvency II, MiFID (EU)	All consumers, financial services' companies, institutions, intermediaries and banks	Best practice / execution for clients' best interests, standards' uniformity and transparency

The mandates below (in alphabetical order) are covered, in the Chapters that follow, reflecting their relevance and importance to this book:

- Basel II
- Federal Deposit Insurance Corporation (FDIC)
- Gramm-Leach-Bliley Act (GLBA)
- Health Insurance Portability & Accountability Act (HIPAA)
- IFRS (International Financial Reporting Standards)
- MiFID (Directive on Markets in Financial Instruments)
- Sarbanes-Oxley Act (SOA or SOX)
- Solvency II

Various Compliance mandates together, are like handling different size eggs in one basket....

Figure 1.1: Compliance eggs in one basket

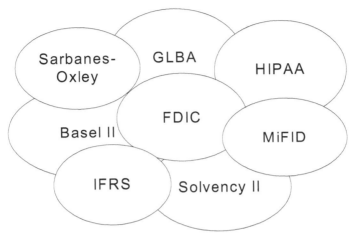

Ask yourself some 'eggy-questions':

1. Do you know how to tread carefully within those eggs without breaking them?
2. How do you deliver with multi-Compliance projects, and avoid overlaps and replication of efforts?
3. Can you prove that your products and services are compliant with relevant mandates?
4. How do you certify this proof?
5. Which methods do you employ to deliver Compliance and change projects?
6. Do you have too many eggs in one basket?
7. If 'yes' have you assessed the risks and mitigation?

2.   Basel II Accord

Coverage

Basel II Accord, introduced from the end of 2006, is a round of deliberations by central bankers from around the world.
It is under the auspices of the Basel Committee on Banking Supervision (BCBS) in Basel, Switzerland, aimed at producing uniformity in the way banks and banking regulators approach risk management across national borders.
The Bank for International Settlements (BIS) supplies the secretariat for, but is NOT the BCBS itself.
Basel II applies a three pillars' concept:

1.   Minimum capital requirements
2.   Supervisory risk review requirements
3.   Market discipline requirements

The first diagram illustrates of the 3 pillars of Basel II – supporting the roof of capital adequacy, being the kingpin of the Accord.

The interplay between risk factors, risk events, impact, probabilities and loss consequences are modelled and analysed by risk analysis tools depicted in the second diagram.

Figure 2.1: Three Basel II pillars under one roof

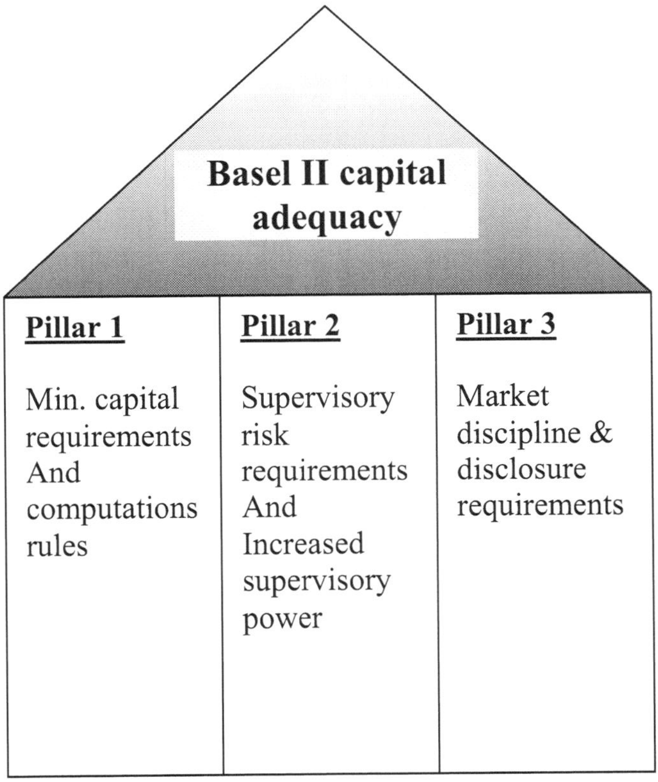

Pillar 1	Pillar 2	Pillar 3
Min. capital requirements And computations rules	Supervisory risk requirements And Increased supervisory power	Market discipline & disclosure requirements

Basel II capital adequacy

The 3 Pillars

1 - <u>Minimum capital requirements</u> - provides improved risk sensitivity in the way that capital requirements are calculated in three of the components of risk that a bank faces: credit risk, operational risk and market risk.
In turn, each of these components can be calculated in between two or three ways of varying sophistication.
Other risks are not considered fully quantifiable at this stage. Risk-Adjusted Return On Capital (RAROC) etc.

Technical terms in the more sophisticated measures of credit risk include EL (Expected Loss) whose components are PD (Probability of Default), LGD (Loss Given Default), and EAD (Exposure At Default).
Calculation of these components requires advanced data collection and sophisticated risk management techniques.

2 - <u>Supervisory risk view requirements</u> - deals with the regulatory response to the first pillar, giving regulators much-improved 'tools' over those available to them under Basel I.
It also provides a framework for dealing with all the other risks that a bank faces, such as name risk, liquidity risk and legal risk, which the accord combines under the title of residual risk.

3 – <u>Greater disclosure requirements</u> - greatly increases the disclosures that the bank must make. This is designed to allow the market to have a better picture of the overall risk position of the bank and to allow the counterparties of the bank price and deals appropriately.

Shortcomings and Fixes

There are four main shortcomings or criticisms in the Basel II accord, namely:

The first is that Basel II excludes reputation-loss risk (damage to an organisation through loss of its reputation or standing) although it is understood that a significant but non-catastrophic operational loss could still affect its reputation possibly leading to a further collapse of its business and organisational failure.

Also, Basel II definition includes legal risk, but excludes strategic risk: i.e. the risk of a loss arising from a poor strategic business decision.

The second is that the more sophisticated risk measures are, the more they unfairly advantage the larger banks that are able to implement them.

The third is that developing countries generally do not have large banks, so Basel II will disadvantage them economically by restricting their access to credit or by making it more expensive.

Experience with United States and the United Kingdom banks and financial institutions, however, shows that the improved risk sensitivity means that banks are more willing to lend to higher risk borrowers, just with higher prices.

Borrowers previously 'locked out' of the banking system have a chance to establish a good credit history.

The fourth and more serious one is that the operation of Basel II might lead to a more pronounced business cycle of expansion, shrinkage, losses, gains, recovery and prosperity.

This criticism arises because the credit models used for pillar 1 - typically use a one-year time horizon.

This could mean that, during a downturn in the business cycle, banks would need to reduce lending as their models forecast increased losses, increasing the magnitude of the downturn, a sort of a chain-reaction.

Regulators should be aware of this risk and can be expected to include it in their assessment of the bank models in use, which could be self-defeating.

Summary of deficiencies fixed in Risk/Control/Assurance Management Identified by the Basel Committee on Banking Supervision[3], which led to Basel II are:

1. Board of Directors and senior management did not establish strong control cultures.
2. Senior management failed to emphasize the importance of a strong control culture through their words and actions and, most importantly, through the criteria used to determine compensation and promotion.
3. Senior management failed to ensure that the organization structure and management accountabilities were well defined.
4. Senior management weakened the control culture by promoting and rewarding managers who were successfully generating profits but failed to implement control policies or address audit findings.
5. Accountabilities were not clearly defined.
6. Inadequate risk recognition and assessment processes.
7. Some banks failed to observe certain key internal control principles especially segregation of duties.
8. Senior management did not respond appropriately to information they were receiving.
9. High-level reviews were not being done. Situations that should have been flagged, as senior management did not investigate abnormalities.

---

[3] Source: Supervisory Lessons Learned from Internal Control Failures, Appendix II, Framework for Internal Control Systems in Banking Organizations, Basle Committee on Banking Supervision, Basle, September 1998, Bank for International Settlements **www.bis.org/publ/bcbs40.htm**

10. Information was not reliable or complete and communication was not effective.
11. Banks failed to adequately communicate employee's duties and control responsibilities or disseminated policies though channels, such as electronic mail, that did not ensure that he policy was read, understood and retained.
12. Lines of communication did not exist for the reporting of suspected improprieties by employees.
13. Banks did not effectively monitor their risk/control systems. The systems did not have the necessary built-in ongoing monitoring processes and the separate evaluations performed were either not adequate or were not acted upon appropriately by management.
14. There was a failure to consider and react to day-to-day information provided to line management and other personnel indicating unusual activity.
15. Failure to react to situations indicating a heightened level of risk.
16. Internal audit was not effective in many problem-banking organizations. This was caused by piecemeal audits, lack of a thorough understanding of business processes, and inadequate follow-up when problems were noted.
17. Fragmented audit approaches resulted because the internal audits were structured as a series of discrete audits of specific activities within the same division or department, within geographic areas, or within legal entities.
18. Inadequate knowledge and training of internal audit staff in trading products and markets, electronic information systems, and other highly sophisticated areas.
19. Internal audit staff was hesitant to ask questions when they suspected problems, and when questions were asked, they were more likely to accept an answer than to challenge it.

20. Management did not accept the role and importance of internal audit and did not appropriately follow-up on issues identified.
21. Senior management failed to receive timely and regular tracking reports that indicated critical issues and the subsequent corrective actions taken by management.

Benefits of Basel II

The greater financial stability benefits are summarised by the Figure below.

Figure 2.2: Basel II benefits' circle

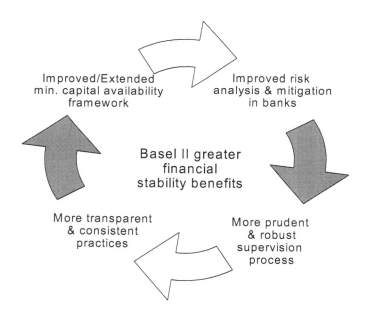

Basel II Accord benefits in more detail:

1. The Accord synergises 3 pillars, more potent and effective combined together
2. The Accord forces banks and financial institutions to hold sufficient capital reserves to cover their risks, as part of an extended triple-protection
3. The Accord improves the dialogue between the industry and their supervisors
4. The Accord enhances greater consistency and supervisory consistency
5. The Accord improves the level playing field and financial stability
6. The Accord has more and better checks and balances
7. The Accord, although complex, has a clearer purpose and framework
8. The Accord exploits best practices of the industry, leading to a more efficient and effective regulation, from an economic stand-point
9. The Accord has potentially more flexibility to accommodate small and big banks
10. The Accord has potentially more flexibility for emerging and developing markets
11. The Accord recognises and encourages developments in risk analysis, mitigation and management - together with enhanced supervisory practices
12. The Accord creates an extended framework and greater incentives to adopt more sophisticated analytical and objective approaches to make better/safer decisions
13. The Accord is a good banking-business practice tool with added value
14. The Accord will be adopted by more than 100 countries - probably more than any other regulatory mandate
15. The Accord encourages a common reporting requirements and model validation

16. The Accord contains guidelines to enhance co-operation and exchange of information between authorities
17. The Accord helps dialogue and interaction with market participants and end-users, including a Consultative Panel

At the heart of Basel II benefits are 3 major components:

1. The people who implement it and held accountable,
2. Credit/market/operation risk evaluations, see example below,
3. The internal controls – the glue and lubricating oil;

Which make it all work together to increase confidence and success probability for the banks and their customers, a win-win situation.

An essay about proactive market risk analyses, applying statistical-probabilistic analysis techniques, such as Monte Carlo simulation, is described to give the reader an idea of the complexity involved in such computations and evaluations, including value at risk.

Applying Proactive Financial Market Risk Management

Introduction

The information below is illustrative of risk computations and is not necessarily representing all of Basel II mathematical details.
There is an expectation on the part of shareholders that financial institutions assume, intermediate and advise on financial and other risks. Organisations appropriately expect that line managers possess the risk management skills, either intuitively or by incorporating formal risk

analyses, necessary for their risk taking business activities.

Consequently, organisations have traditionally spent the greater part of their analytical and technology budgets on expertise and tools to help these managers make money rather than to minimize losses or comply with regulatory requirements.

Risk management systems were too often viewed by these organisations as a costly control function mandated by regulatory authorities with little or no benefit to the bottom line.

In fact, an appropriately implemented and utilised risk management function can help organisations better align their expected returns for the risks and costs undertaken in order to increase the bottom line and ultimately enhance shareholder value.

While risk management has traditionally been viewed as a methodology for preventing large losses and appeasing regulators (capital preservation), it is also a continuous process of balancing risk taking and capital.

Presented below are some high level observations on proactive market risk management and Asset-Liability Management (ALM) at capital markets entities, banks, and insurance companies.

Value at Risk (VaR)

An example of proactive risk management is the Risk-Adjusted Return On capital (RAROC) methodology developed by Bankers Trust two decades ago. RAROC balances return with risk measurements, such as Value at Risk (VaR), simulation, deterministic/scenario risk forecasting, and other risk measurement tools. The ultimate goal of RAROC methodologies is to provide a uniform measure of performance that management can use to compare the correlated economic as opposed to the uncorrelated accounting profitability of businesses.

RAROC calculations include other sources of risk besides market - credit, country, and specific/business risk - but this paper is limited to a discussion of market risk. Another example is the Return on VaR (ROVaR) market risk measure, which utilises estimates of future returns and volatility. The ROVaR ratio (expected return/risk contribution to portfolio) is based on ex-post performance measurement ratios developed by William Sharpe.

ROVaR allows a financial institution to allocate firm capital only to those businesses and transactions whose estimated ROVaR exceeds the firm mandated hurdle ROVaR on an ex-ante basis. For example, Business A may provide an expected return of 30% on capital versus Business B's 12%.
But Business A's contribution to risk is 35% of capital (0.86 ROVaR) versus the latter's 10% (1.20 ROVaR). Consequently, Business B may be a more attractive business viewed purely on a risk-adjusted basis.

The expected return side of ROVaR and RAROC measures should be adjusted for funding, credit, operational costs and associated expenses. If transfer pricing is structured appropriately, such costs could vary greatly between businesses and thus significantly impact comparative ROVaR calculations. For example, a bank's consumer loan portfolio may return higher margins than commercial and mortgage loans, but the associated costs of servicing such loans may reduce their relative appeal. RAROC and the related ROVaR measure integrate risk-taking and capital preservation functions, which usually work independently in most organisations, into the overall corporate objective of optimising total risk-adjusted performance.
Proactive Market Risk Management For Capital Markets Activities Risk Management Units Many entities with

capital markets activities have independent risk management units (RMUs) that measure and monitor risk. RMU staff is often highly quantitative and generally possess appropriate skills to monitor traders and ensure that limits and approved trading strategies are adhered to. But a closer look reveals that not all RMUs are alike or necessarily analyse transactions on a risk-adjusted basis. Once RMU procedures and modelling methodologies have been established, most of the work involves daily transaction monitoring and participation in new product development. For these independent RMUs, true independence means there is no cross fertilization of staff between trading and risk management and that compensation is absolutely independent of trading profits.

Decomposing Risk & Proactive Reporting a proactive reporting and risk analytic infrastructure allows managers and traders to easily view the marginal impact to the firm's risk of potential transactions. For example, if a trader knows that a particular transaction will reduce the firm's or desk's total correlated risk, the trader may be more willing to proceed than if the trade will increase total risk. Of course, performance measurement and compensation should encourage this risk/return trade-off. Otherwise, such reports may serve as strictly a management information piece and risk not being utilised by traders. Clarifying the sources of risk in the portfolio and what trades will provide effective ways to reduce risk can provide help in making appropriate trading decisions. In essence, risk management requires more than a single VaR calculation representing the potential loss amount under a certain confidence level. Risk management requires a decomposition of risk, an ability to find potential hedges, and an ability to find key drivers of portfolio profit and loss on a correlated basis.

The sources of a firm's largest correlated risks determine the composition of the most efficient hedges.

For example, a hypothetical money market desk may estimate that the key driver in its European money market portfolio is the $/Euro FX rate.

Though the desk has no position in the FX markets, the link between money markets and FX may drive its P&L. Consequently, the desk may be most concerned with the $/Mark rate's direction.

Further, the desk might decide that trading in the FX market to either increase or decrease (hedge) its money market portfolio is more efficient than trading in disparate money market instruments.

Proactive Limit Setting The limit setting process must support the firm's risk appetite and mission yet remain flexible enough to permit capture of short-lived return opportunities.

A profitable trade opportunity may require reallocating risk limits. For example, an arbitrage deal in Market A may demand exceeding risk limits by as much as 50%. But because the deal is quite lucrative and may enhance a customer relationship, the deal may be consummated cautiously by reducing risk in products or markets highly correlated to Market A.

Regulatory Pressure Regulators have influenced much of banks' trading risk management practices. For market risk in the trading portfolio, banks must allocate capital according to a combination of Bank for International Settlement (BIS) and US bank regulatory rules. Currently, the Basle Capital Accord of July 1988 requires that banks allocate capital strictly for credit risks. Effective end-1997, the "BIS Amendment to the Capital Accord to Incorporate Market Risks" requires additional capital for market risks in trading portfolios. In September 1996, the US bank regulators issued a joint rule, "Risk-Based Capital Standards: Market Risk" also effective end -1997, requiring banks with significant exposure to market risk to measure that risk using their own internal VaR model and to hold a commensurate amount of capital.

Business Strategy Capital markets entities are beginning to base compensation and business strategy on RAROC. In these cases, the risk/return relationship drives business strategy. For instance, if expected profitability in Business A is disproportionate to potential risk, management may downsize Business A. Fee-based businesses, many of which do not involve any direct use of capital at all, may have significant risks. For example, fee-generating businesses, like corporate financial advisory and asset management, have risks, which may be difficult to quantify.
Advisory is often difficult to leverage since the work can be labour intensive and competitive pressures can force executive compensation to high levels. On the other hand, asset management can be heavily leveraged, as raising additional money requires decreasing marginal expenditures. Yet, in general, acquired money management businesses fetch tremendous premiums, while start-ups require an acceptable three to five year track record to begin acquiring significant mandates.

Proactive Asset Liability Management (ALM) at Banks

Proactive ALM requires an accurate depiction of risk and the communication of such risk to product managers. Often, the major challenge for bank management is addressing the natural tension between loan and deposit product managers and ALM managers.
While product managers may be constantly meeting customer demand by innovating more sophisticated product, ALM managers carefully update their models to measure and control these new risks.
RAROC methodologies encourage product managers to price competing products with these risks in mind so as to maximize profits for a given level of risk.

ALM managers measure and monitor interest rate risk for all on- and off- balance sheet instruments from two perspectives: earnings and market value (see diagram).

The earnings perspective focuses on the impact of interest rate changes on a bank's near-term earnings; while the market value perspective focuses on a bank's underlying value.
The interest rate sensitivity of financial instruments depends on many factors, including duration; yield curve, basis, re-pricing characteristics, and embedded options affecting the timing of cash flows.

Risk Measurement Tools

Event-Driven, Risk-Measurement's Monte Carlo[4] engine, is based on a generic valuation approach involving the revaluation of all securities at each time step along each path of the Monte Carlo scenario.

All cash flows are accurately calculated by the model (i.e. no cash flow compression techniques are utilised), so that intermediate cash flows occurring during the simulation period are captured for all instruments.
A base case mark-to-market (valuation) is performed using internally developed pricing models and, where necessary, third party pricing models. Individual positions are re-valued for each path, the changes in mark-to-market value are calculated and the results are aggregated and ordered to obtain the P&L distribution for the portfolio.

By calculating the P&L distribution (rather than using an approximated distribution, as is the case with an analytic technique) Risk-Measurement enables clients to view non-normality in the P&L distributions.

---

[4] A unique statistical modelling-simulation technique.

Similarly, changes in the P&L distribution as a function of time can also be analysed. VaR results are reported for a specified confidence level and holding period (e.g., 95%for a one month time horizon).

The varieties of VaR are:

Absolute VaR - VaR can be presented in absolute currency amounts or in percentage terms.
VaR as percentage of portfolio market value permits VaR comparisons between other portfolio segments, benchmarks, accounts, etc.

Marginal VaR - Marginal VaR captures the contribution of a specified portfolio, asset class or risk factor to the total risk. Calculating the VaR for the overall portfolio and then systematically removing accounts from the overall portfolio and re-calculating the VaR determine marginal VaR. The difference between the overall portfolio VaR and the VaR less a specified account provide the marginal contribution of that account to the portfolio risk. Marginal VaR facilitates the optimal allocation of risk capital and portfolio rebalancing.

Tracking Error VaR - Tracking Error (Relative) VaR measures how closely a portfolio's risk matches its corresponding benchmark. VaR is first calculated for the benchmark (e.g., the S&P 500). Subsequently, the benchmark is shorted against the actual portfolio and VaR is recalculated. The resulting tracking error (or R-VaR) reflects how well the portfolio tracks (i.e. under or over performs) the benchmark.

Stress Testing - Stress testing is provided as a complement to Risk-Measurement VaR models to allow clients to perform "what if" analyses. These tests enable the calculation of "tail" events (events resulting in loss occurrence in the tail of the P&L distribution, i.e. outside of the specified VaR confidence level) that could create losses under extreme market conditions. Risk-Measurement provides standard (e.g., Fed Tightening, NASDAQ Correction, Asian Flu, etc.) as well as customized scenario analyses.

A typical analysis tool is for example, Derivative-Tool, which is a set of Microsoft Excel add-in functions that values derivative and cash instruments using Monte Carlo simulation. Typical users are traders, risk managers, quantitative researchers, auditors, corporations, investment funds, financial institutions, insurance companies, and energy firms.

Users who want to create new structured deals will benefit from Derivative-Tool. Its component-based approach to instrument modelling and pricing gives the user maximum flexibility to be creative in designing and structuring instruments including, but not limited to, the inclusion of risk factors other than price.

The flexible scripting language built into Derivative-Tool allows users to model almost any deal. The software library option of the product permits models written using Derivative-Tool to be plugged into most other risk analytics packages, enabling holes in portfolio coverage to be filled. Derivative-Tool supports a range of different valuation models.

An appropriate model can be chosen, depending on the underlying commodity and user preference.

Derivative-Tool is typically written in C++ and provides extremely fast calculations. It includes Excel add-in functions (XLL files), customisable Excel templates, and documentation.

When installed, Derivative-Tool adds functions to Excel that are used like the built-in worksheet functions, so you can customize the Derivative-Tool templates or create new ones.

Derivative-Tool can be used to price instruments directly, or it can be used to generate raw scenario values for external computation and analysis, allowing you to do the following:

- Create and utilise a financial instrument
- Create and utilise term structures corresponding to: forward-price curves, foreign and domestic interest-rate curves, convenience-yield curves, spot and forward asset volatilities, and forward asset-pair correlations
- Create and utilise financial models of assets underlying an instrument, including: simple normal and lognormal models, one-factor mean-reverting normal and lognormal models for price and exogenous underlyings, and the one-factor Hull-White interest-rate model
- Create or modify a holiday calendar
- Display the raw scenario results of a Monte Carlo simulation, including user-defined cash flow events and instrument payoff
- Display the summary statistics and histograms of a Monte Carlo simulation, including those of the total payoff, theta risk measure, standard "Greeks," hedge and gamma curves, custom risk measures, and simulated cash flows
- Write results in XML format

Here are some of the instruments Derivative-Tool can value:
- Asset swaps
- Average-price options
- Average-strike options
- Barrier options
- Basket options
- Dividend-paying equity options

55

- Equity-linked securities
- Foreign exchange options
- Forward price options
- Interest rate derivatives
- Energy derivatives
- Electricity Load contracts
- Weather contracts
- Banks

Banks and Risk Management

Risk management is a central concern of every bank. Though few would disagree with this statement, difficulties arise when one attempts to define and implement risk management strategies across the bank.
The problem facing a typical bank risk manager lies in assimilating information from across the entire organisation.

Not only do banks deal with many diverse instruments (from bonds to swaps, loans to commodities), but managers of each asset type general maintain their own trading operation and have their own way of viewing risk. For example, whereas a bond trader may talk about duration and convexity, an equity trader will view his book in terms of alpha and beta.

The key to successful risk management is the ability to create reports in a timely and informative manner. The table below shows some of the types of risk measurements and reports required by a typical bank, each of which are built into leading risk software and data services, which typically exploit the Monte Carlo statistical method.

Table 2.1: Risk requirements

Business Unit	Risk Requirement
Proprietary Trading	Value-at-Risk and VaR Limits. How much can a portfolio lose? How diverse is the portfolio? How can risk be reduced on an instrument basis?
Swaps Desk	Credit Exposure. What are long-term profiles of obligations? How is risk subject to netting agreements?
Credit Officers	Counterparty Risk. How concentrated is risk to specific counter parties. How diverse are these risks?
Financial Control	Regulatory Capital. How is it best managed and requirements reduced?
Credit Portfolio Managers	Credit Risk. How is portfolio affected by credit quality changes and defaults?
Market Risk Committee	Summary Risk Reports. How is risk distributed by currency, asset type, region, desk, etc.?
Corporate Risk Management	Stress Testing. How sensitive are asset values to extreme market moves? What if interest rates should rise or the stock market fall?

Monte Carlo Simulation

The name "Monte Carlo" appeared in the World War II times, and sometimes is attributed to the researcher Nicholas Metropolis, inspired in the interest of S. Ulam, his colleague of Manhattan Project, in the poker game.

Monte Carlo, the capital of Monaco, was a known reference for gambling.

Winston (1996, p.22) wrote that mathematicians S. Ulam and J. von Neumann in the feasibility project of atomic bomb coined the term by simulations of nuclear fission, and they given the *code name* Monte Carlo for these simulations.

The first Monte Carlo paper, "*The Monte Carlo Method*" by Metropolis & Ulam, was published in 1949 in the *Journal of the American Statistical Association*.

Since then, several different areas have been using the Monte Carlo simulations.

With the advent of personal computers and the popularisation of faster computational machines, the Monte Carlo simulations have been increasing popular as an important alternative for the solution of complex problems.

The Monte Carlo statistical method solves a problem by simulating directly the physical process, and is not necessary to write down the differential equations that describe the behaviour of the system.

This is very general and is valid not only for our real options problem as in other areas of knowledge like energy, physics, chemistry, project management, financial analysis, return on investment (ROI) etc.

For several sources of uncertainties, such as investment banking, real options models suffer the problem of the *shortcoming of dimensionality*, which limit the model solution with others methods. For example, for more than three or four state variables, both lattice and finite-difference methods face several difficulties and are not practical.

Therefore, the Monte Carlo simulation must be used together with some optimisation method in order to get the threshold curve, as is the case with the leading edge tools' construction and risk analysis methodology.

A typical statistical distribution modelling with Monte Carlo simulation is shown by the sample graph below, indicating parameters' probabilities of occurrences according to different formulae algorithms.

Monte Carlo simulation has a huge number of modelling scenario uses - from financial to engineering, from agriculture to banking, from social sciences to medicine and so on and so forth.

Figure 2.3: Monte Carlo simulation, typical distribution curves

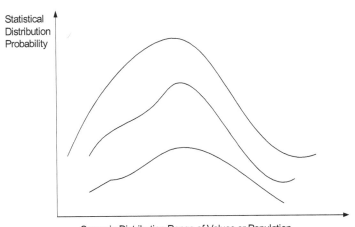

Basel II vs. Sarbanes-Oxley: Which Wins?[5]

The new Basel capital accord on bank safety - Basel II - is a clear winner in the corporate governance cup stakes over the flawed US Sarbanes-Oxley (SOX) regime, which is particularly defective in the area of control effectiveness reporting.

My view is based on comparing the forms of these two entrants for the corporate governance stakes, the one sired by banking supervisors seeking a stable global banking system and the other by the US Congress in response to the series of colossal corporate governance failures exemplified by the Enron scandal and similar disasters.

Basel II clears all but one of seven major hurdles, ranging from the role of directors to incentives to comply, where Sarbanes-Oxley stumbles from a lack of clarity.
Only on timelines does Sarbanes-Oxley have the advantage. Sarbanes is already law, whereas Basel II's timetable remains under threat.

In 1998 the Basel Committee on Banking Supervision, the body of senior banking supervisors from the leading economies that in effect regulates international banking, put forward a framework to help banks and their supervisors strengthen internal control procedures. Deficiencies in internal controls were seen as a source of major problems and significant losses for banks globally.

[5] Reprinted with kind permission of Tim Leech, Paisley Consulting, who compares corporate governance provisions of the Basel II bank accord and Sarbanes-Oxley Act and applies seven tests of effectiveness - see Acknowledgement at the end of this Chapter. This paper was originally published in 2003.

The core elements of the 1998 framework are contained in the new Accord, the Basel II upgrade of international capital rules for bank safety that the Basel Committee wants to bring into effect for the world's major banks by the beginning of 2007.

Basel II has a three-pillar regulatory structure of capital charges against credit, market and operational risk, supervisory review of bank risk management policies and greater information disclosure requirements.

The US Congress passed the Sarbanes-Oxley Act, which sets some of the stiffest corporate governance rules in the world, in July last year with the aim of protecting investors by improving the accuracy and reliability of corporate disclosures. Responsibility for implementing the act is assigned to the Securities Exchange Commission (SEC), the US investment markets regulator, and the new Public Company Accounting Oversight Board (PCAOB) that's charged with policing the accounting industry.

Both the Basel reforms and Sarbanes-Oxley are intended to prevent major corporate control failures. Basel focuses on ensuring the overall safety and soundness of banks. The SOX Act focuses on restoring investor confidence in the integrity and fairness of financial disclosures to regulators and current and prospective investors.

Although both governance reform regimes are focused on achieving similar outcomes, the route chosen to accomplish the task varies widely. What are the similarities and differences? Which approach is most likely to achieve the stated aims? We compare the two regimes in seven areas: the role of the Board of Directors; the regulator's role; the role of management; internal and external audit; reporting requirements; incentives to comply and timeliness of solution.

Board of Directors

The 1998 Basel internal control framework says directors should have responsibility for approving and periodically reviewing the overall business strategies and significant policies of the bank; understanding the major risks run by the bank; setting acceptable levels for these risks and ensuring that senior management takes the steps necessary to identify, measure, monitor and control the risks, approving organisational structure; and ensuring that senior management is monitoring the effectiveness of the internal control systems.

The message that regulators should carefully examine and score the oversight diligence of the board is repeated in numerous places in the draft Basel accord documentation.

Sarbanes-Oxley is largely silent on what is expected from the board of directors and audit committee, other than stating the audit committee should comprise independent directors who should review information they are provided with including whistle-blower reports. Although the 1987 Treadway Commission on fraudulent financial reporting in the US, and numerous other studies around the world since then, have all commented on the key role that should be played by boards and audit committees, Sarbanes did little to specify expectations in this area.

My pick: the Basel reforms

The Regulator

The Basel reforms lay out a fairly detailed set of expectations that bank regulators will use to assess whether an organisation has met risk control requirements. The emphasis is on proving that an effective overall system exists to identify, measure, monitor and mitigate risks. The criteria are clearly described and linked to well-accepted and current best practices.

By contrast, Sarbanes only lays out fairly specific recommendations in some areas; such as whistle blowing, independence of directors and fraud involving accounting personnel. But on the central requirement of reporting on the effectiveness of control systems, it encourages companies to use the 1992 Committee of Sponsoring Organizations ('COSO") control criteria as reporting criteria.

This now dated and somewhat obsolete control framework was never intended as a scoring grid for pass/fail analysis and is not well suited to objectively grade the quality of a company's external disclosure system.

Although COSO 1992 represented a milestone when it was released, in 1992, many major advances have been made in the area of risk and control management since that time.

A new "ERM" (Enterprise Risk Management) version of COSO provides limited help when attempting a pass/fail examination.

The SEC will find it very difficult to confirm or refute representations from chief executive officers and chief financial officers that a company has an effective control system in accordance with either the 1992 or the new COSO framework - despite investors paying billions of dollars for the information!

My pick: the Basel reforms.

Management

The Basel II reforms crystallised in the operational risk provisions of Basel II, focus on the elements of an effective risk management system and the role senior management must play to create and sustain it.

Specific qualitative and quantitative requirements are described depending on the risk management qualification sought, namely the basic indicator approach, the standardised approach or Advanced Measurement Approaches (AMA).

Under AMA, the most sophisticated of the options; a bank will have to show that its op risk measurement system is closely integrated into the day-to-day risk management processes of the bank.
Its output must be an integral part of the process of monitoring and controlling the bank's operational risk profile.
Sarbanes-Oxley by contrast focuses on forcing CEOs and CFOs to state that they have an "effective" system of control to ensure reliable financial disclosures.

The representations must be made against the old 1992 COSO framework or, presumably, against the new 2003 COSO ERM framework. CEOs and CFOs will have to decide if they have passed or failed using vague and loosely defined criteria. The notion of reporting on the degree of conformity with control criteria selected is not an option.
My pick: the Basel reforms

Internal and External Audit

Under Basel II the internal and/or external auditors must regularly review the op risk management processes and measurement systems.
The review must include both business units and the op risk management function.
The new regime is expected to play a lead role helping to create and sustain a bank's op risk management system.
To qualify for AMA, the validation of the op risk management system by external auditors and/or supervisory authorities is required to verify that internal

validation processes are satisfactory and make sure that data flows and processes associated with the risk measurement system are transparent and accessible. In particular, auditors and supervisors must have easy access to the system's specifications and parameters. Again Sarbanes-Oxley is largely silent on the issue. It's not clear whether the PCAOB will accept the premise advanced by many companies that, when an effective and independent internal audit exists, external audit should focus on evaluating and reporting on the reliability of the system that produces the control effectiveness representations.

The big four audit firms have lobbied hard for the right to evaluate independently and test all the processes that produce the external disclosures.
The audit fees for examining all the systems that support external disclosures, versus examining the quality of the system that produced the CEO/CFO representation, will be much higher.
My choice: again, the Basel II reforms.

Reporting Requirements

Under Basel II banks can select the level of risk management sophistication they wish to qualify for, unless regulators force them to qualify for AMA status. They will then have to make the appropriate filings with the regulators in the jurisdictions they operate in. Sarbanes-Oxley requires quarterly pass/fail reports on control effectiveness from CEOs and CFOs in SEC filings. Annual external audit opinions on those control effectiveness representations using the COSO control criteria will be required starting in 2004. Companies do not have to positively report on Compliance with the other sections of Sarbanes-Oxley. Reporting requirements are defined in the Act, in SEC final rules, and soon, by the PCAOB.

My pick: the Basel II reforms

Incentives to Comply

Basel II allows banks that can prove they have effective and sophisticated risk management systems to reduce their level of protective buffer capital, freeing up potentially hundreds of millions of dollars for investment in profitable activities.

The reforms also suggest that once a bank convinces regulators it has an effective and disciplined approach to enterprise risk management, it should attract less regulatory oversight.

Sarbanes-Oxley has created a range of incentives for companies to comply.

These include personal fines and jail sentences for senior executives, denial of an opinion on control effectiveness representations by external auditors, obtaining restitution from offending organisations for victims, and additional ammunition to de-list offending public companies.

But there are no positive benefits under Sarbanes-Oxley for public companies to distinguish themselves by having particularly good risk and control governance systems.

My choice: the Basel II reforms

Timeliness of Solution

Basel II has been under construction since the 1998. Implementation dates continue to be delayed and affected by political lobbying around the world by a range of groups with vested interests in delaying or altering the proposed reforms.

Sarbanes-Oxley was developed and passed into law in a political frenzy in a matter of months, supported by both Democrats and Republicans alike.

Large portions of the legislation became effective immediately. In spite of its failings in some areas, it has had an immediate and profound positive impact on the behaviour of companies, their officers, their boards, their auditors, their lawyers, investment advisors and others in a very short space of time.

My pick: on this it's Sarbanes-Oxley

The winner is...Basel II

There's still time to rectify the failings of Sarbanes-Oxley by moving to a regime that informs investors of the degree to which a public company manifests an "ideal" risk and control system to support reliable external disclosures.

The Malcolm Baldrige quality assessment system in the U.S. developed to improve the competitiveness of U.S. companies provides all the basic structure components necessary to implement such a system.

The 2003 COSO ERM framework provides the core raw material to build appropriate and specific evaluation criteria using modern and well-accepted principles of good governance that are highly compatible with the core components of Basel II.

The implementers of Sarbanes-Oxley can learn from the careful and practical thought contained in Basel II. The Basel supervisors should learn from Sarbanes-Oxley and recognise solutions are needed now, not sometime in the distant future.

ACKNOWLEDGEMENT AND THANKS:
The book's Author acknowledges and thanks Tim Leech,
Chief Methodology Officer of Paisley Consulting, for
contributing his White Paper to the book, as follows:

Paisley Consulting
Corporate Headquarters
400 Cokato Street East
P.O. Box 578
Cokato, MN 55321 USA
Toll free: 888.288.0283 (U.S. and Canada)
Phone: 320.286.5870 (All Other Countries)
Fax: 320.286.6196
E-mail: Tim.Leech@paisleyconsulting.com
Web: www.paisleyconsulting.com

3. Federal Deposit Insurance Corporation (FDIC)

The Federal Deposit Insurance Corporation (FDIC)[6] since 1934 preserves and promotes public confidence in the U.S. financial system by insuring deposits in banks and thrift institutions for up to $100,000; by identifying, monitoring and addressing risks to the deposit insurance funds; and by limiting the effect on the economy and the financial system when a bank or thrift institution fails. FDIC does not protect against losses due to fire, theft, or fraud, which are subject to other protections such as hazard and casualty insurance.
FDIC also does not insure Non-Deposit Investment products (such as Stocks, Mutual Funds, and Annuities) that may be sold at a bank or savings institution.

When an institution is closed by its Chartering or Primary Regulating authority, the FDIC makes payment of insured deposits to all of the failed institution's depositors as soon as possible, usually on the next business day after the closing.

Those depositors who have funds in excess of the insurance limits receive the insured portion of their funds as described above.
They also may receive a portion of their uninsured funds either at that time or as the assets of the failed institution is liquidated.

The FDIC receives no Congressional appropriations – it is funded by premiums that banks and thrift institutions pay for deposit insurance coverage and from earnings on investments in U.S. Treasury securities. With insurance funds totalling more than $44 billion, the FDIC insures

---

[6] See **www.fdic.gov** for more information

more than $3 trillion of deposits in U.S. banks and thrifts – deposits in virtually every bank and thrift in the country.

The FDIC directly examines and supervises about 5,300 banks and savings banks, more than half of the institutions in the banking system.
Banks can be chartered/licensed by the states or by the federal government. Banks chartered/licensed by states also have the choice of whether to join the Federal Reserve System.

The FDIC is the primary federal regulator of banks that are chartered/licensed by the states that do not join the Federal Reserve System.
In addition, the FDIC is the back-up supervisor for the remaining insured banks and thrift institutions.

FDIC Law, Regulations, Related Acts; Table of Contents by Category, cover:

- Section 1000 Federal Deposit Insurance Act
- Section 2000 FDIC Rules and Regulations
- Section 4000 Advisory Opinions
  Section 5000 FDIC Statements of Policy
- Section 5500 FDIC General Counsel's Opinions
- Section 6000 Bank Holding Company Act
- Section 6500 Consumer Protection
- Section 7500 FRB (Federal Reserve Bank) Regulations
- Section 8000 Misc. Statutes and Regulations

Equal Credit Opportunity (Regulation B):

In March 2003, the Federal Reserve Board adopted a final rule amending Regulation B, which implements the Equal Credit Opportunity Act (ECOA).

The ECOA prohibits discrimination in any aspect of a credit transaction on the basis of race, colour, religion, sex, national origin, age, marital status, receipt of public assistance, or the exercise of a right under the Consumer Credit Protection Act.

In addition, FDIC deals with issues concerning:

- Receivership Management
- Resolving Financial Institution Failures
- Protecting Insured Depositors Through Asset Marketing
- Customer Service Center Enquiries
- Receivership Terminations
- Protecting Insured Depositors Through Asset Marketing
- Lessons Learned Symposium

4.   Gramm-Leach-Bliley Act (GLBA)

Coverage

The law applies to about 9,500 U.S. based financial
institutions that offer financial products and services such
as securities, banking, loans and insurance.
The law impacts banks, insurance companies, mortgage
companies, securities brokers, loan brokers, some
financial or investment advisors, tax preparers, providers
of real estate settlement services and debt collectors.

GLBA defines security guidelines for bank and financial
service organizations regarding privacy of customer
information, and it have a number of specific security
objectives, to:

- Ensure security and confidentiality of customer
  information.
- Protect against anticipated threats or hazards to
  security or integrity of information.
- Protect against unauthorized access to or use of the
  customer information.

In order to attain regulatory Compliance, financial service
organizations must apply appropriate technology and
procedures to secure access and usage of data, to
ensure the physical protection of data and to create an
audit trail, showing who has had access to the data, by
what means, when information was accessed, and for
what purpose.

Compliance Requirements

Here's a brief look at the basic financial privacy
requirements of the law that financial institutions must

comply with, according to the Federal Trade Commission[7]:

Financial Institutions

The GLB Act applies to "financial institutions" - companies that offer financial products or services to individuals, like loans, financial or investment advice, or insurance.

The Federal Trade Commission has authority to enforce the law with respect to "financial institutions" that are not covered by the federal banking agencies, the Securities and Exchange Commission, the Commodity Futures Trading Commission, and state insurance authorities.

Consumers and Customers

A company's obligations under the GLB Act depend on whether the company has consumers or customers who obtain its services.
A *consumer* is an individual who obtains or has obtained a financial product or service from a financial institution for personal, family or household reasons.
A customer *is* a consumer with a continuing relationship with a financial institution.
Generally, if the relationship between the financial institution and the individual is significant and/or long-term, the individual is a customer of the institution.

For example, a person who gets a mortgage from a lender or hires a broker to get a personal loan is considered a customer of the lender or the broker, while a person who uses a check-cashing service is a consumer of that service.

---

[7] See **www.ftc.gov** for more information

The Privacy Notice

The privacy notice must be a clear, conspicuous, and accurate statement of the company's privacy practices; it should include what information the company collects about its consumers and customers, with whom it shares the information, and how it protects or safeguards the information.
The notice applies to the "non-public personal information" the company gathers and discloses about its consumers and customers; in practice, that may be most - or all - of the information a company has about them.

For example, non-public personal information could be information that a consumer or customer puts on an application; information about the individual from another source, such as a credit bureau; or information about transactions between the individual and the company, such as an account balance.

Opt-Out Rights

Consumers and customers have the right to opt out of - or say no to - having their information shared with certain third parties.
The privacy notice must explain how, and offer a reasonable way, as to how they can opt out.
For example, providing a toll-free telephone number or a detachable form with a pre-printed address is a reasonable way for consumers or customers to opt out; requiring someone to write a letter as the only way to opt out is not.

Receiving Non-public Personal Information

The GLB Act puts some limits on how anyone that receives non-public personal information from a financial institution can use or re-disclose the information.

Take the case of a lender that discloses customer information to a service provider responsible for mailing account statements, where the consumer has no right to opt out.
The service provider may use the information for limited purposes - that is, for mailing account statements. It may not sell the information to other organizations or use it for marketing.

Other Provisions

Other important provisions of the GLB Act also impact how a company conducts business.

For example, financial institutions are prohibited from disclosing their customers' account numbers to non-affiliated companies when it comes to telemarketing, direct mail marketing or other marketing through e-mail, even if the individuals have not opted out of sharing the information for marketing purposes.

Another provision prohibits "pretexting" - the dishonest practice of obtaining customer information from financial institutions under false pretences.

5. Health Insurance Portability and Accountability Act (HIPAA)

Coverage

According to the Centers for Medicare and Medicaid Services' (CMS) website[8], Title I of HIPAA protects U.S. based health insurance coverage for workers and their families when they change or lose their jobs.
The Administrative Simplification Provisions (ASP) requires the establishment of national standards for electronic health care transactions and national identifiers for providers, health insurance plans, and employers.

The ASP provisions also address the security and privacy of health data. The standards are meant to improve the efficiency and effectiveness of the nation's health care system by encouraging the widespread use of electronic data interchange in health care.

HIPAA's Administrative Simplification Provisions (ASP)

The ASP are only applicable to "covered entities", which include healthcare providers (e.g. doctors, clinics and hospitals) which engage in electronic transactions subject to the HIPAA / EDI (Electronic Data Interchange) rules below, health plans, including health insurance companies and employer-sponsored "group health plans", and also healthcare clearinghouses.

A clearinghouse is an agency that is responsible for settling health insurance related accounts, collecting and maintaining margin cash, regulating delivery and reporting data. The clearinghouse becomes the buyer to each seller

---

[8] See http://en.wikipedia.org/wiki/HIPAA for more information

(and the seller to each buyer) and assumes responsibility for protecting buyers and sellers from financial loss by assuring performance on each contract.

HIPAA's Privacy Provision (PP)

The PP measures include:

- Individuals must be able to access their record and request correction of errors
- Individuals must be informed of how their personal information will be used.
- Individuals "Protected Health Information" (PHI) cannot be used for marketing purposes without the explicit consent of the involved patients.
- Individuals can ask their covered entities which maintain PHI about them to take reasonable steps to ensure that their communications with the patient are confidential.
- Individuals can file formal privacy-related complaints to the Department of Health and Health and Human Services (HHS) Office for Civil Rights.

Key EDI Transactions (and related information)

These measures concern:

- 837: Medical claims with subtypes for Professional, Institutional, and Dental varieties.
- 820: Payroll Deducted and Other Group Premium Payment for Insurance Products
- 834: Benefits enrolment and maintenance
- 835: Electronic remittances
- 270 / 271: Eligibility inquiry and response
- 276 / 277: Claim status inquiry and response
- 278: Health Services Review request and reply

HIPAA's Administrative Safeguards

Covered entities (entities that must comply with HIPAA requirements) must adopt a written set of privacy procedures and designate a privacy officer to be responsible for developing and implementing all required policies and procedures.
The policies and procedures must reference management oversight and organizational buy-in to Compliance with the documented security controls.

Procedures should clearly identify employees or classes of employees who have access to Protected Health Information (PHI). Access to PHI in all forms must be restricted to only those employees who have a need for it to complete their job function.
The procedures must address access authorization, establishment, modification, and termination, and related business and IT processes and controls.

Entities must show that an appropriate ongoing training program regarding the handling PHI is provided to employees performing health plan administrative functions.
Covered entities that out-source some of their business processes to a third party must ensure that their vendors also have a framework in place to comply with HIPAA requirements.

Companies typically gain this assurance through clauses in the contracts stating that the vendor will meet the same data protection requirements that apply to the covered entity. Care must be taken to determine if the vendor further out-sources any data handling functions to other vendors and monitor whether appropriate contracts and controls are in place.

A contingency plan should be in place for responding to emergencies. Covered entities are responsible for backing up their data and having disaster recovery procedures in place.

The plan should document data priority and failure analysis, testing activities, and change control procedures.

Internal audits play a key role in HIPAA Compliance by reviewing operations with the goal of identifying potential security violations. Policies and procedures should specifically document the scope, frequency, and procedures of audits. Audits should be both routine and event-based.

Procedures should document instructions for addressing and responding to security breaches that are identified either during the audit or the normal course of operations.

HIPAA's Physical Safeguards

Controlling physical access to protect against inappropriate access to protected data
Responsibility for security must be assigned to a specific person or department. This responsibility includes the management and oversight of data protection and personnel conduct with respect to data protection.

Frequently, a Chief Security Officer (CSO) position is established to fulfil this requirement. This position typically reports to executive level management.

Controls must govern the introduction and removal of hardware and software from the network. (When equipment is retired it must be disposed of properly to ensure that PHI is not compromised.)

Access to equipment containing health information should be carefully controlled and monitored.

Access to hardware and software must be limited to properly authorized individuals.
Required access controls consist of facility security plans, maintenance records, and visitor sign-in and escorts.

Policies are required to address proper workstation use. Workstations should be removed from high traffic areas and monitor screens should not be in direct view of the public.
If the covered entities utilize contractors or agents, they too must be fully trained on their physical access responsibilities.

HIPAA's Technical Safeguards

Controlling access to computer and IT systems and enabling covered entities to protect communications containing PHI transmitted electronically over open networks from being intercepted by anyone other than the intended recipient.

Information systems housing PHI must be protected from intrusion. When information flows over open networks, some form of encryption must be utilized.
If closed systems / networks are utilized, existing access controls are considered sufficient and encryption is optional.

Each covered entity is responsible for ensuring that the data within its systems has not been changed or erased in an unauthorized manner.
Data corroboration, including the use of check sum, double keying, message authentication, and digital signature may be used to ensure data integrity.

Covered entities must also authenticate entities it communicates with. Authentication consists of corroborating that an entity is who it claims to be.

Examples of corroboration include: password systems, two or three-way handshakes, telephone call back, and token systems.
Covered entities must make documentation of their HIPAA practices available to the government to determine Compliance.

In addition to policies and procedures and access records, information technology documentation should also include a written record of all configuration settings on the components of the network because these components are complex, configurable, and always changing.
Documented risk analysis and risk management programs are required. Covered entities must carefully consider the risks of their operations as they implement systems to comply with the act.
(The requirement of risk analysis and risk management implies that the act's security requirements are a minimum standard and places responsibility on covered entities to take all reasonable precautions necessary to prevent PHI from being used for non-health purposes.)

The following Chapter outlines a typical application to assist IT Compliance with HIPAA.

6. Ecora's Practical Guide To Implementing HIPAA IT Security Standards[9]

Introduction

HIPAA, the Health Insurance Portability and Accountability Act of 1996, has probably already had a significant impact on your IT department. The 45 CFR Part 164 security regulations and the April 21, 2005 deadline have broad implications to corporate policies regarding the security and confidentiality of individual health information managed by your IT staff.

To ensure Compliance and meet federally mandated Compliance requirements; organizations must formally evaluate their administrative procedures, networks, and applications to meet HIPAA requirements.

Many health-related businesses have been working to achieve Compliance over the past few years. They have parts of the Compliance model in place but continue to struggle to build a comprehensive sustainable system. A review of the security standards shows that many of the requirements can be filled with accurate documentation of information held within the configuration data of your infrastructure.

Automation of the IT infrastructure documentation process, with the right tools, can significantly reduce the cost and time of Compliance. This paper is about documenting your IT infrastructure as part of a "best business practice" plan for Compliance with HIPAA security standards.

[9] This White Paper was reprinted with some editing by kind permission of Ecora Software Corporation - see Acknowledgement at the end of this Chapter.

IT Documentation: How it applies to HIPAA

The inevitable evolution of the information age within the health care industry was secured by the passage of HIPAA (Public Law 104-191).

The Final Rule adopting HIPAA standards for the security of electronic health information was published in the Federal Register on February 20, 2003. This final rule (45 CFR Part 164) specifies a series of administrative, technical, and physical security procedures for covered entities to assure the confidentiality of electronic protected health information.
These regulations are far-reaching and require due diligence to Compliance on the part of all health care providers, health care plans, and health care clearinghouses, considered "covered entities" under HIPAA.
The security regulations set standards for ensuring a secure Information Technology (IT) enterprise-wide network on which the individual identifiable health information is housed.
Compliance can be viewed as an insurmountable task or as an opportunity to develop enterprise-wide solutions to standardize and simplify health information networks.
Although this is not a "technology" law, an integral part of Compliance to the privacy standards is Compliance with the security standards for electronic health information.
The protection of private medical information, as covered by the privacy rules, falls under the security rules.

The IT architecture within the Information System (IS) plan of an organization is key to the success and Compliance of the business.
Building the security strategy of IT networks protects the privacy of individual health information and avoids potential civil and criminal penalties, while reducing the organization's potential security breaches, liability, and

possible loss to business reputation. Negative publicity in local and national news compromises a health care organization's standing in the industry and the public's view.

Organizational policies and procedures need to be enterprise-wide to ensure an effective security plan. Individual departmental policies for the secure and confidential handling of private medical information will not meet Compliance with HIPAA. Accrediting agencies look for documentation to prove that policies exist and are followed as written.
In accreditation terms: "If it isn't documented, it isn't done."

What is IT Documentation?

IT documentation is a written record of all the configuration settings on the components of a network. These components include servers, applications, routers, switches, databases, and more. Documentation is needed because these components are extraordinarily complex, configurable, and always changing.

Technical staff is often responsible for large numbers of servers and devices, each with a complex collection of settings. IT documentation can provide a central repository of all the relevant information for these settings, their impact, and their values or options.

IT Documentation General Benefits

A thorough understanding of your existing systems significantly improves your planning and management of the IT infrastructure.

This process starts with detailed documentation and has not always been a priority because it requires time and resources.

Most organizations rarely (if ever) document IT infrastructures because, until now, system documentation could only be done manually. By the time a system was entirely documented, the process had to begin all over again to stay current.

Good IT documentation lets you:

- Create "Auditor-Ready" documents on demand
- Detect security vulnerabilities
- Simplify server consolidation and network servers
- Understand dependencies between parts of the network
- Optimize network and system configuration
- Standardize configuration settings across all networks and systems
- Accelerate problem resolution and troubleshooting
- Migrate to new platforms: knowing that baseline and subsequent changes are critical
- Manage and preserve system knowledge despite IT staff changes
- Speed up Disaster Recovery
- Educate new staff and consultants on the organization's IT infrastructure
- Create a standardized "workbook" for outside consultants

Documentation helps streamline migration to new information management applications and new platforms. These products depend on a well-designed network infrastructure. Studying the existing environment prior to migration helps to plan how you want to reconfigure it to make it more efficient.

IT Documentation Cost/Benefits

- One of the highest costs of Information Systems is the IT staff. Trying to deal with the tasks associated with the initial and continual documentation of network servers can keep IT staff from completing higher priority projects. Software that automatically documents current network server configurations in minutes in plain-English reports can be less than 10% of the cost of hiring an IT professional to do the same and requires virtually no time / attention from your current staff.
- The quality, utility, and consistency of the information collected are critical for disaster recovery, IT audits, IT staff training, and certification or accreditation agencies.
- Downtime is minimized because current, consistent, and accurate documentation is available for reference. IT systems should be available at all times to provide real-time availability of patient health information to those authorized to access it.
- Due to the increasing demand for a decreasing supply of trained IT professionals, staff turnover can be high.
- Therefore, an efficient method of knowledge retention and transfer is crucial. The right documentation becomes the basis for training new staff with up-to-date information.
- Security skills and resources are scarce. As organization's move from HIPAA awareness to assessment, development, and finally implementation of Compliance plans; demand for these resources will only increase as the 2005 Compliance deadline nears. The sooner core tools are in place, the lower the risk of added expense in a last-minute rush.

The Importance of Server Configuration Settings

Servers are the last line of IT security defences. They are managed through their settings. Documenting server configuration settings provides: a record of how the server is configured, a check for inconsistencies and potential security vulnerabilities, and a useful troubleshooting tool. IT system configurations change regularly.
Since it is essential that all servers and devices are configured to meet corporate HIPAA Compliance plans and policies, IT documentation of server configurations should be a fundamental component of any HIPAA-compliant plan to ensure consistent, documented Compliance.

Network and Server Configuration Documentation

You can document your network and servers manually. However, it is time consuming, seldom current, and often inaccurate. It also uses valuable staff resources for a mundane task.
Prior to automation, if network servers were documented at all, it was expensive and tedious.

Documenting network servers can also be a record-keeping nightmare. The basic steps, in order of occurrence are:

1. Find all the servers on the network.
2. Find the servers' owners and physical locations (this can take days or weeks depending on the size of the organization).
3. Get access to the servers, assuming the owners are cooperative.
4. Locate, record, and examine configuration settings (this requires knowledge of where settings are stored,

access to the data/interfaces, and time to open the applications and files required).
5. Interpret the data and settings gathered. Much or all of the information is in "raw-data" format, requiring definition, organization, and explanation to be comprehensible.
6. Produce a report with varying levels of detail appropriate for various audiences, IT staff, Configuration Auditors, accreditation organizations, and Compliance auditors.
7. Return to step 1 and repeat the process continually.

Today, the above steps can be done in less time than it takes to make a cup of coffee. Automated documentation tools are available that build consistent, current, and comprehensive plain-English reports for you.
These easily attainable and readable reports of network and server configurations provide valuable knowledge of the IT system. This knowledge is crucial for the optimal use of IT staff and IT budgets.

Back-up Tapes and Back-up Documentation for Network Servers

45 CFR 164 requires all covered entities to have in place contingency plans to recover form emergencies or disasters. It requires:

- Data backup plan
- Disaster Recovery Plan
- Emergency mode operation plan

Backup tapes typically record raw data, not core configuration settings. The tapes are usually stored offline or offsite and the data is retrieved in the event of a problem or corruption.

IT system configurations aren't necessarily "backed-up" unless there is a software program on the system specifically designed for this.

Most programs only provide server configuration data in partial or raw-data format and the files require a high-level IT professional to decipher and then reconfigure the servers. If you were not the one who originally installed and configured the servers, you might have quite a time restoring the servers without readily available, readable documentation.

Backing up network servers provides information on configuration settings before a disaster occurs. It is important to bring the servers to a state of known configuration settings that worked within the IT security network environment prior to a disaster event.

For example, one server might have many different applications that require very specific server configurations on one machine, i.e., Windows NT/2000 and Exchange. Reconfiguring a system from memory or multiple incomplete or generic sources is a fast track to a living nightmare.

IT Documentation, Risk Analysis and Management

HIPAA security standards require both risk analysis and risk management.
Risk analysis is the process of selecting cost-effective security/control measures by comparing costs of control measures against losses that would be incurred if the measures were not in place.
During the analysis, it is important to identify any security risks, assess the probability of an occurrence of a security risk, and analyze the potential adverse impact is if a security breach occurs.

Risk management is the process of assessing risk, taking steps to reduce risk to an acceptable level, and maintaining that level of risk.
Using IT documentation data can help you discover security vulnerabilities. An on-going automated configuration management system can help manage and mitigate infrastructure risks.

What is the difference between a Security Audit and an IT audit?

HIPAA defines security as mechanisms to guard data integrity, confidentiality, and availability. The HIPAA Security Matrix is comprised of three categories: administrative, physical, and technical safeguards. Security audits include both physical and informational components of security. Administrative safeguards are information policies such as documenting the IT infrastructure surrounding the data of a healthcare organization: servers, databases, workstations, routers and/or any points of network access.

IT audits encompass some of the physical security audits and all of the information audits. The IT department must have documentation of where hardware components physically exist: the shelf, the room, the floor, the building, the location, the city, and the country.
IT audit trail documentation must provide a snapshot of who has access privileges to which servers and if any changes were made to the servers from one point in time to another.
They must also document everyone who has physical access to those components at those locations.

The IT department must also audit all of their components from a technology perspective. Configuration settings affect how the components of the network interact with each other from both inside and outside the network. The IT audit provides knowledge that is key to how an organization's network is functioning, to the security of the patient information stored there, and to the survival of the business.

Specific HIPAA Security Rules

The security rules required by HIPAA are spelled out in detail in the Federal Register, Part II, Department of Health and Human Services, Office of the Secretary, 45 CFR Parts 160, 162, and 164 Health Insurance Reform: Security Standards; Final Rule.

The closing part of this Chapter segments security standards into Administrative, Physical, and Technical safeguards. IT configuration documentation can provide audit ready Compliance within a number of Administrative and Technical areas.

HIPAA Security Standards

45 CFR 164 requires that covered entities ensure that electronic information is protected in terms of confidentiality, integrity, and availability.
This pertains to protected health information created, received, maintained, or transmitted. It also stipulates that Compliance is required at the workforce level. It's not enough to have a good plan – you need to make it actionable.

Another requirement is that the security measures you implement must be reviewed and modified as needed to "continue provision of reasonable and appropriate protection of electronic protected health information…"This points out the need to build a system that is self sustaining wherever possible.

The record-keeping burden associated with meeting and maintaining Compliance documentation will vary depending upon individual business needs and the size of the organization.

The form, format, or degree of documentation necessary to demonstrate Compliance is relative to the extent of the IT network.

Administrative, Physical, and Technical Safeguards

The HIPAA security standard is defined in three segments of safeguards: Administrative, Physical, and Technical.

Administrative safeguards are policies, procedures, and actions that specify how to define, implement and manage the overall security measures for protected health information. It also includes security management of the workforce.

Physical safeguards cover physical aspects of a covered entity's electronic information systems protection.

Technical safeguards address the technology and the policies and procedures in place to protect the electronic health information it accesses.

IT documentation can play a significant role in preparing covered entities for Compliance in the administrative and technical area.

HIPAA IT Security Standards Compliance and Ecora Auditor

As discussed earlier, IT documentation can help you meet HIPAA Compliance mandates. The Tables below show how, in the areas of administrative and technical safeguards. This data is meant to be a working template rather than a comprehensive solution.

In the following Tables, the first column is a defined security safeguard from 45 CFR164. The second column specifies an action that validates Compliance with the safeguard. Column three shows the Ecora Auditor report that documents validation.

Table 6.1: Administrative safeguards

Security Safeguard	Compliance Validation	Ecora Report For Validation
Information system activity review (Required). Implement procedures to regularly review records of information system activity, such as audit logs, access reports, and security incident tracking reports.	Ensure strong audit policy configured to ensure audit trail of events is recorded to provide audit trail of user activity (e.g. account login events, policy change, object access, process tracking, etc.)	Audit Policy
	Enable audit events to provide audit trail of user activity	Auditing Enabled
	Enable Archive Log Mode to allow point in time recovery to ensure data not lost when recovering	Archive Log Mode
	Ensure event log setting are configured to retain recorded events for appropriate time and prevent guest access to logs	Event Log
Termination procedures (Addressable). Implement procedures for terminating access to electronic protected health information when the employment of a workforce member ends or as required by determinations made	Select sample of terminated employees and determine if their access has been removed	User Access

as specified in paragraph (a)(3)(ii)(B) of this section.		
Access Authorization (Addressable). Implement policies and procedures for granting access to electronic protected health information, for example, through access to a workstation, transaction, program, process, or other mechanism.	Ensure strong password and account lockout policies are implemented.	Password Policy
	Ensure appropriate database authentication mode is configured	Authentication Mode
Protection from malicious software (Addressable). Procedures for guarding against, detecting, and reporting malicious software.	Ensure systems are updated with appropriate service packs and hot fixes	Patch Levels
	Ensure anti-virus software installed on systems	Computer without Ant-virus Installed
	Review installed applications on all relevant systems.	Installed Application by Computer
Log-in monitoring (Addressable). Procedures for monitoring log-in attempts and reporting discrepancies.	Validate that attempts to gain unauthorized access to financial reporting system are logged and followed up.	Failed Login, Frequently Failed Login
Password management (Addressable). Procedures for creating, changing, and safeguarding passwords.	Prove adequate password validation in place	Password Lifetime, Password Grace Period, Password Reuse Time, Failed Login

		Attempts, Password Lock Time
Disaster recovery plan (Required). Establish (and implement as needed) procedures to restore any loss of data.	Restore selected configuration data and compare to see if its accurate	Change Report
	Review selected server configuration data and compare with baseline data	Consolidated Change Report

Table 6.2: Technical safeguards

Security Safeguard	Compliance Validation	Ecora Report For Validation
Access control. Implement technical policies and procedures for electronic information systems that maintain electronic protected health information to allow access only to those persons or software programs that have been granted access rights as specified in § 164.308(a)(4).	Ensure all logins have passwords and not default password	Login Password
	Review role memberships and permissions to ensure appropriate access and privileges to databases	Role Permissions & Memberships
	Select a sample of new users and determine if access granted matches access approved	User Access

	Select a sample of current users and review access privileges to determine if rights are appropriate for job function	User Access
Unique user identification (Required). Assign a unique name and/or number for identifying and tracking user identity.	Ensure Verify Function exists and valid to ensure user passwords are validated and strong password criteria required	Verify Function
Audit controls. Implement hardware, software, and/or procedural mechanisms that record and examine activity in information systems that contain or use electronic protected health information.	Ensure strong audit policy configured to ensure audit trail of events is recorded to provide audit trail of user activity (e.g. account login events, policy change, object access, process tracking, etc.)	Audit Policy
	Enable audit events to provide audit trail of user activity	Auditing Enabled
	Enable Archive Log Mode to allow point in time recovery to ensure data not lost when recovering	Archive Log Mode
	Ensure event log setting are configured to retain recorded events for appropriate time and prevent guest access to logs	Event Log

97

Integrity. Implement policies and procedures to protect electronic protected health information from improper alteration or destruction	Audit and review user privileges on each system	User Privileges
	Audit and review system access permissions to sensitive files	NTFS (NT File System) Permissions
	Ensure systems configured to restrict anonymous remote access to your systems.	Remote Access
	Identify all public database links. Review and replace with private links as appropriate to restrict access to confidential data	Public Links
Mechanism to authenticate electronic protected health information (Addressable). Implement electronic mechanisms to corroborate that electronic protected health information has not been altered or destroyed in an unauthorized manner.	Set Initialization Parameters to provide security and ensure database auditing is active	Initialization Parameters
	Audit and review DB owner for each database	DB Owner

Person or entity authentication. Implement procedures to verify that a person or entity seeking access to electronic protected health information is the one claimed.	Ensure strong password and account lockout policies are implemented.	Password Policy
	Ensure Verify Function exists and valid to ensure user passwords are validated and strong password criteria required	Verify Function
Transmission Security. Implement technical security measures to guard against unauthorized access to electronic health information that is being transmitted over an electronic communications network	Confirm that standard server configuration is documented and implemented	Baseline Report
	Review relevant infrastructure components to determine if they adhere to organization's policies.	OS and Service Pack Report by Computer Role
	Ensure all services are configured appropriately and that only required services are running to protect system from unauthorized access	Services Summary

	If using SNMP ensure appropriate Community String(s) defined to prevent unauthorized users from obtaining systems status information	SNMP

Summary

Until recently, creating comprehensive documentation and keeping it current was tedious, time-consuming, expensive, and not legally mandated.

Federal HIPAA law makes improved data management and the real-time availability of secure and confidential patient information a critical part of doing business in the health care industry.
The common backbone of each of these is the IT systems on which the information resides. The implementation of security matrixes that meet the Compliance requirements of HIPAA is best served by having core tools on which to build and maintain an organization's IT infrastructure.

Being able to provide automated documentation of IT servers, with little human intervention, is a technology value-added solution to the HIPAA security Compliance requirements facing health care organizations.
Best practices need best solutions. Documentation is the key to proving an organization's Compliance with HIPAA.
REMEMBER: IF IT ISN'T DOCUMENTED IT ISN'T DONE.

ACKNOWLEDGEMENT AND THANKS:
The book's Author acknowledges and thanks Ecora
Software Corporation, for contributing the White Paper to
the book, as follows:

Ecora Software Corporation
Two International Drive, Suite 150
Portsmouth, NH 03801 USA
Phone: 877.923.2672
Fax: 603.436.4344
Email: feedback@ecora.com
Web: www.ecora.com

7.   International Financial Reporting Standards (IFRS)

Coverage

International Financial Reporting Standards (IFRS)[10] along with International Accounting Standards (IAS) are a set of accounting standards.

Currently - the International Accounting Standards Board (IASB) issues them.

Although IASs are no longer produced, they are still in effect unless replaced by a new IFRS, either in part or completely.

IFRSs are considered a "principles-based" set of standards, in that they establish broad rules rather than dictating specific treatments.

As of 2002 a number of IFRSs offer the preparer choices of treatments; the IASB's Improvements Project is seeking to reduce these choices.

In addition, the IASB co-operates with national accounting standard-setters to achieve convergence in accounting standards around the world.

IAS Standards

International Accounting Standards (IAS) currently in use:

- IFRS 1 First-time Adoption of International Financial Reporting Standards
- IFRS 2 Share-based Payment
- IFRS 3 Business Combinations
- IFRS 4 Insurance Contracts
- IFRS 5 Non-current Assets Held for Sale and Discontinued Operations

---

[10] See **www.ifrs.co.uk** for more information

- IAS 1: Presentation of Financial Statements
- IAS 2: Inventories
- IAS 7: Cash Flow Statements
- IAS 8: Net Profit or Loss for the Period, Fundamental Errors and Changes in Accounting practices
- IAS 10: Events After the Balance Sheet Date
- IAS 11: Construction Contracts
- IAS 12: Income Taxes
- IAS 14: Segment Reporting
- IAS 15: Information Reflecting the Effects of Changing Prices
- IAS 16: Property, Plant and Equipment
- IAS 17: Leases
- IAS 18: Revenue
- IAS 19: Employee Benefits
- IAS 20: Accounting for Government Grants and Disclosure of Government Assistance
- IAS 21: The Effects of Changes in Foreign Exchange Rates
- IAS 22: Business Combinations
- IAS 23: Borrowing Costs
- IAS 24: Related Party Disclosures
- IAS 26: Accounting and Reporting by Retirement Benefit Plans
- IAS 27: Consolidated Financial Statements
- IAS 28: Investments in Associates
- IAS 29: Financial Reporting in Hyperinflationary Economies
- IAS 30: Disclosures in the Financial Statements of Banks and Similar Financial Institutions
- IAS 31: Financial Reporting of Interests in Joint Ventures
- IAS 32: Financial Instruments: Disclosure and Presentation
- IAS 33: Earnings per Share
- IAS 34: Interim Financial Reporting
- IAS 35: Discontinuing Operations
- IAS 36: Impairment of Assets

- IAS 37: Provisions, Contingent Liabilities and Contingent Assets
- IAS 38: Intangible Assets
- IAS 39: Financial Instruments: Recognition and Measurement
- IAS 40: Investment Property
- IAS 41: Agriculture

IFRS Subject Headings

IFRS – General Purpose subject headings:

- Balance Sheet, Classified Format
- Balance Sheet, Order of Liquidity Format
- Balance Sheet, Net Assets Format
- Balance Sheet, Portfolio Format
- Income Statement, By Function Format
- Income Statement, By Nature Format
- Income Statement, Financial Institutions
- Cash Flow, Direct Method
- Cash Flow, Indirect Method
- Cash Flow, Direct Method, Financial Institutions
- Cash Flow, Indirect Method, Financial Institutions
- Statement of Changes in Equity
- Accounting Policies
- Accounting Policies, Financial Institutions
- Explanatory Disclosures
- Explanatory Disclosures, Financial Institutions
- Classes
- Classes, Financial Institutions
- Current / Non Current Classification
- Net / Gross Classification
- Code Lists
- First Time Adoption of IFRS
- Other

8.   Markets in Financial Instruments Directive (MiFID)

Summary

MiFID is a new regulatory framework for the European Financial Markets (Directive 2004/39/EC), dictated by the EU Commission.
It replaces the Investment Services Directive (ISD), which has been in place since 1993.
The date set for coming into effect is 1 November 2007, in order to give firms more time to prepare for the legislation.

MiFID has the following major objectives:

- Market transparency and greater protection of the retail investor will become dominant
- Investment firms authorized to operate within one regulatory jurisdiction in one country in Europe can do so across all EU jurisdictions.
- All EU regulatory standards between those jurisdictions will become harmonised and uniform for the sake of equality, standardisation and transparency.

Investors and investment institutions can transact freely across borders under the same terms and conditions, and issuers can have access to wider, deeper and more liquid markets, and hidden liquidity would be shown to all participants.
MiFID includes over 70 articles, which will impact trading exchanges, banks, brokers, pension and asset managers, issuers, investment and financial service providers, and regulators operating within the EU.

Entities external to the EU will also need to consider their position, because the new Compliance rules are designed to be attractive to investors worldwide. Should investors from the US or Australia, for example, wish to trade in the EU, they may do so with EU registered entities instead of using their local service providers in their own home countries.

This is both a similar and reverse scenario, whereby an SEC registered entity from the UK or Europe, must comply with Sarbanes-Oxley Act (for example) and possibly other mandates in order to trade in the US. Likewise, foreign firms from outside the EU, who have local registered entities in the EU, must comply with MiFID and possibly with other European mandates.

With globalisation very much evident and still growing, it is highly likely that any new EU or US mandate or directive will become international and impact firms trading across the globe, almost regardless where they are physically based.

MiFID's scope and level of detail are very comprehensive and the majority of these obligations cover:

- All financial instruments, including equities, bonds, and money market instruments, Foreign Exchange, and all types of derivative.
- Multi-lateral Trading Facility (MTF), Over The Counter (OTC) and Systematic Internalizer (SI) to cover the activities of institutions that effectively act like exchanges.
- Banks within the EU will be able to trade shares internally and off an exchange respectively but will be required to publish the prices of intended trades to the rest of the market beforehand.
- Much greater transparent conduct and openness than ever before.
- Best practice in the interest of investors and interfacing institutions.

MiFID Impact and Key Issues

MiDIF will affect financial organisations and entities throughout the EU, and possibly world wide, in a number of ways, which are short listed below:

- The impact of MiFID will vary for different firms, depending on how well the companies have prepared themselves
- Current national and possibly international market practice and accepted norms will be effected
- An investment firm in a specific regulatory jurisdiction and existing standard of best practice may already be close to complying with certain elements of the directive whereas other firms may not
- The effort to comply with the requirements of MiFID for each type of investment firm and financial marketplace will vary in differing regulatory jurisdictions
- Key issues concerning MiFID are:
  - Type of customer (i.e. private/retail, professional, Eligible Counter-Party [ECP] classification)
  - More obligations will be imposed on firms doing business with professional customers
  - Compliant entities will adhere in particular to business conduct rules when providing investment advice to ECPs
  - Customers may be classified according to different products or services
- Pre- and post-trade transparency obligations will initially be limited to equities but subsequently the mandate may be extended to the other asset classes
- Categorises pre- and post-trade regimes will include Regulated Markets (RMs) and Multilateral Trading Facilities (MTFs)
- Firms' best-practice-execution obligations will ensure the best possible deal for customers, taking into account not just price (as of now) but also other

parameters, such as cost, speed, and the likelihood of execution and settlement

- Firms will be required to establish and implement an order execution policy to allow them to obtain best possible execution
- Investment entities will have to monitor the efficacy of their chosen execution venues to achieve best execution compared to alternatives at least to an annual basis
- Investment entities will be required to advise their customers of any material changes to their execution venues
- Customers must receive from the firm adequate reports on the service provided and these reports should include the costs associated with the transactions and services undertaken on behalf of the customer
- This will result in increase of trade reporting obligations for equities in the first instance and other asset classes in due time
- Entities must have suitable frameworks and controls in place to prevent a conflict of interests adversely affecting their clients' best interests to ensure that these interests are not compromised and customers must be notified accordingly

IT Aspects

Sophisticated and costly data management and information reporting systems will be required to cope with MiFID.
An all embracing applications' platform that enables access to, and process messages for the world's leading back-office and real-time data feeds in an automated fashion will be needed, with huge investment costs.

Typically, such a platform will involve:

- Day-to-day Data transactions and Management
- Automation (routing, reporting, on-screen display)
- Task Scheduling / Workflow
- Data Requests
- Data Downloads
- Data Communications
- Data Conversions
- Data Storage and Retrieval
- Data Search Engine
- File Transfer Protocol (FTP) (see below)
- Metadata and Process Mapping (see below)
- Data Mutation and Management (see below)
- Data Reformatting
- Data Cleansing
- Exception Handling
- Reconciliation
- Security Master File (see below)
- Golden Copy File Management (see below)
- Export into target and out of source applications

Metadata and Process Mapping

Metadata is a definition or description of data and information and how it hangs together. This includes object links and relationships, both hierarchical and sideways, and how data process mapping illustrate the manipulation of such objects or data elements, depending on preset conditions, process and exception rules.
In information manipulation and data processing, metadata is definitional data that provides information about, or documentation of, other data managed within an application or environment.

For instance, metadata would document data about data elements or attributes, (name, size, data type etc.) and data about records or data structures (length, fields, columns etc.) and data about data (where it is located, how it is associated, ownership, etc.). Metadata may

include descriptive information about the context, quality and condition, or characteristics of the data.
For instance, the data of a report is the headline and actual content, whereas the metadata describes who wrote it, when and where it was published, and so on and so forth.

Data Mutation and Management

In biology, cell mutations are changes to the genetic material (usually DNA or RNA) – life building blocks. Mutations can be caused by copying errors in the genetic material during cell division and by exposure to radiation, chemicals, or viruses, or can occur deliberately under cellular control during the corruption processes.
In multicultural organisms, mutations can be subdivided into *germ line-sequential mutations,* which can be passed on to progeny; and *somatic mutations,* which cannot be transmitted to the offspring.

Mutations, when accidental, often lead to the malfunction or death of a cell and can cause cancer.
Some as the driving force of evolution considers mutations, where less favourable (*deleterious*) mutations are removed from the gene pool by natural selection, while more favourable (*beneficial* or *advantageous*) ones tend to accumulate.
Neutral mutations are defined as mutations whose effects do not influence the fitness of either the species or the individuals who make up the species, at least in the short term.
Likewise, data corruption or mutations act in a somewhat similar way to the biological model discussed above, and if remained unchecked and not corrected, it could cause havoc in financial markets, systems and records world wide, and involve huge costs and non-Compliance.
See also STP below.

THIS IS A CENTRAL ISSUE NOT JUST FOR MiFID BUT ALSO FOR ALL OTHER COMPLIANCE MANDATES, AND IT MUST BE MANAGED AND MITIGATED EFFECTIVELY AND EFFICIENTLY.

Security Master File (SMF) and FTP

The Security Master File (SMF), among other things, is central to MiFID and other relevant regulatory measures, because it provides detailed information[11] concerning:

- Date of Issue and Incorporation Date
- Eligibility Status and Custodian Information (location and type of custody, e.g., book-entry-only)
- Restriction Indicators (deposit, withdrawals, trade reporting, settlement)
- Security Features (which trigger the automated creation of entitlement, including corporate action etc.)
- A database file (called the 7030 file) of electronic text files of securities information, including: a detail record, market/symbol record or ticker, restriction and feature records relevant to different types of securities. For example, identifying distribution frequency, effective date, expiry date, period and interest compounding method
- An update file (called the 7031 file) sent daily to subscribers with updates and additions to the SMF, identifying: new preliminary issues (entered on the previous day but not yet confirmed), deleted preliminary issues (deleted overnight), new confirmed issues, changes in status of confirmed issues (changed to inactive or deleted), changes to details of confirmed issues.

---

[11] See: **http://www.cds.ca/cdshome.nsf** - The Canadian Depository for Securities Limited (CDS)

111

The 7030 and 7031 file feeds can be provided virtually anywhere in the world by File Transfer Protocol (FTP) through a secure connection over a leased line for clearing and settlement processing.

Straight Through Processing (STP)

According to the Tower Group, corporate action processing is still seen as a significant problem. Almost 80% of the firms surveyed cite "inconsistent, inaccurate and incomplete reference data as the major cause of internal Straight Through Processing (STP) failure".

According to a 2003 study, reference data is characterized as 'decentralized' (respondents had an average of 43 systems containing client and counterparty data and 37 systems containing securities data)!
Lacking automation is another issue (respondents cite an average 58 FTEs – Full Time Equivalent staff - to maintain reference data).
It is expensive too, and cost an average of US $3.2 million per year to acquire and maintain data!
It is causing increased operational risk (30% of trade failure is a direct result of inaccurate reference data).
Accordingly, reference data projects were being considered a top or high priority by over 60% of respondents.

Golden Copy File

According to the University of Edinburgh's Records Management Section, Freedom of Information (Scotland) Act 2002, the Data Protection Act 1998, and records management, FAQ[12]:

---

[12] See: **http://www.recordsmanagement.ed.ac.uk**

"The 'golden copy' is the official, master version of a record. There can only be one golden copy of each record. A golden copy exists from the point of creation of a record not just once the record is no longer used. It is important to remember that the golden copy of a record exists for all stages of its development.

Therefore, during the early stages of a records development the golden copy may be a draft. When a record is superseded by an updated version a golden copy may still exist for the previous version, for example with assessment regulations which are updated every year, it is not just the current regulations which have a golden copy – a golden copy should exist for each previous set of regulations, and there will also be a golden copy of the draft of the next year's regulations."

Financial Services Authority (FSA)[13] on MiFID

MiFID is a major part of the European Union's Financial Services Action Plan (FSAP), which is designed to create a single market in financial services. MiFID comprises two levels of European legislation. 'Level 1', the Directive itself, was adopted in April 2004. In several places, however, it makes provision for its requirements to be supplemented by 'technical implementing measures', so-called 'Level 2' legislation.
Formal Commission recommendations for the Level 2 measures were published on 6 February 2006.

In addition to the services covered by the Investment Services Directive (ISD), MiFID:

---

[13] Extracts reprinted by kind permission of The Financial Services Authority, 25 The North Colonnade, Canary Wharf, London E14 5HS, Tel. 020 7066 3302, web site: http://www.fsa.gov.uk

- Upgrades advice that involves a personal recommendation to a core investment service that can be passported on a stand-alone basis;
- Introduces operating a multilateral trading facility (MTF) as a new core investment service covered by the passport; and
- Extends the scope of the passport to cover commodity derivatives, credit derivatives and financial contracts for differences for the first time
- It sets more detailed requirements governing the organisation and conduct of business of investment firms, and how regulated markets and MTFs operate. It also includes new pre-and post-trade transparency requirements for equity markets; the creation of a new regime for 'systematic internalisers' of retail order flow in liquid equities; and more extensive transaction reporting requirements
- It improves the operation of the 'passport' for investment firms by more clearly delineating the allocation of responsibility between home state and host state for passported branches and generally clarifying some of the jurisdictional uncertainties that arose under the ISD.

Most firms that fall within the scope of MiFID will also have to comply with the new Capital Requirements Directive (CRD), which will set requirements for the regulatory capital which a firm must hold. Those firms newly covered by MiFID will be subject to directive based capital requirements for the first time.

Impact on firms

In general, MiFID will cover most if not all firms currently subject to the ISD, plus some that currently are not. This will include:

- Investment banks;

- Portfolio managers;
- Stockbrokers and broker dealers;
- Corporate finance firms;
- Many futures and options firms; and
- Some commodities firms.

In some areas, the position for firms will be less clear-cut. For instance, Retail banks and building societies will be subject to MiFID for some parts of their business – for example, selling securities, or investment products which contain securities, to customers - but not others.

Implementation timetable

The UK Presidency tabled a proposal last year that would give industry an additional six months in which to finalise their preparations, resulting in an implementation date of 1 November 2007. The revised draft-amending Directive also sets 31 January 2007 as the date by which national authorities in Member States must transpose MiFID's requirements into domestic law.

In the meantime, the FSA has published a "Planning for MiFID" document. This is a short factual document, whose purpose is to encourage the senior management of firms to begin planning for MiFID implementation. It aims to highlight some of the likely key impacts of MiFID, and those areas where review of firms' operations, systems, business practices and procedures is likely to be necessary, and for which firms will need to budget in the coming financial year.

Key provisions

Scope

New developments include bringing investment advice within the scope of EU regulation. Commodity derivatives are now a financial instrument for the purposes of MiFID but not all firms trading commodity derivatives are within the scope of the directive. This will depend on whether they fall within an exemption contained in MiFID.

Organisational Requirements

The MiFID requirements are more extensive than the FSA's Handbook in this area. The Handbook will therefore be amended to reflect this.
The requirements are likely to cover Compliance arrangements, internal systems and controls, outsourcing, record keeping, management of conflicts of interest, and safeguarding of client financial instruments or money held by firms.
Much of the detail in these requirements is subject to the final Level 2 measures.

Conduct of Business

Common conduct of business standards is established in MiFID. These standards are extensive and will require significant changes to the FSA's Handbook. The starting point for many of these changes is the introduction of a new client classification regime, which, while presenting similarities with the current FSA regime, differs in some aspects (see below).

Best Execution

The MiFID requirements on best execution will mean some important changes to the current FSA regime. Firms will be required to take all reasonable steps to obtain the best possible deal for their clients taking not just price into consideration, but other factors such as cost, speed and likelihood of execution and settlement. The proposals are broadly consistent with the FSA's CP 154 (October 2002) proposals on best execution.

Passporting Rights

MiFID improves the operation of the single passport for investment activity.
Firms will be able to establish branches in other member states and offer cross-border services in a wider range of cases, following the increase in the scope of the directive. Where a firm establishes a branch in another member state, the host country is responsible for ensuring Compliance with conduct of business requirements where services are provided within its territory.

Client Classification

MiFID establishes a common EU framework for classifying counterparties between professional clients, market counterparties and retail clients. The FSA will have to adjust its current counterparty classification system to the new framework in a number of areas.

Regulated Market and MTF Standards

MiFID establishes new minimum standards for regulated markets (i.e., exchanges) and for multilateral trading facilities (MTFs). FSA's existing standards for recognised investment exchanges and ATSs will require changes (as will the legislative underpinning in the FSMA).

Pre-trade Equity Transparency

MiFID establishes minimum standards of pre-trade transparency for shares traded on regulated markets and MTFs. It also obliges an investment firm that is a 'systematic internaliser' to undertake what is effectively a public market-making obligation. That is, the firm must provide a definite bid and offer quotes in liquid shares for orders below 'standard market size'.

Post-trade Equity Transparency

All types of trading in shares, whether on regulated markets, MTFs or OTC, are subject to a post-trade transparency obligation. Exemptions for block trades and the mechanics of publication are detailed in Level 2.

Transaction Reporting

Transaction reporting refers to post-trade reporting to regulators and does not refer to the publication of trades. While MiFID requirements will shift the reporting emphasis to the competent authority of the home/host state of firms and not to the competent authority of the regulated markets on which the instrument is traded. While current reporting requirements extend to debt and equity related products, MiFID will require transaction reports for any instrument admitted to trading on a regulated market – including commodity instruments admitted to trading on exchange.

CNET[14] on MiFID

Cheat Sheet: MiFID
Banks get miffed at new regulation
By Steve Ranger
Published: Monday 31 October 2005

Sounds okay so far. Where does the IT come into this? Firms will have to be able to prove 'best execution' on deals - which is likely to have to take into account issues

---

118

such as price, venue, cost and speed. And they will have to keep records for five years.

Lots of the firms that currently trade off-book just don't have the systems to record and store this information and prove that they are providing best execution.

Firms will also have to publish much more information than before, which will mean new communications infrastructure. And they'll have to build new business processes to deal with all this. Analysts are predicting £10m for IT and £12m for new processes - costing the industry around £1bn.

Ouch.

Yup. And many players - including the Financial Services Authority in the UK - are warning that the costs of Compliance may well outweigh the benefits. It could also lead to a wave of mergers of the smaller players in Europe. And as the deadline is pretty soon, we could see an outbreak of poaching as banks get desperate to have the best workers in place.

Don't let MiFID delays stop IT work
Short deadline will cause skills shortage, says IT chief
By Steve Ranger
Published: Tuesday 31 January 2006

Banks will have to spend big to get their IT systems in place to cope with the change - analyst TowerGroup predicts that a typical medium-sized European broker will have to spend $22m to get compliant - although on the plus side all this spending will lead to $1.5m in annual savings.

But the Level 2 implementation measures for MiFID - which provide the actual detail of what companies will have to do to comply - still haven't appeared.

FSA to do minimum for EU Compliance
Could cut costs for companies
By Dan Ilett - Published: Monday 5 December 2005

The UK Financial Services Authority (FSA) has said it will only implement the minimum requirements for European Compliance regulations.

Earlier this year the FSA criticised the European Union for failing to provide a cost-benefit analysis for the Markets in Financial Instruments Directive (MiFID), a regulation that will allow financial institutions to establish branches in other European states. Analysts claim it would cost firms $1bn in IT restructuring.

The FSA has now hinted it will do only what it must to comply with EU requirements.

A statement from the organisation said: "[The] FSA is committed to implementing directives in a sensible and proportionate way. It is obliged to implement the minimum requirements, even if these would fail a cost-benefit analysis from the UK's viewpoint, but it will not 'gold-plate' EU requirements. It will add requirements only when they are justified in their own right."

FSA slams EU over IT burden
Euro-regulations to cost IT €1bn.
By Dan Ilett
Published: Monday 25 July 2005

The UK's Financial Services Authority (FSA) has blasted the EU for imposing complicated regulations that could land European banks with a €1bn technology bill.

Chairman of the FSA Callum McCarthy has attacked the EU, saying it is "deeply unsatisfactory" that UK banks have to implement more IT equipment when no cost-benefit analysis has been carried out.

McCarthy said in his AGM statement: "That kind of approach to policy-making cannot be sensible. Going forward we will do all we can alongside a growing band of regulators who share our commitment to assessing costs and benefits, to support Commissioner McCreevy's determination to make rigorous impact assessment a vital determinant of EU legislation.

"But it is already clear that the MiFID changes will impose significant costs on the UK market including, for example, through systems changes and IT upgrades. Industry is understandably concerned about the potential scale of these costs - and I share those worries. It is far from clear that the benefits to the UK will outweigh the costs."

Financial analyst Celent has said that MiFID would force European financial firms to spend €1bn on IT.

The analyst's report said: "Most financial institutions remain totally unprepared for MiFID and are only in the earliest of stages of even understanding what the directive entails... Under MiFID, exchanges will lose significant revenues in terms of market data, print fees for off-exchange trades and trade fees.

The total annual lost revenues will be over €300m annually. MiFID will require significant IT investments by market participants, totalling over €1bn."

ACKNOWLEDGEMENT AND THANKS:
The book's Author acknowledges and thanks John Shelly, Marketing Executive, Strategy & Marketing, CNET Networks UK, for contributing these articles to the book, as follows:

CNET Networks UK, International House,
1 St. Katharines Way, London E1W 1UN
Tel: 0207 903 6800
E-mail: enquiries@silicon.com
www.silicon.com

9. Sarbanes-Oxley Act

Coverage

This Act (abbreviated to SOA or SOX) is by far the most draconian of all Compliance mandates, carrying with it the most severe threat of prison sentence for non-Compliance, and also probably the most complex, difficult and costly to implement.

The U.S. federal government's Sarbanes-Oxley Act[15] was established in 2002 to protect investors by improving the accuracy and reliability of corporate disclosures.
The act covers issues such as establishing a public company accounting oversight board, auditor independence, corporate responsibility and enhanced financial disclosure.

SOX act was designed to review the dated legislative audit requirements, and is considered the most significant change to United States securities laws since the New Deal in the 1930s.
The act came in the wake of a series of corporate financial scandals, including those affecting Enron, Tyco International, and WorldCom (now MCI).

3 years after the passing of this law, according to a poll conducted by The Wall Street Journal and Harris Interactive;

"55 percent of U.S. investors believe that financial and accounting regulations governing publicly held companies are too lenient."

---

[15] See http://en.wikipedia.org/wiki/Sarbanes-Oxley and Abe Abrahami's ARTICLE; Sarbanes-Oxley Act (SOA) Compliance, Management Services magazine, Autumn 2005

"41 percent say they are not sure about the effect Sarbanes-Oxley has had on communication transparency."

This statistics suggests that many investors don't understand the legislation and its impact on businesses.

The Sarbanes-Oxley Act's major provisions include:

- Certification of financial reports by CEOs and CFOs
- Ban on personal loans to any Executive Officer and Director
- Accelerated reporting of trades by insiders
- Prohibition on insider trades during pension fund blackout periods
- Public reporting of CEO and CFO compensation and profits
- Additional disclosure as appropriate and relevant
- Auditor independence, including outright bans on certain types of work and pre-certification by the company's Audit Committee of all other non-audit work
- Criminal and civil penalties for violations of securities law
- Significantly longer jail sentences and larger fines for corporate executives who knowingly and wilfully misstate financial statements.
- Prohibition on audit firms providing extra "value-added" services to their clients including actuarial services, legal and extra services (such as consulting) unrelated to their audit work.
- A requirement is that publicly traded companies furnish independent annual audit reports on the existence and condition (i.e., reliability) of internal controls as they relate to financial reporting.

In connection with SOX, 'Auditing Standard No. 2' of the Public Company Accounting Oversight Board (PCAOB) has the following key requirements:

- The design of controls over relevant assertions related to all significant accounts and disclosures in the financial statements
- Information about how significant transactions are initiated, authorized, supported, processed, and reported
- Enough information about the flow of transactions to identify where material misstatements due to error or fraud could occur
- Controls designed to prevent or detect fraud, including who performs the controls and the regulated segregation of duties
- Controls over the period-end financial reporting process
- Controls over safeguarding of assets
- The results of management's testing and evaluation.

Internal Controls

Under Sarbanes-Oxley, two separate certification sections came into effect – one civil and the other criminal. See 15 U.S.C. § 7241 (Section 302) - civil provision, 18 U.S.C. § 1350 (Section 906) - criminal provision.

Section 302 of the Act mandates a set of internal procedures designed to ensure accurate financial disclosure.
The signing officers must certify that they are "responsible for establishing and maintaining internal controls" and "have designed such internal controls to ensure that material information relating to the [company] and its consolidated subsidiaries is made known to such officers by others within those entities, particularly during the

period in which the periodic reports are being prepared."
See 15 U.S.C. § 7241 (a)(4).

Section 409 mandates that companies disclose any material changes in their financial conditions or operations on a "rapid and current basis." This means real-time disclosure.
Section 409 ultimately requires immediate access to information, open lines of communication and a fast response time.
If a company is already struggling to monitor Sarbanes-Oxley activities and progress, Section 409 will only compound these problems.
Companies that fail to immediately grasp changes will be in no position to quickly apprise the public of them, as mandated.
Section 409 requires that a company maintain a clear view of their end-to-end business performance and records.

Section 802 raises issues for both business and technical groups.
From a business perspective, one needs to determine what to retain, how long to keep a document, a record, an object, and its final disposal.
On the technical side, companies are challenged to provide content management type capabilities for the variety of documents and formats.
Another component of Section 802 is that companies should establish emergency policies for retention in the event of legal inquiry.
Section 802 has critical implications so far as reliance on information retention and retrieval policies and practice, including - audit trail, integrity of related document/object links, data storage and lifecycle management, proof of authenticity etc.

Section 1001 concerns corporate tax returns (including consistent / transportable electronic file formats exchanged between companies, tax authorities and advisors).

It has wide-ranging implications for ERP – Enterprise Resource Planning applications (such as SAP and ORACLE).

The impact extends to ERP interfaces, for example - CRM – Customer Relationship Management (such as Siebel) and banking/treasury applications (such as Globus).

In particular; data archiving and information retention, retrieval and display formats and the speed and cost for doing it.

While Section 401 deals with disclosure requirements, *Section 404* of Sarbanes-Oxley mandates that companies put into place what's called "internal controls" to insure the accuracy of their financials.

The officers must "have evaluated the effectiveness of the [company's] internal controls as of a date within 90 days prior to the report" and "have presented in the report their conclusions about the effectiveness of their internal controls based on their evaluation as of that date."

Section 404 has serious effects on those found to have material weaknesses in internal control. In this act, companies must, for the first time, provide attestation of internal control assessment.

This presents new challenges to businesses, specifically, documentation of control procedures related to information technology.

Moreover, under Section 404 of the Act, management is required to produce an "internal control report" as part of each annual Exchange Act report. See 15 U.S.C. § 7262.

The report must affirm "the responsibility of management for establishing and maintaining an adequate internal

control structure and procedures for financial reporting."
See 15 U.S.C. § 7262 (a).

The report must also "contain an assessment, as of the end of the most recent fiscal year of the [Company], of the effectiveness of the internal control structure and procedures of the issuer for financial reporting." Additionally, PCAOB has issued guidelines on how management should render their opinion.

The main point of these guidelines is that management should use an internal control framework such as COSO (Committee of Sponsoring Organizations of the Treadway Commission).

It describes how to assess the control environment, determine control objectives, perform risk assessments, and identify controls and monitor Compliance.

Companies have almost uniformly elected COSO as the standard when choosing an internal control framework.

COSO is sponsored and funded by 5 main professional accounting associations and institutes; American Institute of Certified Public Accountants (AICPA), American Accounting Association (AAA), Financial Executives Institute (FEI), The Institute of Internal Auditors (IIA) and The Institute of Management Accountants (IMA).

Audit, IT Controls and Section 404

The PCAOB suggests considering the COSO framework in management / auditor assessment of controls. Auditors have also looked to the IT Governance Institute's "COBIT - Control Objectives of Information and Related Technology" - for more appropriate standards of measure. This framework focuses on IT processes, while keeping in mind the big picture of COSO's "control activities" and "information and communication". However, certain aspects of COBIT are outside the boundaries of Sarbanes-Oxley regulation.

128

Likewise for ITIL -Information Technology Infrastructure Library – is also relevant.
It is highly unlikely that a company that has to comply with SOX would not implement COBIT and/or ITIL.
COBIT and ITIL are not magic bullets but implementing them goes a long way towards Compliance, they are briefly described below.

COBIT

Control Objectives for Information and related Technology (COBIT) is a framework for information (IT) management risks created by the Information Systems Audit and Control Association (ISACA), and the IT Governance Institute (ITGI).

Control Objectives for Information and related Technology, or COBIT, provides managers, auditors, and IT users with a set of generally accepted information technology control objectives to assist them in maximizing the benefits derived through the use of information technology and developing the appropriate IT governance and control in a company.

In its 3rd and 4th editions, COBIT has 34 high level control objectives that cover 318 control objectives categorized in four domains: Planning and Organization, Acquisition and Implementation, Delivery and Support, and Monitoring.
It comprises six elements: management guidelines, control objectives, COBIT framework, executive summary, audit guidelines and an implementation toolset. All are documented in separate volumes.
The IT GOVERNANCE INSTITUTE and the Information Systems Audit and Control Foundation developed it in 1992 when the control objectives relevant to information technology were first identified.

The first edition was published in 1996; the second edition in 1998 - the third edition in 2000, the on-line edition became available in 2003, and in 2005 the fourth edition was published. It has more recently found favour due to external developments, especially the Enron scandal and the subsequent passage of the Sarbanes-Oxley Act.

The COBIT mission is "to research, develop, publicize and promote an authoritative, up-to-date, international set of generally accepted information technology control objectives for day-to-day use by business managers and auditors."
Managers, auditors, and users benefit from the development of COBIT because it helps them understand their IT systems and decide the level of security and control that is necessary to protect their companies' assets through the development of an IT governance model.

The two cornerstones of COBIT are KPIs and delivery framework.

COBIT criteria of KPIs, consists of:

1. Availability
2. Compliance
3. Confidentiality
4. Effectiveness
5. Efficiency
6. Integrity
7. Reliability

COBIT framework, consists of:

1. Planning and organization
2. Acquisition and implementation
3. Delivery and support – covered by ITIL
4. Monitoring

ITIL

The Information Technology Infrastructure Library (ITIL) is a customizable framework of best practices that promote quality-computing services in the information technology (IT) sector.
ITIL addresses the organisational structure and skill requirements for an IT organisation by presenting a comprehensive set of management procedures with which an organisation can manage its IT operations. These procedures are supplier independent and apply to all aspects of IT infrastructure.

Since the mid 1990's, ITIL has been promoted as a standard for IT Service Management and is similar to Information Services Procurement Library (ISPL), the Application Services Library (ASL), Dynamic Systems Development Method (DSDM), and Control Objectives for Information and related Technology (COBIT).
ITIL is built on a process-model view of controlling and managing operations.

ITIL is published in a series of books, each of which covers one topic. The names ITIL and IT Infrastructure Library are Registered Trade Marks of the UK Office of Government Commerce (OGC), which is an Office of the United Kingdom's Treasury.

The recommendations of ITIL were developed in the late 1980's by the Central Computer and Telecommunications Agency (CCTA), which merged into the OGC in April 2001 and disappeared as a distinct organization in the UK.

The two cornerstones of ITIL are service support and service delivery.

Service Support consists of:

1. Configuration Management
2. Change Management
3. Release Management
4. Incident Management
5. Problem Management
6. Service Desk

Service Delivery consists of:

1. Service Level Management
2. Capacity Management
3. Financial Management for IT Services
4. Availability Management
5. IT Service Continuity Management

In addition to COBIT and ITIL, British Standard BS 7799, and QCR 3000™ (Quality Compliance-Cost Reduction) methodology are very helpful to attain Compliance. The ratings from these may be applied to derive the overall BBS - Business-balanced Scorecard – rating of the organisation - although one does not have to use them all, as there are overlaps between them.

In today's business environment, the financial reporting processes of most organizations are driven by Information Technology (IT) systems.
Few companies manage their data manually and most companies have moved to electronic management of data, documents, and key operational processes.

Therefore, it is apparent that IT plays a vital role in internal control. As PCAOB's "Auditing Standard 2" states: "The nature and characteristics of a company's use of information technology in its information system affect the company's internal control over financial reporting."

Chief information officers are responsible for the security, accuracy and the reliability of the systems that manage and report the financial data.

Systems such as ERP (Enterprise Resource Planning) are deeply integrated in the initiating, authorizing, processing, and reporting of financial data. As such, they are inextricably linked to the overall financial reporting process and needs to be assessed, along with other important process for Compliance with Sarbanes-Oxley Act.

So, although the Act signals a fundamental change in business operations and financial reporting, and places responsibility in corporate financial reporting on the Chief Executive Officer (CEO) and Chief Financial Officer (CFO), the Chief Information Officer (CIO) plays a significant role in the signoff of financial statements.

With the widespread use of Information & Communication Technology (ICT) systems, evaluating and monitoring the effectiveness of internal control over financial reporting. For most organizations, the role of IT will be crucial to achieving these objectives.

Some of the key areas of responsibility for ICT include:

- Understanding the organization's internal control program and its financial reporting process.
- Mapping the IT systems that support internal control and the financial reporting process to the financial statements.
- Identifying risks related to these IT systems.
- Designing and implementing controls designed to mitigate the identified risks and monitoring them for continued effectiveness.
- Documenting and testing IT controls.

- Ensuring that IT controls are updated and changed, as necessary, to correspond with changes in internal control or financial reporting processes.
- Monitoring IT controls for effective operation over time.
- Participation by IT in the Sarbanes-Oxley project management office.

To comply with Sarbanes-Oxley, it is critical that organizations must understand how the financial reporting process works and must be able to identify the areas where technology plays a critical part. In considering which controls to include in the program, organizations should recognize that IT controls could have a direct or indirect impact on the financial reporting process. For instance, IT application controls that ensure completeness of transactions can be directly related to financial assertions.

Access controls, on the other hand, exist within these applications or within their supporting systems, such as databases, networks and operating systems, are equally important, but do not directly align to a financial assertion.

Application controls are generally aligned with a business process that gives rise to financial reports. While there are many IT systems operating within an organization, Sarbanes-Oxley Compliance only focuses on those that are associated with a significant account or related business process.

SOX Implementation Costs

One key area of cost is the updating of information systems to comply with the control and reporting requirements. Systems, which provide document management, access to financial data, or long-term storage of information must now provide auditing capabilities.

In most cases this requires significant changes, or even complete replacement, of existing systems, which were designed without the needed level of auditing details.

Costs associated with SOX 404 Compliance have proven to be higher than first anticipated. According to the Financial Executives International (FEI), in a survey of 217 companies with average revenue above $5 billion, the cost of Compliance was an average of $4.36 million.

The survey also indicated actual costs of to be approximately 39% higher than companies expected to spend. The high cost of Compliance throughout the first year can be attributed to the sharp increase in hours charged per audit engagement.

PCAOB has concluded that auditors may have been overly harsh in applying auditing guidelines. However, non-Compliance comes with an even higher cost in terms of stiffer penalties and jail sentences.

Year One Resources Spent on Section 404 Compliance, Roundtable Survey, December 2004, by Revenue[16]:

---

[16] See http://www.answers.com/topic/sarbanes-oxley-act-of-2002-sox

Table 9.1: Typical SOX Compliance costs

Company Revenue	< $5 B	$5 B - $10 B	$10 B – $50 B	> $50 B
Average Additional Audit Hours	6,285	20,756	11,540	19,000
Average Total Compliance Cost per Billion Dollars in Revenues (millions)	$1.9	$1.1	$0.6	$0.3

Summary of the Act Critical Sections

201: Auditor's independence (cannot provide non-audit and/or consulting services)
302: A set of internal procedures designed to ensure accurate financial disclosure and Corporate Responsibility (honesty, integrity, transparency, accountability).
404: Management Assertion of Internal Controls (robust procedures, audit independence versus consulting engagement of advisors, conflict of interests etc.)
409: It requires immediate access to information, open lines of communication and a fast response time – a great challenge for information content management.
802: Reliance on Information Retention Policies (audit trail, document links etc.)
906: All periodic reports containing financial statements filed with the SEC come with a written statement of the CEO and CFO.
1001: Corporate Tax Returns (consistent / transportable electronic file formats exchanged between companies, tax authorities and advisors).

SOX Compliant Architecture and Philosophy

SOX and other Compliance mandates, business change and transformation, together with business-balance scorecards, IT infrastructure and information warehouse architecture, must be in sync with one another to work correctly, effectively and efficiently.

A change in one area or component has an impact or a domino affect on other areas or components, business procedures and processes, quality, availability and integrity of data and information.

The Figures below illustrate Compliance together with business-balance scorecards, information warehouse, and governance frameworks, and also the 'tip of the iceberg' phenomenon of the '80-20 rule'.

Many companies implement Compliance mandates without due diligence and connectivity to performance indicators and benchmarks, this is a fundamental and monumental error that cost them many millions in lost revenues or extra costs.

Figure 9.1: Compliance, IT and business-balance scorecards

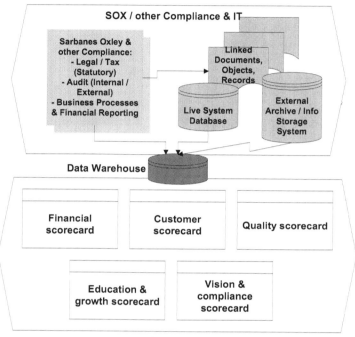

Benchmarks

Figure 9.2: Tip of the Compliance iceberg

TIP OF THE COMPLIANCE ICEBERG
APPARENT TOP 20%:

- Sarbanes-Oxley Act compliance rules

- Interpretation / Understanding of SOA rules

80% IN-DEPTH ANALYSIS & SOLUTION DEVELOPMENT:

Translation of SOA, data, system and process analysis,
change delivery and training scope of work in relation to:

- Finance dept. procedures
- Audit dept. procedures
- Sales and CRM procedures
- Product delivery and service engagement procedures
- Taxation / Statutory compliance procedures
- VAT compliance procedures
- Business organisation, governance and procedures
- HR structure, governance and procedures
- IT dept. governance, procedures and changes
- System application changes
- Third party involvement

- Visibility of connection threads from lower level
system-business processes and transaction results
all the way up to financial and audit reporting
including P&L and balance-sheet facts and figures

Ten Cardinal Sins of SOX Non-Compliance

1. Record and document management policy and applications are not linked to regulatory requirements and mandates
2. Document and record retention schedule is incomplete, vague, or no longer reflective of the law and departmental procedures

3. Formal policies and procedures are nonexistent or inconsistent across departments
4. Record and document management covers paper records only or electronic data only, without a connective information warehouse to integrate both
5. No one is directly responsible for administering and delivering results from the Compliance programme
6. Information retention periods are not integrated with document and record management to purge obsolete information and save storage space and system maintenance fees
7. Employees are unaware of, or vague about Compliance policy and practices.
8. There are no tools and authority in place for deleting obsolete documents and records
9. There is no audit process in place to track what happened with Compliance and related issues.
10. There is no intuitive or comprehensive indexing, so it is impossible or extremely difficult to retrieve documents when required.

QCR 3000™ Roadmap to Deliver SOX and Other Compliances

The following 15 steps are typically involved in successful implementation of SOX and other Compliance:

1. Questionnaire-template construction
2. Information gathering, workshops, interviews
3. Business process, data, system and application analysis
4. Project planning, objective briefings, education and presentations
5. PIQD (project implementation & quality document) preparation
6. Project scope, work package/element definitions - Project Management Structure (PrMS)

7. Agree roles & responsibilities; SPOC (single point of contact)
8. Deliverable progress reporting and outline solution formulation
9. Working with Finance & Accounting auditors, business people, IT dept., system application users, third party suppliers and outsource service providers
10. Solution build and initial testing
11. Quality assurance
12. Re-testing and fixing
13. Training & web info.
14. Solution rollout
15. *Evaluation, remedial actions.*

Step 15, according to QCR 3000™, post delivery of SOX and/or other Compliance mandates, is broken down below into a 10-fold criteria and parameters to evaluate and measure resultant business transformation and performance for effectiveness and efficiency.

1/ Price and Delivery
Select company products and services, plus key contractors and suppliers will be assessed for Compliance.

2/ Quality and Reliability
Quantitative and qualitative measurement of Mean Time Between Failure (MTBF) of IT systems and the organisation itself will be conducted.

3/ Performance to Cost Ratio
PCR will be derived, including cost of quality and Compliance from KPIs.

4/ Service Level and Customer Satisfaction
Service Level Agreement / Contract (SLA / SLC) will be studied.

5/ Training and introduction of new Practices and new Technology

The company's training policy and practices, together with course sample material will be evaluated.

6/ Measure of perceptions of the company and its culture

Select people will be requested to discuss frankly issues, challenges and proposed remedies.

7/ Workable contingency and recovery procedures being in place

Evidence will be sought to illustrate that workable plans are in place, which are visible to the work force.

8/ Management style and leadership by personal example

Measure of employee perceptions of the company's management and its culture, and the reverse will be sought.

9/ Interfaces between different parts of the company

Assessment of linkages between company departments and how they interact will be conducted.

10/ Linkage between personnel performance and reward

HR, select management and staff performance will be assessed against financial and other rewards.

As a result of the above, proposed recommendations and actions should be annotated with traffic light indicators:

1. Green/Blue – fine, leave alone for now
2. Amber – requires attention later on
3. Red – immediate action required

In addition, risk management and assurance of the organisation should be scored as discussed next.

SOX Risk Management Capability Assessment Criteria[17]

1. Risk Assessment How do you identify and measure the threats/risks that could impact on the achievement of your business objectives?	SCORE: 10
2. Control Assessment How healthy are your control frameworks? How long has it been since you evaluated their effectiveness?	SCORE: 10
3. Control Cost Optimization Could you eliminate some controls and still have an acceptable residual risk level at a lower overall cost?	SCORE: 10
4. Risk Testing the Future Do you consider and evaluate risks when making important business decisions and preparing strategic plans?	SCORE: 10
5. Planning for Serious Risk Situations Do you have contingency plans in place to deal with low probability, high-risk situations that could cripple your unit or the company? Do you periodically revisit these plans to reassess their adequacy?	SCORE: 10
6. Worst Case Scenarios Have you considered the possibility of high-risk situations, which, if they occurred together, could have a devastating effect on the company?	SCORE: 10

---

[17] Reprinted with kind permission of Tim J. Leech, FCA·CIA, CCSA, CFE, Principal Consultant, Chief Methodology Officer, Paisley Consulting, Author of a White Paper: Sarbanes-Oxley, Sections 302 & 404: Proposing Practical, Cost Effective Compliance Strategies **www.paisleyconsulting.com**

	SCORE:
7. Early Warning Systems Do you regularly monitor your risk status for early warning signs that changes are needed to your controls and/or objectives?	10
8. Risk Transfer/Financing Options Have you considered risk transfer and insurance options available to avoid or reduce the consequences of specific threats/risks to your business objectives?	SCORE: 10
9. Regular Re-evaluation Do you periodically reassess the acceptability of your risk acceptance decisions?	SCORE: 10
10. Oversight Process Does Senior Management and the Board of Directors understand the major risks the company faces and take steps to ensure work units are identifying, measuring, controlling and monitoring risks?	SCORE: 10
TOTAL RISK FITNESS SCORE:	100

ACKNOWLEDGEMENT AND THANKS:
The book's Author acknowledges and thanks Tim Leech, Chief Methodology Officer of Paisley Consulting, for contributing his White Paper, as follows:

Paisley Consulting
Corporate Headquarters
400 Cokato Street East
P.O. Box 578
Cokato, MN 55321 USA
Toll free: 888.288.0283 (U.S. and Canada)
Phone: 320.286.5870 (All Other Countries)
Fax: 320.286.6196
E-mail: Tim.Leech@paisleyconsulting.com
Web: www.paisleyconsulting.com

SOX and Total Asset Management[18]

Abstract

This paper shows a real example of where a common IT Asset Management auto-discovery concept – the concept of using auto-discovery to validate the presence of network-connected PCs in the enterprise – can cause concern for internal and external auditors when considering Sarbanes-Oxley.
It shows the auditor's perspective and the trap that an IT Asset Manager can fall into if not careful. Finally, this paper gives a recommendation on how to proceed.

A Real Life Example

Consider a large company whose asset manager recently underwent an internal audit. The auditor was shown a report that documented a percentage of PCs whose whereabouts could not be definitively stated and that had not "checked in" via network login in over 90 days.

The internal auditor wrote a comment in his report citing the lack of definitive knowledge of the whereabouts of the PCs as an issue, which then spawned an intensive set of internal initiatives aimed at reducing that percentage to something more reasonable.

"More reasonable", as it turns out, is a relative term. To an asset manager, who knows the difficulty in attaining, and sustaining, definitive location knowledge of a high percentage of all PC assets, 3% may seem entirely reasonable – even a stretch.

---

[18] Sarbanes-Oxley and the Autodiscovery "Watchdog" Process, A MANAGEMENT WHITE PAPER BY: WILLIAM B. HUSSELBAUGH and FRANK KASSEL - an excerpt reprinted with kind permission of the Authors - see Acknowledgement at the end of this Chapter.

To an auditor, concerned about the misappropriation of sensitive information that may be on the local PC hard drives, or password or URL history information that could be used to hack into corporate systems, 0% is the only reasonable response.

Herein lies the trap – beware and do not fall into this trap as the large company in the example did. As a seasoned asset manager knows, it is practically impossible to hope for sustaining positive location knowledge of 100% of all PC assets, so there is little hope of satisfying the auditor. There is a way to avoid this trap, so read on.

The Auditor's Perspective

Sarbanes-Oxley (7/02) Sec. 404 requires management to internally document, assess, test and report on the adequacy of internal control (design and operating effectiveness) over financial reporting, asset acquisitions and dispositions, and asset safeguarding (prevent/detect unauthorized acquisition, use, disposition - ref. Sec. 103 and SEC Rule 33-8238).

Once management has done that, the external auditors will test management's documentation, assessments and assertions, and will issue their own audit opinion report as to whether internal control is adequate.
Internal control deficiencies that do not provide reasonable assurance (low risk) that material misstatements in the financial statements, via errors or fraud, will be prevented or detected on a timely basis during the ordinary course of business are known as "Material Weaknesses".

Material Weaknesses must be disclosed in management's internal control report. If a deficiency exists that is less serious but still allows more than an inconsequential misstatement, this is known as a "Significant Deficiency". Significant Deficiencies that are related must be aggregated to determine whether the aggregation is, in and of itself, a "Material Weakness". When a "Material Weakness" exists, the external auditor must conclude that the company's internal control is "not effective" in its report to the SEC and investment/creditor community.

Frequently, when a Material Weakness is reported, CFOs get fired, CIOs get fired, the company's stock price takes a hit, and the Directors & Officers insurance cost goes sky high.

On the surface, not being able to account for 10% of all PCs might not seem like such a big deal quantitatively. Sure, the fixed asset "existence" and "valuation" assertions will require an adjustment to the fixed asset subsidiary ledger and related general ledger accounts for the carrying amount of the missing PCs.

In many companies, this adjustment will not be deemed "material", because from a money standpoint, the carrying amount of the lost PCs relative to all other corporate assets is relatively small. If the adjustment is not made, the potential adjustment will be tracked and could, along with other potential adjustments, tip the aggregate adjustment threshold and require a larger financial statement adjustment be made. The lack of PC fixed asset accountability could, therefore, still get the blame, but the blame would be greater for tipping a much larger adjustment.

However, a lack of sufficient accountability over asset acquisitions and dispositions may be a direct violation of Sec. 404 and related SEC rules in cases where, even though the quantitative amount of the assets involved is small, the qualitative value of data directly associated with the asset is large.

In these cases, it is reasonable to suggest that the "materiality factor" for establishing accountability (acquisition, disposition, unauthorized use or access) over these assets is "smaller rather than larger", such that a lack of sufficient accountability over such assets might, at a minimum, constitute a "Significant Deficiency" and could very well be a "Material Weakness" under Sec. 404.

From a Sec. 404 standpoint, however, the larger problem is likely the lack of internal control (general controls and application controls) over the information on the PCs. PCs typically have URL histories, saved passwords, and local data (data files and e-mail) stored on them. Consider what could happen if a "lost PC" fell into the wrong hands:

- Saved passwords could allow access to ERP/servers where fraudulent transactions could be entered undetected and sensitive data compromised (customer data exposed to competitors, payroll data scanned for social security numbers and sensitive salary data, financial data leaked before public release)
- URL history could allow a hacker-undetected access to ERP/server log-ins, where password-cracking software could be used to gain ERP/server access
- Local data could include customer data, payroll data, and financial data. In the wrong hands:
    - That data could be manipulated such that fraudulent transactions could be entered
    - Confidential customer, payroll or patient data could be compromised such that laws could be violated (HIPAA, Gramm-Leach-Bliley, California SB 1386)
    - Data that represents documentation (books, records, memoranda) that must be retained via Sec. 802 could be lost

To illustrate the seriousness of the situation, consider for example if a company could not track:

- 1% of its PCs. On the surface, 1% of a company's PCs might not sound like a big deal from a money standpoint, but consider if that 1% were in the Payroll department, the Finance department, the Sales department, the Credit Department or the Procurement department.
- Unauthorized ERP/server and local data access could be a real problem, such that controls over the unaccounted for or "lost" PCs do not provide reasonable assurance (low risk) that material misstatements in the financial statements, via errors or fraud, will be prevented or detected on a timely basis. And that, my friends, is the definition of a "Material Weakness" in internal controls (due to weak PC physical access control over data, weak PC logical access control to ERP/applications and data).

How to Proceed

To avoid falling into the trap described earlier in this article, consider following these points of advice:

- Join forces with IT security. The ideal answer is to be able to demonstrate, to the satisfaction of an internal or external auditor, that sufficient access security or compensating controls exist to negate any risk to the corporation should a PC fall into the hands of an individual with mal intent. For example, as compensating controls, all PCs could have their URL-histories automatically erased during boot-up, password saving could be disabled, server/application passwords could be rotated frequently, restrictions via job-description could be placed on what data could be stored on local PCs, ERP/network hack detection software could be installed, and ERP access/violation

149

detection software installed (attempts to gain unauthorized access to incompatible functions monitored and reported).

- Consider setting up different "risk" classes for PCs, which might mean a different disk image based on "risk" class. Conceptually, a high "risk" class PC would be highly controlled to the extent that it is physically impossible for it to contain sensitive data locally have passwords stored locally, or past URLs stored locally.
- This class of PC would be issued to employees who do not possess a need to have potentially compromising information stored locally – they do all their work on the network. It may be time to reconsider "thin clients". That would arguably leave a smaller percentage of PCs in the higher "trust" classes, creating a smaller and more manageable population to track.
- Be proactive. Work with internal auditing to construct a go forward plan that is practical, yet satisfies the concerns of all involved. Don't wait to get audited and
- Hope for the best. Don't automatically assume that sufficient compensating controls exist to mitigate PC access control weaknesses. What you don't know can hurt you.
- Wait until all parties involved, to, have completed all phases of the plan
- Publish any reports from your watchdog process.

Sarbanes-Oxley is simultaneously raising the importance of ITAM (IT Asset Management) as well as challenging it. Some IT asset managers, especially hardware IT asset managers, may now have a new catch point to consider as a result – internal audit. Embracing this new catch point appears to be the best course of action.

ACKNOWLEDGEMENT AND THANKS:
The book's Author acknowledges and thanks W. Brett Husselbaugh, for contributing this White Paper to the book, as follows:

W. Brett Husselbaugh
727-521-9585 (office)
727-415-6444 (cell)
727-521-0394 (fax)
E-mail: brett@husselbaugh.com
Web: www.husselbaugh.com

KPIs and Sarbanes-Oxley Act Sections

One of the key pints of SOX Compliance is added value, not simply ticking the boxes of self-assessment and audit questionnaires, because this is an ongoing process, which requires time and effort for the overall and greater good of the enterprise.
But how can this be? We usually look upon such measures in a negative light, after all it's expenditure and a headache, we would rather not encounter.
However, if you look at SOX Compliance right in the face, and brave the early upheaval, you may discover that there is a silver lining, in the form of increasing added value, and greater value for money with improved KPIs- Key Performance Indicators, see more below.

Section 100 - Public Company Accounting Oversight Board
Nine subsections - dealing with accounting firm and audit provisions, admin-control, quality, inspections, investigations, independence, accounting standards etc.
This is an opportunity to improve audit efficacy KPI.

Section 200 - Auditor Independence
Nine subsections - dealing with pre-approval requirements, auditor's scope of practice, partner's rotation, auditor's comments to audit committees, conforming agreements, conflicts of interest etc.
This is an opportunity to improve audit efficacy KPI.

Section 300 - Corporate Responsibility
Eight subsections - dealing with public company audit committee, financial report corporate responsibility, and improper influence on audit conduct, bonuses and profits, officer and director penalties, insider trades, attorney's responsibility etc.
This is an opportunity to improve trading integrity and client confidence KPI.

Section 400 - Enhanced Financial Disclosures
Nine subsections - dealing with disclosures in periodic
reports, enhanced conflicts of interest provisions,
transaction disclosures involving management and
principal stakeholder, management assessment of
internal controls, code of ethics for financial officers,
disclosure of audit committee financial expert etc.
This is an opportunity to improve trading integrity and
client confidence KPI.

Section 501 - Analyst conflicts of interest
Treatment of securities analysts by registered securities
associations and national securities exchanges
This is an opportunity to improve trading integrity and
client confidence KPI.

Section 600 - Commission resources and authority
Four subsections - dealing with authorisation of
appropriations, appearance and practice before the
commission, federal court authority to impose penny stock
bars, qualifications of associated persons of brokers and
dealers etc.
This is an opportunity to improve trading integrity and
client confidence KPI.

Section 700 - Studies and reports
Five subsections; dealing with General Accounting Office
(GAO) study and reporting concerning consolidation of
public accounting firms, commission study and report
concerning credit rating agencies, violators and
enforcement actions, investment banks etc.
This is an opportunity to improve quality, extent and depth
of reporting KPI.

Section 800 – Corporate and criminal fraud accountability
Seven subsections; dealing with criminal penalties for
altering documents, debts non-dischargeable if incurred in

violation of securities fraud law, status of limitations for securities fraud, review of federal sentencing guidelines, protection of employees who provide evidence, criminal penalties etc.

This is an opportunity to improve trading honesty and client's goodwill KPI.

Section 900 - White-collar crime penalty enhancements
Six subsections; dealing with attempts to commit criminal fraud, criminal penalties for mail fraud, criminal penalties for violations of employee retirement income security act, amendment to sentencing guidelines, corporate responsibility of financial reports etc.

This is an opportunity to improve trading honesty and client's goodwill KPI.

Section 1000 - Corporate tax returns
One subsection; dealing with corporate tax returns
This is an opportunity to improve IRS e-tax filing efficiency and archiving KPI.

Section 1100 - Corporate fraud accountability
Seven subsections; dealing with tampering with records or impeding an official proceeding, temporary freeze authority for the SEC, amendment to the federal sentencing guidelines, authority of the commission to prohibit persons from serving as officers or directors, increased financial penalties, retaliation against informers etc.

This is an opportunity to improve trading honesty and client's goodwill KPI.

The 11 SOX Sections above are summarised below in terms of 5 major KPIs and their respective challenges.

The company executives and senior management should apply SOX Compliance wisely, to better understand and manage the enterprise operations, to enhance business honesty and integrity and increase income while reducing overheads, which are key business objectives.

After the Table below, the following Chapter outlines a typical application to assist IT Compliance with SOX.

Other tools deal with accountancy, audit, balance sheet, sales, purchase, and similar financial issues.

Table 9.2: KPI Challenges and answers to SOX

Challenge KPI	Meeting the KPI challenge with
1. Greater transparency, openness and accurate reporting with robust supply-chain management	Effective/Transparent enterprise-vendor-client contract management solution that contains functionality that automatically alerts company executives when contract milestones are either met or missed, as required by SOX.
2. Evidenced financial statements of income, expenses, off-balance sheet commitments with robust supply-chain management	Evidenced enterprise-vendor-client contract management solution that has the functionality to monitor company performance to contract, and highlight potential deviations to management, whereas a 1-5% increase in Compliance can mean millions of saved dollars
3. Effective IT applications and infrastructure embracing real-time financial/business unit/operations' reporting	Effective enterprise-third party contracts and relationships management system, together robust procedures and process flow diagrams underpinned by a suitable information warehouse system that comes with a set of best-practice tools to manage update and expand, can save millions of dollars in rework and fixes
5. Greater audit efficacy and independence, less chances to cheat, greater investor confidence	Cascaded reporting and transparency; up, down and sideway, helps to increase confidence and goodwill and reduce costs of non-Compliance and rework

10. Ecora's Practical Guide to Sarbanes-Oxley IT Internal Controls[19]

Introduction

The Sarbanes-Oxley Act of 2002 was written and enacted in response to some rather large and public failures of corporate governance. Enron. WorldCom, and Tyco became well known brand names for all the wrong reasons. Scenes of C level executives being arrested and "perp-walked" in handcuffs became common TV news fare.
Sarbanes-Oxley was fashioned to protect investors by requiring accuracy, reliability, and accountability of corporate disclosures. It requires companies to put in place controls to inhibit and deter financial misconduct. And it places responsibility for all this – unambiguously – in the hands of the CEO.

Failure to comply with Sarbanes-Oxley exposes senior management to possible prison time (up to 20 years), significant penalties (as much as $5 million), or both. Historically, Sarbanes-Oxley is one of the most complete American corporate anti-crime laws ever. It focuses on and proscribes a range of corporate misbehaviour such as, altering financial statements, misleading auditors, and intimidating whistle blowers. It doles out harsh punishments and imposes fines and prison sentences for anyone who knowingly alters or destroys a record or document with the intent to obstruct an investigation.

Sarbanes-Oxley is clear on what it disallows, and sets the tone for proper corporate conduct. It does not, however, detail how to become compliant. It leaves the bulk of that

---

[19] This White Paper was reprinted with some editing by kind permission of Ecora Software Corporation - see Acknowledgement at the end of this Chapter.

decision and definition in the hands of individual businesses. This flexibility is a plus in that it provides wide latitude in Compliance. At the same time this lack of detail has created some confusion as to what constitutes appropriate controls. Much of the discussion about Sarbanes-Oxley as it relates to IT focuses on two sections: 302 and 404.

Section 302: Corporate Responsibility for Financial Reports

Sarbanes-Oxley 302 specifies that certifying officers are responsible for establishing and maintaining internal control over financial reporting.

302 requires:

- A statement that certifying officers are responsible for establishing and maintaining internal control over financial reporting
- A statement that the certifying officers designed internal controls and provide assurance that financial reporting and financial statements were prepared using generally accepted accounting principles.

A statement that the report discloses any changes in the company's internal control over financial reporting that have materially affected those internal controls.
This section makes corporate executives clearly responsible for establishing, evaluating, and monitoring internal control over financial reporting. For most companies the IT department is crucial to achieving this goal. IT is the foundation of any system of internal control.

Section 302 effectively puts IT in the Sarbanes-Oxley Compliance game. CEOs, CFOs and CIOs, who bear full responsibility for Sarbanes-Oxley Compliance, quickly find that IT departments are where internal controls at a material level can be implemented, managed, and documented.

Section 404 - Management Assessment of Internal Controls

When the Sarbanes-Oxley Act was signed into law, it was obvious Compliance would require significant effort from financial executives. An area of particular concern was Section 404, Management Assessment of Internal Controls.

Section 404 of Sarbanes-Oxley requires companies that file an annual report to include an internal control report that states the responsibility of management for establishing and maintaining an adequate internal controls structure and procedures for financial reporting.

It also requires an annual assessment of the effectiveness of the internal control structure and procedures of the issuer for financial reporting. Section 404 also requires the company's auditor to attest to, and report on, management's assessment of the effectiveness of the company's internal controls and procedures for financial reporting in accordance with standards established by the Public Company Accounting Oversight Board.

Compliance with Section 404 originally became effective on June 15, 2004, for all SEC reporting companies with a market capitalization in excess of $75 million. That was later extended to November 15, 2004. For all other companies that file periodic reports with the SEC, the Compliance deadline was April 15, 2005.

Compliance with Section 404 requires companies to establish an infrastructure to protect and preserve records and data from destruction, loss, unauthorized alteration, or other misuse. This infrastructure must ensure there is no room for unauthorized alteration of records vital to maintaining the integrity of the business processes.

This involves establishing the necessary controls, engaging in risk assessment, implementing control activities, creating effective communication and information flows, and monitoring.

When developing this infrastructure the organization must follow a structured internal control framework, such as the Internal Controls – Integrated Framework of the Committee of Sponsoring Organizations (COSO) of the Treadway Commission.

The COSO framework applies to operations, finance, and Compliance in the following five areas:

1. The control environment
2. Risk assessment
3. Control activities
4. Information and communication
5. Monitoring

The Public Company Accounting Oversight Board (PCAOB) clearly states in its Auditing Standard No. 2 (March 9, 2004) that,

"Management is required to base its assessment of the effectiveness of the company's internal control over financial reporting on a suitable, recognized control framework established by a body of experts that followed due-process procedures to develop the framework…Although different frameworks may not contain exactly the same elements as COSO, they should have elements that encompass all of COSO's general themes."

Based on PCAOB guidance this document will use the COSO standard in discussing SOX IT controls.

While most provisions of Sarbanes-Oxley focus on financial records, it is clearly not meant to stop there. For example, during an investigation, discovery requests can be submitted to IT departments. In addition, such requests could require access to all e-mail communication. There needs to be a good faith effort to attain this Compliance by the businesses affected by the act.

The focus of this paper is to give an overview of IT Compliance as it relates to Sarbanes-Oxley.

Impact on IT

One particularly challenging area of Sarbanes-Oxley 404 involves IT controls, a key area since so many of today's business processes are IT driven. Corporate Sarbanes-Oxley Compliance Teams should include a core team member with an IT background to ensure IT issues are considered during implementation. And a general IT controls section should be included in the documentation of each process and must be completed by a person with an IT background.

Due to the availability of reliable technology, most companies have already regulated themselves to a degree. And have also instituted some form of financial oversight in the form of independent audits.

Since financial data rests on servers, the security and documentation of IT systems is imperative to ensure the integrity of the data placed there. The corporation must have reliable, replicable, and audit proof detail about control of, and access to, the infrastructure that supports financial data.

So what exactly is needed – in an IT sense – to get ready for Sarbanes-Oxley?

Organizations are mandated to implement a series of 'internal controls' and procedures to communicate, store, and protect that data. In other words, you need to lock down the IT environment and clearly document how this is done and how it is monitored. Underneath that simple statement lays a wide range of tasks involving a great deal of work. The types and frequency of reports you'll need to create will be dictated by the complexity of your business processes and your company's specific audit and Compliance structure/definition.

What are 'Internal Controls'?

Defined by COSO, Internal controls are the exercise of best practices. More formally, an internal control is broadly defined as a process, affected by an entity's board of directors, management, and other personnel, designed to provide reasonable assurance regarding the achievement of objectives in the following categories:

- Effectiveness and efficiency of operations
- Reliability of financial reporting
- Compliance with applicable laws and regulations.

Controls over IT Systems

With IT playing a fundamental role in most business processes, controls are needed over all systems. IT controls generally cover IT environments, access to systems, programs, and data, computer operations and change management.
IT governance is an essential piece and contributor to overall financial governance.
Control frameworks exist that can facilitate Sarbanes-Oxley Compliance efforts.

COSO, Committee of Sponsoring Organizations, *Internal Control – Integrated Framework* and CobIT's *Control Objectives for Information and Related Technology* are excellent references for IT controls.

Regardless which framework you select, organizations must select accounts that are material to financial reporting.

This involves mapping control objectives for financial reporting to IT control objectives. Which means that IT management must become intimate with and conversant in common financial concepts such as:

- Existence and occurrence – controls should address the possibility of duplicate, retransmitted, or fictitious transactions during all processing stages.
- Measurement – measurement criteria should be tailored to the requirements on the basis of relevance to financial reporting.

Many internal controls for financial reporting are IT dependent. In defining internal controls it is important to articulate the central technology components of business processes and increase the understanding between IT and business members of the Sarbanes-Oxley team. It is also critical to determine if an IT process or component is relevant to Sarbanes Compliance.

Evaluating IT Relevance

While many IT controls are essential to smooth functioning of IT itself, they may have little or no bearing on Sarbanes-Oxley Compliance. To add value to Sarbanes-Oxley initiatives, IT controls need to help meet act's requirements. Some questions to consider when evaluating IT control relevance include:

- Is the computer processing directly or indirectly related to the timely production of financial reports?
- Is an IT process critical to the business?
- Is an IT activity connected with an important account?
- Are there known deficiencies or material weaknesses in a technology?

- Is this a high-risk computer operation?
- Is the financial application a feeder system to several system interfaces — from transaction origination to final destination — in a major general ledger account?
- Is the application characterized by: high-value and/or high-volume transactions, automated computation and reconciliation, straight-through processing, and a high volume of non-routine procedural bypasses/overrides?
- Do many business units share the application across the enterprise?
- Is this IT process dependent on manual controls to complete the end-to-end process?
- Is this IT process managed by a third-party outsourcer?

Questions such as these can help place relevance boundaries around your IT operations and infrastructure.

Internal Control Model

A good model to use in looking at internal controls is contained in IT Control Objectives for Sarbanes-Oxley by the IT Governance Institute.

From an overall view this model helps define the internal control universe needed for IT controls. If you identify the significant accounts in financial statements and the processes and applications you've put some real limitations on your scope of work.

It should be noted that from a control perspective all other controls are dependent on IT general controls which reside on the bottom tier of the Figure below.

Figure 10.1: Internal Control Model for defining IT Controls

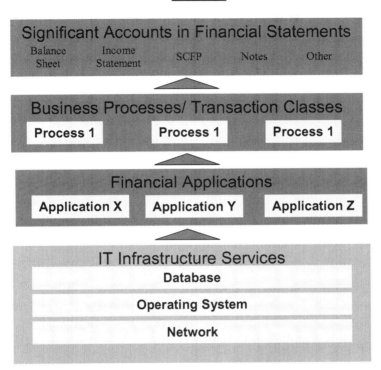

IT general controls cover a wide range of behaviours and systems at the infrastructure level. This includes program development, change management, computer operations, and access to programs and data.

If you have sound IT general controls you, by definition, limit the exposure of all the controls on the other levels – especially application controls. The reason for this is that the amount of testing required at the application level diminishes if you demonstrate that controls at the network, database, and OS level are sound.

Scope of Internal Controls

Based on Ernst & Young data there is a wide range in the number of processes being documented and the number of controls being documented within each process. Companies are documenting anywhere from five to 50 processes per location with 2/3 evaluating less than 25, which highlights the confusion around 404 internal controls.

It seems the PCAOB went out of their way to be as vague as possible as to what internal controls are necessary. They defaulted to:

"Internal control is not "one-size-fits-all" and the nature and extent of controls that are necessary depend, to a great extent, on the size and complexity of the company." Consequently, companies and auditors are both struggling to determine what an appropriate level of internal control is, and to what level must they be defined and tested.

Testing Internal Controls

Remember, Sarbanes-Oxley is all about financial reporting. A company's management needs to decide which controls it depends on to detect material errors in financial statements. They need to decide which combination of controls and testing will provide the right level of assurance.

Again, there is no pat answer. Each company needs to develop a testing program that management believes in. After all the intent of Sarbanes-Oxley is to have senior management own and manage the control process – form design to implementation to assessment.

Today many companies are executing to an internally manageable level in terms of resource, cost, and risk. Then waiting until they experience their first audit to determine an on-going action plan.

However, the "control – test – document" model is one that will become ingrained in companies as Sarbanes-Oxley establishes itself as an on-going Compliance requirement.

How to Structure IT General Controls

As we've pointed out repeatedly, Sarbanes-Oxley is about financial reporting. When you are defining IT general controls it is to your benefit to make sure that you clearly define the systems and processes that touch your company's financial reporting universe.

In COSO there are two broad groupings of IT internal controls:
- Application Controls - apply to business processes they support and designed within the application to prevent and detect unauthorized transactions
- General Controls - apply to all information systems, support secure and continuous operation
- In order to construct IT general controls, functional areas can be delineated to provide a suitable template for specific controls. These include:
    - Systems Security
    - Configuration Management
    - Data Management
    - Operations

Each of these areas has multiple controls – some of them logical documented policy statements, others more concrete data measurable processes.

For each internal control single or multiple tests can exist to demonstrate the controls' validity. In many policy instances a copy of a written plan is an acceptable test.

In other cases such as security or configuration, documented reports showing appropriate data points from a system will be required.

In the section that follows we have developed a template of IT General Controls for multiple functional areas. In each template we will:

- Define a series of internal controls
- Defines tests for those internal controls
- Identify an Ecora report that documents the test

In some cases there will be no Ecora report because the control is a broad written policy.

Systems Security

Probably the most visible area of IT is security. Many companies have security officers and many audit security of a regular basis.
However, specific to Sarbanes-Oxley, security internal controls aim to provide reasonable assurance that the systems supporting financial reporting are secure against unauthorized use, manipulation, or loss of data.
This means both physical and logical controls that support the overall security environment where deficiencies could impact financial reporting (see Tables below).

Table 10.1: System security

Internal Control	Test of Internal Control	Ecora Report for Test
An IT security policy is in place and approved by senior management	Review a copy of the security policy. Evaluate specific areas for Compliance.	Not Applicable
	Review security plan to insure relevant financial reporting systems are adequately covered.	Not Applicable
User authentication procedures are followed to insure transaction validity	Ensure strong password and account lockout policies are implemented.	Password Policy
	Ensure appropriate database authentication mode is configured	Authentication Mode
	User session timeout is defined and in place for authorized users	
	Audit and review user privileges on each system	User Privileges
	Audit and review system access permissions to sensitive files	NTFS Permissions

A process exists to review and maintain access rights effectiveness.	Ensure each DBA has own account and no generic accounts used to bypass audit trail of DBA activity	DBA Accounts
	Ensure all logins have passwords and not default password	Login Password
	Review role memberships and permissions to ensure appropriate access and privileges to databases	Role Permissions & Memberships
	Set file system privileges to prevent unauthorized access to database server data files, log files, and backup file	System Privileges
	Ensure Verify Function exists and valid to ensure user passwords are validated and strong password criteria required	Verify Function
	Prove adequate password validation in place	Password Lifetime, Password Grace Period, Password Reuse Time, Failed Login Attempts,

		Password Lock Time
Procedure exists to insure timely action on user account activity: issuing, closing, adjusting	Select sample of terminated employees and determine if their access has been removed	User Access
	Select a sample of new users and determine if access granted matches access approved.	User Access
	Select a sample of current users and review access privileges to determine if rights are appropriate for job function	User Access
	Validate that attempts to gain unauthorized access to financial reporting system are logged and followed up.	Failed Login Frequently Failed Login
A control process exists to review and confirm access rights.	Audit and review user privileges on each system	User Privileges
	Audit and review system access permissions to sensitive files	NTFS Permissions

	Ensure systems configured to restrict anonymous remote access to your systems.	Remote Access
Appropriate controls exist to review and manage remote network access	Audit and review list of linked and remote servers	External Servers
	Identify all public database links. Review and replace with private links as appropriate to restrict access to confidential data	Public Links
	Ensure anti-virus software installed on systems	Computer without Ant-virus Installed
IT Security administration monitors and logs security information and violations reported to management	Determine that a security office or function exists and monitors/reports on security vulnerabilities	Not Applicable
	Review security notable events over past year and management's response.	Not Applicable

172

| Access to facilities is restricted to authorized people and requires identification and authentication | Review written policies and procedures to determine appropriateness. | Not Applicable |

Configuration Management

Configuration Management controls ensure that systems are set up and maintained to protect the security, availability, and processing integrity of financial reporting.

Table 10.2: Configuration management

Internal Control	Test for Internal Control	Ecora Report for Test
Only authorized software is in use on company IT systems.	Review installed applications on all relevant systems.	Installed Application by Computer
System infrastructure is configured to prevent unauthorized access	Confirm that standard server configuration is documented and implemented	Baseline Report
	Review relevant infrastructure components to determine if they adhere to organization's policies.	OS and Service Pack Report by Computer Role
	Ensure all services are configured appropriately and that only required services are running to protect system from unauthorized access	Services Summary

	If using SNMP ensure appropriate Community String(s) defined to prevent unauthorized users from obtaining systems status information	SNMP
Procedures for protection against malicious programs are in place through the use of anti-virus and other software and measures	Ensure systems are updated with appropriate service packs and hot fixes	Patch Levels
	Ensure anti-virus software installed on systems	Computer without Ant-virus Installed
Applications and data storage systems are properly configured to ensure appropriate access control	Evaluate management's frequency of configuration management review	Not Applicable
	Review configuration changes to see if they have been properly approved based on policy.	Consolidated Change Report

Operations

Managing operations addresses how your company maintains reliable systems in support of financial reporting processes.

174

Table 10.3: Operations

Internal Control	Test for Internal Control	Ecora Report for Test
Management establishes, documents, and maintains standard policies and procedures for IT operations.	Review documented policies and determine if they are reviewed periodically.	N/A
Appropriate audit mechanisms are in place to allow detail event tracking	Ensure strong audit policy configured to ensure audit trail of events is recorded to provide audit trail of user activity (e.g. account login events, policy change, object access, process tracking, etc.)	Audit Policy
	Enable audit events to provide audit trail of user activity	Auditing Enabled
	Enable Archive Log Mode to allow point in time recovery to ensure data not lost when recovering	Archive Log Mode
	Ensure event log setting are configured to retain recorded events for appropriate time and prevent guest access to logs	Event Log
Controls exist to ensure data is collected for tracking user activity	Set Initialization Parameters to provide security and ensure database auditing is active	Initialization Parameters

175

	Audit and review DB owner for each database	DB Owner

Data Management

Data management controls are used to support information integrity, completeness, and accuracy.

Table 10.4: Data management

Internal Control	Test for Internal Control	Ecora Report for Test
Policies exist for handling, distribution and retention of data and financial reporting output.	Review documented policies and determine if they are adequate and reviewed periodically.	Not Applicable
Retention periods and storage terms for all incoming and outgoing data are clearly defined.	Review written procedures for completeness and adequacy	Not Applicable
A backup and recovery plan has been implemented	Review plan for completeness and relevance.	Not Applicable
	Restore selected configuration data and compare to see if its accurate	Change Report
Confirm no unauthorized changes occur in financial relevant infrastructure	Review selected server configuration data and compare with baseline data	Consolidated Change Report

Summary

Sarbanes-Oxley is a complex and demanding legal requirement. One piece of it is demonstrating IT internal controls.

To comply with the Sarbanes-Oxley Act you need to establish internal controls and procedures. Accurate reporting and record keeping are the 'best practices' for IT organizations and business operations.
Manually collecting this critical configuration information from your servers is time consuming and relies on a human-based process.

Companies utilizing a human-based process invest enormous resources and allow tremendous room for human error.
Therefore, we highly recommend that you use an automated process, configuration management tool using Ecora Enterprise Auditor.

Ecora Enterprise Auditor can help you quickly and simply demonstrate internal controls with comprehensive reporting and change management processes.
It is an indispensable tool for documenting and managing your IT environment. If you're addressing Sarbanes-Oxley, HIPAA, CFR Part 11, or other regulatory Compliance acts, Ecora automates and delivers audit-ready reports that improve accuracy and, save time and money. Ecora supports enterprise platforms: Cisco Systems, Lotus Domino, Microsoft, Novell, Oracle, HP-UX, IBM, Sun Microsystems, Red Hat, and Citrix.

Ecora provides total configuration management solutions that automate multi-platform configuration reporting, change monitoring, and patch management.
Ecora's solutions (see below) enhance efficiency and reduce the costs associated with IT Compliance, business

continuity, and vulnerability assessment while providing the means to monitor change and plan for recovery.

Ecora Patch Manager – Don't let researching and manual patching take over your time – Know You're Patched, Today! Save time and reduce costs with a focused patch management solution featuring an optional-agent technology for the automated deployment of critical patches and unique reporting capabilities for both, IT administrators and managers.

Ecora Dr. Wi-Fi - Continuously monitor the availability and performance of mission critical Wi-Fi networks. Dr. Wi-Fi provides IT managers' real-time data with easy-to-read "dashboard" reports and proactive alerts.

Ecora DeviceLock - Prevent users with USB drives from stealing your data. Halt unauthorized Wi-Fi networks from gaining access to your valuable information and manage user access to devices.

ACKNOWLEDGEMENT AND THANKS:
The book's Author acknowledges and thanks Ecora Software Corporation, for contributing this White Paper to the book, as follows:

Ecora Software Corporation
Two International Drive, Suite 150
Portsmouth, NH 03801 USA
Phone: 877.923.2672
Fax: 603.436.4344
Email: feedback@ecora.com
Web: www.ecora.com

11. Solvency II

Meaning of Solvency

Solvency refers to the strength and capacity of a business to remain in active in business. We assess how certain risks may harm the firm's ability to keep operating, as its financial figures and ratios relate to debt and liabilities. An organization is said to be "insolvent" when it is no longer able to profit or when liabilities outweigh assets. Insolvent businesses either operate at a loss or become bankrupt.

Therefore, the firm's financial ability to pay debts or insurance policy claims, when they become due; is critical to solvency. The solvency of a company tells an investor, a policyholder or a scheme-member whether a company can pay its debts. To find the solvency of a company, liquidity ratios are typically used, such as, Acid-Test Ratio (ATR) or Current Ratio (CR).

These ratios are used to measure a company's ability to pay its liabilities using assets that are cash or very liquid. ATR is computed by subtracting current assets by inventory; then divide by current liabilities. A ratio of 1.0 or greater may be recommended, but an acceptable value will largely depend on the industry a company is in - it's also called Quick Ratio.

Acid-Test Ratio = [Current Assets – Inventory] / Current Liabilities

As a common financial ratio CR is used to measure a company's liquidity, or its ability to meet short-term debt obligations. A higher ratio indicates that a company is more liquid, therefore better able to service short-term debt. However, too high a ratio indicates an over-conservative utilization or under-utilization of finance.

Current Ratio = current assets / current liabilities.

Various rules and regulations mandate solvency Compliance and applications in each country, however in recent years, many of these have come together internationally.

Coverage of Solvency II

An insurance company should have a solvency position that is sufficient to fulfil its obligations to policyholders and other parties[20]. It is important that insurance undertakings in the EU are subject to same solvency margin requirements to provide the same protection of policyholders' interests as well as to create a level-playing field between undertakings.

The current solvency regime was created in the 1970's and it has recently been amended and updated as part of the "Solvency I" package.
In addition to these amendments, the Commission Services, in co-operation with the Member States, have started "Solvency II project" to assess whether more fundamental changes to the EU insurance solvency regime would be needed.
This very comprehensive project should analyse and bring together subjects such as a more risk-based approach, harmonisation of the establishment of technical provisions, new risk transfer techniques and recent developments in financial reporting.

The Solvency II Directive proposal will be accompanied by an impact assessment report, which explains the need for legislative action, outlines the objectives of the work

---

[20] For more information go to
http://europa.eu.int/comm/internal_market/insurance/solvency_en.htm

and the various options available to meet these objectives.

An impact assessment report measures in a qualitative and quantitative way the various options taking account of stakeholders' comments.
The Quantitative Impact Studies run by the Committee of European Insurance and Occupational Pensions Supervisors (CEIOPS) will be a key input in assessing the quantitative impact of the proposal.
Significant developments have taken place in the insurance market as well as in supervisory practice, since the rules were created, and there is consequently a need to analyse whether the rules still serve their purpose.

Three Pillars of Solvency II

Solvency II will offer protection to policyholders against failure of insurance companies and be in force for all insurance companies in the EU after transforming the directive into national law, effective from 2007, to be implemented probably in 2009/2010. It will also apply to foreign companies operating in the EU.

The 3 pillars, similar to Basel II, which include; 'fair value', insurance risk, investment / market risk, credit risk, asset-liability mismatch, and operational risk, are (see Figure below):

1 - Financial resources; embracing:
- Technical provisions
- MCR: Minimum Capital Requirements
- SCR: Solvency Capital Requirements
2 – Regulatory review; embracing:
- Internal controls
- Risk Management
- Measures of supervision
3 – Market discipline; embracing:

- Disclosure of information on risks
- Scenario analysis of assets
- Technical provisions

Solvency II Project

Solvency II project has a much wider scope than
Solvency I.
It contains a fundamental and wide-ranging review of the
current regime in the light of current development in
insurance, risk management, finance techniques, financial
reporting, etc.
One the key objectives of Solvency II are to establish a
solvency system that is better matched to the true risks of
an insurance company.
The new Solvency regime will be developed using the
Lamfulussy framework's four level-approach:

- Level 1 – Primary legislation to define broad
  "framework" principles
- Level 2 - Technical implementing measures to be
  adopted by the Commission with the assistance of a
  regulatory committee and an advisory committee
- *Level 3 – Cooperation among national regulators to
  ensure consistent interpretation of Level 2 rules*
- Level 4 – Enforcement to ensure consistent
  implementation of EU legislation.

Useful links concerning Solvency II Project are:

- EU Commission Solvency II Page
- CEIOPS

Solvency II Project Supervisors are:

- International Association of Insurance Supervisors
  (IAIS)
- The UK Financial Services Authority (FSA)

- The Dutch Supervisory Authority (DNB)
- The Swiss Supervisory Authority (FOPI)
- Canadian Office of the Superintendent of Financial Institutions (OSFI)
- Australian Prudential Regulation Authority (APRA)
- Monetary Authority of Singapore (MAS)
- National Association of Insurance Commissioners (NAIC)

Other stakeholders:

- Groupe Consultatif Actuariel Européen
- International Actuarial Association

The Solvency II framework for enhanced European insurance solvency rules is currently under preparation, and a draft EU published directive is expected in mid-2007. Even prior to its formal implementation, Solvency II will dominate the European insurance industry's agenda in the next few years.

The new EU solvency framework is based on a three-pillar approach similar to the Basel II accord designed for banks. This project addresses several key areas of regulatory Compliance, including risk management and disclosure.
The project also tackles the issue of asset and liability valuation, and links to the accounting treatment of insurance contracts under International Financial Reporting Standards (IFRS).

As a risk-based solvency regime, Solvency II encourages the use of internal models.
Some countries such as the UK and Switzerland have anticipated such a risk-based solvency framework and already started to implement Solvency II-type regulatory requirements.

12.   Redwood Blueprint for Sustainable Compliance Solutions[21]

Executive Summary

Around the globe corporations are facing increasingly demanding requirements to comply with governmental regulations. The impact of Compliance on the enterprise can
be far-reaching - from issues of corporate governance in the board room to the information privacy needs of individual customers.

Compliance with the United States Public Company Accounting and Investor Protection Act of 2002, better known as the Sarbanes-Oxley Act, has created a substantial burden on all US public companies and on foreign companies with corporate interests in the U.S. As organizations struggle through the process of meeting the demands of Sarbanes-
Oxley, many have found inadequacies and inefficiencies in their internal controls for financial reporting, which are the focus of the legislation.
While most companies will meet the first deadlines, the requirement to sustain Compliance year after year is causing executives to seek more effective and less costly solutions than those employed during the initial rush to Compliance.

At this critical stage companies have an opportunity to transform the Compliance burden into business value with the solutions they put into place. The weaknesses and inefficiencies in internal controls exposed during the initial

[21] Reprinted from a White Paper with some editing by kind permission of Redwood Software Inc. - see Acknowledgement at the end of this Chapter.

Compliance project can now be identified as areas for process improvement.
Companies that take advantage of this information can improve risk management, create better executive visibility across the enterprise and produce more agile control processes capable of better responding to the demands of both regulation and competition.

Redwood Software uses its unique combination of process automation and information management technologies to provide practical solutions for sustainable Compliance that also deliver measurable business value. The blueprint that we offer here promises a sustainable solution for Compliance with Sarbanes-Oxley and other corporate governance requirements while taking advantage of both the lessons learned during the first phases of Compliance and the processes and systems that are already in place.

Compliance and Business Value - Not a Contradiction

Every corporation is now facing Compliance with industry regulations and laws regarding corporate governance.
In the United States, public companies are required under Section 404 of the Sarbanes-Oxley Act to establish internal controls that ensure timely and accurate financial reporting.

Sarbanes-Oxley also has implications for organizations, which have corporate interests in the US even if they are not US companies. Securities firms are instituting information retention systems to meet the mandates of SEC Rule 17.

Healthcare organizations are protecting confidential patient information under the HIPAA requirements. International banking institutions are preparing to comply with reporting standards mandated by the Basel II Capital Accord.

For corporations trying to manage the immediate burdens of regulatory Compliance, notion related to return on investment and improving business performance may seem wildly optimistic.
However, at Redwood we know from experience that solutions which help enterprises comply with current and approaching regulations can at the same time make organizations more responsive and create business value.
With deadlines either past or fast approaching, the case for the Sarbanes-Oxley (SOX) Act is particularly relevant. SOX is forcing companies to rethink and refine their processes around financial reporting and enterprise risk management.

According to a survey published in July 2004 by PricewaterhouseCoopers, 79 percent of senior executives said that their company must make improvements in order to comply with Section 404 of Sarbanes-Oxley. This reflects the process of discovery that Compliance forces on organizations.
Compliance causes examination of existing internal controls and business processes. The result is inevitable - gaps and weakness in existing processes are found. The PwC survey indicates that internal controls requiring remediation include financial processes, computer controls and internal audit effectiveness.

With the appropriate solutions to close these gaps, determined companies have the opportunity to use their investment in Compliance to build a more transparent, responsive and competitive business. However, the initial push to Compliance at the first deadline has generated solutions that are proving to be expensive, inefficient and inflexible for sustaining Compliance year after year.

In the PwC survey, 93 percent of executives expect their company to launch process improvement initiatives to streamline future Compliance.
Compliance projects to meet the deadlines were not enough - Compliance programs are now required.

Some of the key areas of process improvement that have been exposed by SOX Compliance initiatives are:

- Risk identification and mitigation
- IT operations
- Information sharing
- Document management and retention
- Financial reporting

Report2Web

Report2Web is a Web-based document management and distribution solution that enables the secure, automated publishing and delivery of business information. By treating the Web as an automation platform, Report2Web connects employees, partners, and customers to the information they need day-to-day.

Report2Web modules include:

- Report2Web server
- Extranet Edition
- Bundler
- Burster
- Router
- Archiver
- Forms designer.

The Report2Web Server manages documents in a document repository, which automatically catalogues and secures all documents according to rules established by system administrators.

Report2Web Extranet Edition utilizes the reach of the Internet in securely publishing reports to end-users, customers and business partners located beyond the firewall without exposing internal systems to unauthorized access.

Report2Web Bundler creates personalized report bundles to suit individual end-user requirements.
Instead of searching through reams of irrelevant output dispersed across multiple print files, end-users only need open their report bundle to find all the information they need to perform a particular task.

Report2Web Burster creates personalized documents that feature context sensitive hyperlinks, highlighting of significant field values and helpful annotations. In addition, report content can be converted into Excel spreadsheet format as well as XML documents.
(See Figure below)

Report2Web Router enables you to control the routing and distribution of output files created by any application. The moment a report arrives; it is processed and delivered to the people that need it.

Report2Web Archiver delivers seamless, Web-based access to aged reports. End-users become more productive with Report2Web Archiver, while at the same time important documents are retained for long-term retrieval, enabling regulatory requirements to be met. Historic information remains accessible through a single click for each archived report within Report2Web.

Report2Web Forms Designer transforms application output into high quality business documents through electronic forms processing

Stored softcopy versions of reports are an exact match of hardcopy documents, enabling customer service agents to become more efficient when dealing with customer billing and invoicing inquiries.

Output created by any existing system, such as mainframe, ERP or CRM solutions can be enhanced without any application changes using Report2Web Forms Designer.

Redwood is no stranger to building Compliance solutions that also create business value. Our Report2Web for Healthcare solution has assisted hundreds of public and private healthcare organizations, and major insurance and pharmaceutical companies to meet and exceed the mandates for document retention and personal health information privacy and security of the US Healthcare Insurance Portability and Accountability Act of 1996 (HIPAA).

For example, when Wake Forest University Baptist Medical Centre implemented Report2Web for Healthcare they found that the Finance Department was able to shave 3 days off of their month-end closing activities, and eliminated over 1.5 million pages of printing and paper costs per month.

The same solution also provided internal controls for information sharing and security required by HIPAA and enabled the medical centre to meet Federal regulations for 7-year retention of patient information.

Charles Ware, Director of Computer and Communications Services, concluded: "HIPAA does change the way we do business in most cases, but in the case of Report2Web we are already there."

Redwood has taken this same approach - supporting Compliance together with business value - and applied it to our Sarbanes-Oxley solution.

By following Redwood's SOX Blueprint, companies can build sustainable Compliance solutions, gain better visibility for corporate governance, create more effective and efficient operations and build more responsive business processes.

The Key Provisions of Sarbanes-Oxley At the heart of the Sarbanes-Oxley act are Sections 302 and 404. Section 302 focuses on the transparency, reliability, timeliness and accuracy of a company's financial statements.

Section 404 requires certification of the internal controls and business processes that support the accuracy of financial reports. Since all public companies in the United States must comply with Sections 302 and 404 in the near term, most have a sense of urgency in documentation, remediation and testing of internal controls related to financial reporting.

Auditors are also being guided by regulations and their interpretation by the PCAOB (Public Company Accounting Oversight Board) to assess each company's management of information and communications, and the company's ability to monitor the effectiveness of their control activities.

Perhaps even more demanding in terms of sustainable Compliance is Section 409, which requires companies to urgently disclose material changes to their financial condition or operations, usually within 4 days.

At the same time, the U.S. Securities and Exchange Commission (SEC CFR Release 33-8128) is accelerating quarterly and annual financial reporting requirements from 90 to 60 days for large companies and from 45 to 30 days for smaller ones.

The requirements of real-time disclosure and accelerated period-end reporting create.

The Redwood Blueprint for Sustainable Compliance Solutions Coverage

- Corporate Risk
- Improved Operational
- Efficiency
- Automate Systems & Processes
- Establish Information & Communications Controls
- Decreasing Risk
- Increasing Value

If that is not enough, Sections 802 and 1102 of Sarbanes-Oxley dramatically increase the scope of documents that must be retained and accessible for auditing purposes. The PCAOB has indicated that a company's period-end close documentation is subject to audit under their interpretation of SOX regulations.

And auditors are now required to maintain all audit or review work-papers and other records for 7 years. Further, under threat of stiff criminal penalties, companies must institute internal controls to protect documents from improper alteration or destruction.

Redwood Software's Sarbanes-Oxley Blueprint addresses the key provisions of SOX and future Compliance demands by providing a methodology, which supports the application of Redwood's cost-effective software solutions to either replace or assist manual and automated processes for internal controls.

The Blueprint helps identify weaknesses in information management and IT controls and uncovers high-value areas where automation can support document and process management to minimize risk and avoid costly testing of controls each year.

Companies that already have automation solutions in place can typically use these existing systems and add value through integration with Redwood solutions.
In short, the Redwood SOX Blueprint provides a practical plan for taking the internal controls and processes you already have in place and improving their effectiveness and business value over time.

The 6 steps in the Redwood SOX Blueprint

- Step 1 - Inventory documents and IT processes that support financial reporting.
- Step 2 - Improve control of information aggregation, access and retention.
- Step 3 - Strengthen control of IT processes across applications and systems.
- Step 4 - Automate period-end close controls.
- Step 5 - Institute more effective real-time alerts and notifications.
- Step 6 - Expand use of the Redwood Blueprint beyond financial reporting.

IT General Controls

In their July 2004 "Sarbanes-Oxley Act Section 404 Practical Guidance for Management2", PricewaterhouseCoopers identifies that general controls for computer operations are a key requirement for Sarbanes-Oxley Section 404 Compliance.
According to PwC, system and application processing must be appropriately authorized and scheduled, and the control objective is that "processed deviations or problems from scheduled processing are identified and resolved."

Controls must be put in place to "record, analyze and resolve incidents, problems, and errors for systems and applications in a timely manner. System jobs, including batch jobs and interfaces, for relevant financial reporting applications or data must be processed accurately, completely, and in a timely manner."

Additional general controls are recommended for the backup of production data and the scheduling of production jobs.
To reach the goal of sustainable Compliance, a process control and management system must be put in place to control and monitor complex, distributed IT operations.

The 1st Step of the Redwood SOX Blueprint is intended to build upon what the organization has learned in its initial project for Sarbanes-Oxley Compliance, where internal control processes have been documented, remediated and tested.
In this step, your organization identifies and inventories the information resources (reports, records and documents) and IT general controls that are part of your internal control processes.

By listing and examining IT controls at this level in Step 1 of the Redwood Blueprint, some key IT control deficiencies could be exposed such as:

- Procedures for manual and system processes do not exist, or do not match reality
- Automated processes can be changed without authorization and without traceability.
- Posting periods are not restricted
- Production transactions are accessible to large numbers of users
- Many people can run business transactions in production
- Unidentified or unresolved segregation of duties.

Particular attention should be paid to the period-end closing process. Because of Sarbanes-Oxley, auditors are now paying attention to monthly, quarterly and year-end closes and consolidations. Since most closes and consolidations involve multiple IT applications, cross application processes must be completed on schedule. Operations controls should be identified such that corrections must be managed at the source rather than by top line entries accomplished by management overrides.

By identifying, listing and documenting these and other weak manual and automated operations in Step 1, the important gaps in IT general controls are uncovered so that sustainable controls can be put in place in subsequent steps of the Blueprint.

The 2nd Step is to improve control of information aggregation, access and retention.
Step 2 of the Redwood SOX Blueprint uses Redwood's enterprise information management solution to collect and aggregate the documents listed in the first step, from the variety of corporate systems, into an enterprise document repository.
Once secured in the repository, the solution facilitates search and retrieval controls, traces information access, and automates document retention.

For example:

- Form 10Q (SEC-filed quarterly financial statement/report)
- Form 10K (SEC-filed annual financial statement/report)
- Detail Report
- Notices
- Claims
- Payroll
- Spreadsheets
- Financial Summaries
- Inventory
- Scanned Documents

- Shipping Documents
- Meeting Minutes
- Legal Documents
- Assets & Liabilities
- Bills of Lading
- Confirmations
- Vendor Financial Statements
- Long Term Dept Reports
- Employee Benefit Costs
- Property Reports
- Correspondence
- Statement of Financial Performance
- Time Sheets
- Code of Ethics
- Invoices - Sent & Paid
- Expenses
- Statement of Responsibility
- Sales Orders
- Purchase Orders
- E-Mail
- Quotes
- Price List
- Safety Check Reports
- Cheques - Cancelled, Issued, Stale
- Accounts Receivables
- Contact Logs
- Fax
- Financial Reports
- Insurance Claims
- Bank Statements
- Bonds
- Letters and Memos
- Accounts Receivables
- Contracts
- Scanned Documents
- Taxes
- Policies
- Annual Report

- Cash-flow
- Expenses and Revenue
- Customer Letters
- Authorizations
- Notes Payable
- General Ledger
- Investment Reports
- Credit Memos
- Judgements
- Customer E-Mails
- Certificates
- Early Warning Reports
- Disbursements
- Accounting Records
- Form 8K (SEC-filed corporate changes or material events which are important to investors and not previously disclosed in any other form)
- Transcripts
- Trial Balance
- Order Log

A few of the benefits of the Redwood information management solution are:

- Logically organizes all information that feeds the financial reports
- Saves time and money by enabling authorized personnel to quickly locate the information they need
- Eliminates the cost, maintenance and liability of multiple document archiving and filing systems
- Minimizes the potential for lost and altered documents
- Provides security and traceability of document access
- Low cost integration with existing applications
- Redwood's information management solution enables both electronic and paper documents to be captured, managed and archived in a central location

- Documents are captured with a minimum of change to the systems and applications that generate the information
- Documents from across the organization are captured and centralized, protected from unauthorized access, and every access to the document repository is logged.
- The system automatically catalogues and secures all documents according to rules set by authorized system administrators.

Powerful administration tools simplify the management of:

- User and system security
- Document access rights
- Document data format conversions
- Information search and retrieval functions
- Document storage and delivery operations
- Auditing of document access and system usage

The Redwood solution provides specific features that are important for control of period-end and financial documents.

Classification and Indexing

Every document that is published into the enterprise document repository is classified and indexed.
With appropriate security authorization, a user can find documents in a familiar customizable folder structure.

Documents can be indexed in multiple views so that they are grouped according to what makes sense within each department with specific information being visible to specific individuals or groups.

This multiple indexing and document security based on each user's role makes it easy to locate information, while also enforcing rules for Segmentation of Duties so vital to SOX Compliance.

Sensitive information is secured in a tamper-proof read-only format so that users can easily find what they need, and only what they need, to do their jobs.

Version Control and Snapshot Reports

The Redwood document repository stores snapshot reports generated by ERP systems, BI (Business Intelligence) tools and any other software applications.

If multiple versions of the same report are generated, the repository automatically creates versions and time-stamps the documents so that the versions can be easily compared and tracked with just a few clicks in a browser. Using this solution, uncertainty can be eliminated and the workload of producing documentation during audits and discovery can be significantly reduced.

Annotation and Approval

Often the final approval of financial information is communicated by email or simply in a conversation. An enterprise document repository improves visibility and traceability of signoff and change control.

Holding documents in a centralized repository and requiring any requested changes to be recorded as notes or annotations to the original document can institute better internal controls.

For example, an employee's expense report can be archived upon submission, and any changes to it could be done only by means of notes added and recorded electronically along with the report in the repository. Updated versions of the expense report would also be archived, producing an audit trail of changes to the document. Finally, when the expense report is approved for payment, the approval signoff can be recorded with a digital stamp of the approving manager and the time and date of the approval.

This type of control process is available for any financial document maintained in the repository.

The 3rd Step is to strengthen control of IT processes across applications and systems.

In Step 3, the IT control processes that were identified as being crucial to financial reporting in Step 1 are strengthened by improving systems automation across applications and systems.

The challenge for organizations trying to manage internal controls for financial reporting lies in the back-end integration of legacy, ERP and Web-based applications.

Tighter integration is required because events that occur as part of business transactions, such as creating customer orders, now require multiple applications to complete, such as accounting, manufacturing, shipping and warehouse management, often involving multiple data centres and companies. Enterprise-wide IT process management becomes a necessity for managing risks.

Some of the benefits of using the Redwood IT process management solution are:

- Controls and monitors the applications and systems that feed the financial reports — across applications, systems and data centres
- Saves time and money by automating routine and non-routine IT operations, and optimizing computing resources
- Eliminates errors and controls weaknesses introduced by manual intervention in IT processes
- Speeds detection and correction of IT operations problems and incomplete processes

- Minimizes turnaround time and delayed postings of business transactions
- Strengthens control of system and data backup and recovery operations
- Leverages existing ERP, Accounting Systems, SCM and other IT investments.

The Redwood solution provides specific features that are important for effective control of period-end and financial reporting processes.

Transaction-level Process Management

Redwood provides a dynamic execution environment that enables monitoring and control at the transaction level. Unlike legacy based automation solutions, which create a schedule for a particular time interval that is then loaded on a target server for processing, Redwood loads tasks onto the server at run time.

This means that a new transaction based service can be provided so that a previously unattainable level of real-time systems management is possible. Not only can processes be scheduled to start by calendaring rules such as "every last working day of the month", but system activities can be used to trigger processes based on events such as the completion of a file transfer, a database record update or the completion of a series of processing steps.

Event-based Triggers and Alerts

Events generated by business applications can be used to fully automate back-end business processing, enabling a real-time IT process control and monitoring.

For example, an account update transaction in a CRM application can trigger a set of processes to maintain consistency of the account information in the ERP system.

The arrival of an order file perhaps faxed or web based can also trigger Redwood's solution to start the order fulfilment process and even move the order file to the enterprise document repository for secure archiving for future retrieval.

The system can automatically initiate recovery and restart procedures according to prescribed process flows should failures occur.

If there is no known resolution to the failure, the system can immediately alert appropriate personnel.

Reports can be initiated to document and store failure information in the enterprise document repository.

Redwood not only automates and documents processes but also provides management and auditors with documentation of the process flows and audit trails through comprehensive logging.

The system provides the ability to trace and detect irregularities in the processes and to provide real-time alerts when exceptions are detected.

Ability to Manage Across Existing IT Systems and Applications

For sustainable Compliance, business processes related to financial reporting must be managed across existing IT systems and applications, including legacy systems.

Investments in ERP, CRM and SCM solutions must be leveraged by the system automation solution.

Redwood provides seamless interfaces to strategic business applications such as SAP, Oracle and PeopleSoft.

Redwood IT process management technology has been proven to be more than capable of meeting the largest scale enterprise and Internet application demands on a variety of computing platforms including UNIX, Linux, Windows, J2EE, VMS, AS/400 and z/OS.

The Redwood Process Monitor console provides real-time information about the status of each step within each process, enabling authorized IT administrators to control individual application processes running in real-time on any platform, at any location.

Segregation of Duties

Compliance requires the ability to delegate and control administration so that only authorized users is empowered to work with their own business work units. Redwood implements very granular security based on individual users.
Each user or group of users defined to the system is allocated different responsibilities depending on who they are and what they need to do.

For example you can restrict the ability to define workload, create schedules, and configure events to specific users, while others can perform only day-to-day operational tasks such as monitoring running jobs and responding to messages.
You can also define groups of users who can administer one set of processes (e.g. Manufacturing) but not another, such as Finance or Accounting. This allows a single tool to be used to administer multiple business-critical application processes while securely maintaining SOD controls.

Better Control of System and Data Backup and Recovery Operations

Redwood can help in several ways as part of a corporate data backup and recovery policy.

Corporate planning for disaster recovery will include procedures such as: running background tasks to recover data from backup sources, applying recovered data to applications, instigating 'roll forward' procedures to apply incremental backup data to full backup staging posts, executing test suites to ensure recovery has been successful and so on.

Redwood can bring the disparate recovery actions together - for example detecting when a restore has completed and applying database 'redo log' processing to put individual transactions back in place.
It can also create checkpoints by demanding operator response to system messages before proceeding with the next step, allowing full control both in terms of automation and manual intervention only where it is necessary.

The 4th Step automates period-end close controls. Controls on period-end processes are crucial to the accuracy and reliability of the financial reports, and are not only important for Sarbanes-Oxley Compliance, but also for overall corporate governance and risk management.
Redwood solutions for period-end close provide some of the most significant business value of any activities a company can do related to Sarbanes-Oxley.

Benefits include (see Figure below):

- Management receives accurate financial reports more quickly, enabling quicker decision-making and disclosures
- Processes are monitored in real time. In this example, financial data and orders are being extracted from the data warehouse
- The monitor indicates an error in the data warehouse backup process, and completion of the report

distribution process. Automated notification of the backup error is executed by the error step

- Use of electronic report distribution streamlines operations, saves time and labour for report production and reduces paper, printing, distribution and storage costs
- Enables tighter management and better visibility of the scheduling and execution of the many IT processes that finally produce the financial reports
- Improves traceability for adjustments of accounts and out-of-period postings.

Figure 12.1: Redwood's Sarbanes-Oxley Blueprint

Decreasing risk   Increasing value

| Establish info. & communication controls | Automate systems & processes | Improved operational efficiency |

Redwood's Sarbanes-Oxley Blueprint

Most companies use multiple applications and sources of information to feed the closing process. Native application tools may not be powerful enough to trigger and monitor the appropriate IT and reporting processes across the enterprise.

Take for example, a typical corporation that is composed of several entities (companies), each of which is responsible for closing their financials at the end of each period.

As each company closes, a report is generated by the ERP solution, which indicates a new period from the day before. Rather than a set of people in accounting watching for this change of period and the implied period closure, better internal control is enabled by a period-end close solution that automatically detects the change of period as soon as the report is produced by the ERP system.

The solution then intelligently triggers other processes, such as consolidations across the entities when all of them have closed and manages the subsequent production and distribution of related reports to appropriate personnel.

Control of In-Period Postings

Given the potential for risk, auditors and management alike need better reliability and visibility over in-period and out-of-period postings. These postings need to be identified, controlled, monitored and traced.

Often these are events that span applications; rely on batch journal entries from multiple systems and updates to databases or data warehouses that are used to consolidate the financials.

Using Redwood, these batch processes can be managed as automated job chains and, if processes do not execute according to schedule, the system can endeavour to automatically restart or resume processes that have not completed.

Documents that are awaiting input from various transactions or applications ("parked documents") can be detected and the system can take appropriate action to correct the problem in period, or provide notification of incompletion. In fact, any job chain that does not complete within a specified period of time can automatically issue alerts and notifications to appropriate personnel.

The system maintains logs related to all period-end processes for internal review and auditing after the close. This ability to schedule and monitor batch journal entries from multiple systems and detect incomplete or delayed processes is an important IT control for any period-end close process.

Documenting Adjustments of Accounts and "Over the Top" Entries

Another area where automation improves internal control of the period-end close process is documenting any adjustments of accounts and "over the top" journal entries.
Such adjustments may be communicated by email, on paper, or verbally, with poor management visibility and auditability.
Redwood's solution provides a means of documenting and auditing adjustments of accounts by maintaining financial report snapshots in the enterprise repository. As mentioned above, each report is automatically versioned to enable an historical record of changes.
Since documents are maintained in a centralized repository, there is no question as to what is the "document of record" at any point in time, and all accesses to that document are recorded in auditable log files, along with the identity of the person who viewed it with a digital date and time stamp.
A typical period-end process is to manually run multiple copies of period-end financial reports. Then, IT or accounting staff split the reports into pieces or "sub-reports" for example by department or business unit. These sub-reports are distributed to the appropriate business owners responsible for review.
Then their comments are collected and the financial applications and spreadsheets are updated to reflect their changes. The entire process is reiterated, perhaps several times until the period close is determined.

This inefficient, time-consuming and laborious process can be automated and shortened, sometimes by days. By using Redwood's period-end close solution, companies routinely save time and reduce the cost of their period-end close.

Documents are stored on a centralized web server so that multiple copies and print versions are no longer required.

Reports are automatically split into appropriate sub-reports by the Report Burster tool, and the sub-reports are immediately routed to appropriate personnel, who can receive email notification that they are ready for review. Documents are reviewed and electronic annotations and notes collect comments.

Then, after updates are made to financial applications, new versions of the reports are automatically published into the system.

The review process is more controlled and each iteration is completed more quickly.

The 5th step is to institute more effective real-time alerts and notifications.

Using Redwood's tools has improved the timeliness, reliability and auditability of period-end closes. The next step of the Redwood Blueprint is to identify specific points throughout these and other processes that require faster or more granular notifications or alerts when document content or IT process flow is not within acceptable risk tolerance, or when possible material changes in financial or operational status may require timely disclosure.

Document/Content Alerts

Manual controls for document content introduce risk, especially when there are a large number of transactions. Take for example a cost centre report. Typically, transactions are grouped rather than having people examine each and every transaction. Manual controls for review and comparison of content within or across documents are costly, prone to human error and it may even be difficult to determine whether or not the documents were actually reviewed.

With Redwood's solution, content variations can be detected with tools that scan the content of documents and automatically detect anomalies and variants in financial data that may be missed by manual controls. When such problems are detected, notification and alerts can be immediately issued to appropriate personnel. Intelligent scanning and bursting tools eliminate manual controls such as comparing values across multiple documents to verify, for example, the accuracy of purchase orders and fulfilments, cost centre reports, invalid account codes, etc.

This document/content alert process supports the requirements of Section 409 of Sarbanes-Oxley to notify management of material changes to financial conditions or operations. By identifying key fields in financial reports that can be automatically scanned as soon as they are published, management can be alerted quickly to material changes.
Furthermore the Redwood solution can bundle together relevant documents and route them to appropriate executives to facilitate timely internal review and disclosure.

IT Process Alerts

The accuracy of financial reporting is dependent on the reliability and accuracy of many IT processes. Programmed and configurable IT process controls provide a means of automating the risk management process. With Redwood's process automatically re-starting, process chains can often correct management solution problems reliably and efficiently, or providing alternate process chains in case of specific errors or conditions.

However, not every possible condition can be anticipated. For example, a critical process that doesn't complete in time or a "parked" document waiting for data input can have widespread impact on financial reports.
Problem management procedures are typically a combination of automated and manual controls. Redwood's solution can immediately alert systems administrators or operators if there is no known resolution to a failure and audit trails provide a comprehensive log of all processing.

The 6th Step is to expand use of the Redwood Blueprint beyond financial reporting.
Steps 1 through 5 above represent a Blueprint that creates business value by providing more visibility and better control of financial reporting processes related to Sarbanes-Oxley Compliance.
The same methodology and technologies are providing effective return on investment for other business process management applications beyond financial reporting.

Some representative applications of Redwood's solution are:

- A worldwide distributor of IT and telecommunications products uses Redwood's solution for SAP to speed order fulfilment by better management of the manufacturing cycle and stock control
- A leading office superstore retailer uses Redwood to electronically distribute operational reports produced by AS/400, UNIX and VAX VMS systems to thousands of store managers around the globe, and has reduced the number of pages of paper printed by over 90%
- A major telecommunications company uses Redwood to enable business analysts and financial controllers to continuously monitor the key performance indicators of all major business units

- A financial services company with more than half a million customers uses Redwood solutions to meet frequently changing regulations in the financial industry and to automate operations that increase the responsiveness of its customer management system
- A major bank uses Redwood to automatically split its half-million page monthly general ledger into sub-reports by branch and business unit and distribute the appropriate information to managers at branch banking and regional centres throughout the world.
- A global food company uses Redwood software to automate previously manual batch processing of business processes and document distribution across multiple applications within manufacturing, sales and order processing, finance and logistics.

Conclusion

The accuracy and reliability of a company's financial statements require a complex array of business processes and internal controls to function without failure. This typically involves a wide range of manual and automated processes, documents and IT resources throughout the enterprise. In the effort to comply with Sarbanes-Oxley, most organizations have exposed processes that need improvement.
This provides an opportunity to assess the weaknesses discovered and to apply technology where it can assist to improve business processes and better manage risk.
By using the Redwood Sarbanes-Oxley Blueprint, companies can build sustainable Compliance solutions that also provide business value.
Redwood's information management solution can manage the expanded range of document retention and auditability requirements of Sarbanes-Oxley while providing the business with faster information flow and reduced cost of distribution and storage.

Redwood's process management solution can be used to automate key IT processes across systems, thereby strengthening general IT controls and assisting in the reliability and traceability of information resources that feed the financial statements.

The end result is a more agile enterprise, exploiting an event-driven infrastructure with real-time control and monitoring of systems and information resources - in short, an enterprise with less risk that is better able to respond to the dynamic challenges of today's quickly changing, competitive business climate.

ACKNOWLEDGEMENT AND THANKS:

The book's Author acknowledges and thanks Redwood Software for contributing this White Paper to the book, as follows:

Redwood Software Inc.
3000 Aerial Center,
Suite 115 Morrisville,
NC 27560 USA
Phone: +1-919-460-5400 / 888-425-2235 (toll free)
Fax: +1-919-460-5444
E-mail: info.us@redwood.com
Web: www.redwood.com

13. IBM's Insurance Information Warehouse Support for Regulatory Compliance[22]

Introduction

The purpose of this paper is to review the new insurance regulatory environment and analyze how a solution such as Insurance Information Warehouse (IIW) assists insurers worldwide to address the associated data modelling and data consolidation issues.

The standards and interpretations adopted by the International Accounting Standards Board (IASB) in Bound Volume May 2005, and used in the development of IIW, include:

1. International Financial Reporting Standards (IFRS);
2. International Accounting Standards (IAS); and
3. Interpretations originated by the International Financial Reporting Interpretations Committee (IFRIC), formerly the Standing Interpretations Committee (SIC).

Emerging Solvency II requirements are based on interpretations of existing EU Commission Notes and Consultative Papers on the design of a future prudential supervisory system (refer to http://europa.eu.int/comm/internal_market/insurance/solvency/solvency2-workpapers_en.htm). Also, we have taken into consideration existing European reporting regulations at national level (e.g., Solvency I, UK FSA's Prudential Reporting, German Accounting Standards GAS-5 for risk reporting).

---

[22] This White Paper was reprinted with some editing by kind permission of IBM - see Acknowledgement at the end of this Chapter.

Sarbanes and Oxley Act (SOX) requirements are based on the analysis and interpretation of the forms 10-K and 10-Q defined by the U.S. Securities and Exchange Commission (SEC), on which companies report their annual and quarterly results.

The New Regulatory Environment

The regulatory and reporting environment for insurers is changing at a dramatic pace and will keep changing for the next several years.

High-profile failures of insurance companies in countries worldwide, due to an unfavourable macro-economic environment and major losses caused by natural and man-made catastrophes, underscore the need for regulators to improve solvency regulations, such as the E.U. Solvency II initiative, and for insurance companies to better understand their risks.

On the other hand, companies operating internationally are confronted with a wide range of national accounting standards, which makes consolidated financial reporting a complex task. The International Accounting Standards Board (IASB) has developed a framework for accounting rules known as the International Financial Reporting Standards (IFRS), which is being adopted as the basis for international alignment. IFRS is intended to:

- Enhance transparency by requiring companies to account for transactions in a more consistent way and to disclose new and different aspects of their businesses.
- Enable companies to be compared more easily with their peers.
- Promote efficient cross-border investment and access to capital.
- Facilitate merger and acquisition transactions.

Another factor driving the new IFRS accounting framework was the revelation of accounting scandals in recent years in both the U.S. and Europe, which has undermined public confidence in financial reporting. As a result, the U.S. passed in 2002 the Sarbanes-Oxley Act (SOX), which requires CEO certification of financial statements and introduces several measures aiming to protect investors by improving the accuracy and reliability of corporate disclosures.

The combination of the new IFRS Compliance requirements, the new Solvency II regulations and the renewed focus on corporate governance and risk management, will have a major impact on how insurers manage their business.

Sarbanes-Oxley Act (SOX)

Passed in 2002 in the U.S.A. after a series of corporate scandals, the Sarbanes-Oxley Act (SOX) requires CEO certification of financial statements and other steps aimed to protect investors by improving the accuracy and reliability of corporate disclosures. SOX requirements have an immediate and direct impact on US listed companies, but shortly thereafter will apply to foreign insurers with securities listed in the United States. Particularly relevant to insurers is the SOX Section 404 requirement, effective since June 2004. The main goal is to put in place a process by which insurers can renew and continuously improve financial reporting, governance and enterprise risk management.

More specifically, Compliance with SOX Section 404 requires a fine-grained financial reporting capability, down to the transaction level of every internal business process across the organization. With heterogeneous systems for financial reporting, significant amount of manual reconciliation of transaction data, and numerous data sources, insurers have a huge challenge in order to meet the requirements of financial transparency.

Another key Compliance requirement, under Section 409 effective since 2005, is the real-time reporting on "material" weaknesses, including operational risks such as fraudulent events and systems downtime or failure.

Other important SOX requirements include:

- Section 302: A set of internal procedures designed to ensure accurate financial disclosure and Corporate Responsibility (honesty, integrity, transparency, accountability).
- Section 802: Reliance on Information Retention Policies (audit trail, document links and so on).
- Section 906: All periodic reports containing financial statements filed with the Securities and Exchange Commission (SEC) come with a written statement of the CEO and CFO.
- Section 1001: Corporate Tax Returns (consistent / transportable electronic file formats exchanged between companies, tax authorities and advisors).

International Financial Reporting Standards (IFRS) and International Accounting Standards (IAS)

The implementation since 2005 of the new International Accounting Standards (e.g., IAS 32, 37 and 39) and International Financial Reporting Standards for insurance contracts (IFRS 4) will provide a greater transparency for the insurance industry, because most financial assets are evaluated at fair value and technical provisions are based on best estimate information.

The International Accounting Standards Board (IASB) issued IFRS 4 in March 2004 with the objective to achieve convergence of widely varying accounting practices in insurance industries around the world.

In particular, IFRS 4 introduce disclosure to identify and explain amounts in insurers' financial statements arising from insurance contracts and to helps users (regulators, shareholders, analysts, rating agencies) understand the amount, timing and uncertainty of future cash flows from insurance contracts.

Also, under IFRS4, equalization and catastrophe reserves, used to absorb exceptional losses, are prohibited and some embedded options and guarantees in life insurance contracts must be carried at fair value.

IFRS 4 provides a new definition of an insurance contract:
"A contract under which one party (the insurer) accepts significant risk from another party (the policyholder) by agreeing to compensate the policyholder or other beneficiary if a specified uncertain future event (the insured event) adversely affects the policyholder or other beneficiary".

In essence, an insurance contract requires the presence of significant insurance risk and adverse event that affects the policyholder. Insurance risk is defined as a transferred risk other than financial risk. Financial risks include the risk of a possible change in one or more of a specified interest rate, financial instrument price, commodity price, exchange rate, etc.

The change in the definition of insurance contracts may have a significant impact on recorded premiums.
Policies will need to be unbundled into their insurance and investment aspects, which could result in a significant reduction in reported insurance premiums.

Insurance contracts include term assurance, whole life policies, most general insurance or Property & Casualty

(P&C) insurance contracts, disability and medical insurance. Contracts that contain only financial, lapse or expense risk are treated as investment contracts. Examples include unit-linked contracts or variable contracts with minimum death benefits.

It is important to point out that the definition of an insurance contract distinguishes insurance contracts that are subject to IFRS 4 from investment contracts that are subject to IAS 39. IAS 39 is relevant for financial assets, derivatives (including embedded derivatives), and investment contract liabilities.

IAS 39 requires most financial assets to be carried at fair value in the financial statements, and allows an amortized cost approach for most liabilities. Financial assets (except for loans and receivables) are classified as held-to-maturity (HTM), trading, or available-for-sale (AFS).

IAS 37 focuses on liability adequacy tests. The objective of these tests is to assess whether the liability held makes adequate provision for the obligation of the contract. The liability is compared with the current estimates of future cash flows. It considers all contractual cash flows and related cash flows such as claim handling costs, including cash flows resulting from embedded options and guarantees.

If the liability (less deferred acquisition costs or purchased intangible) is less than the measure of future cash flows, the difference must be recognised in profit or loss in the current reporting period.

The IAS 37 liability adequacy measure is the best estimate of the payment required to settle the obligation. The best estimate used under IAS 37 is different from the typical insurance 'best estimate', as it requires market-related margins for risk and uncertainty. An example of the liability adequacy test for short-term contracts would imply to compare:

- The sum of expected claims costs and claim adjustment expenses; expected dividends to policyholders; unamortized acquisition costs; and maintenance costs;
- To unearned premiums.

For long-term contracts, the best estimate liability is calculated as the present value of projected benefit payments plus the present value of projected expenses minus the present value of projected future receipts (i.e., taking into account investment earnings, inflation, taxation, expenses, mortality and morbidity, policy discontinuance and reinsurance).

Solvency II

The objective of the E.U. Solvency II initiative, with implementation planned for 2008, is to assess the overall financial position of an insurance undertaking from the perspective of prudential supervision. Solvency II aims to protect policyholders against the risk of an individual insurer going bankrupt.

Solvency II requires a consistent valuation of assets and liabilities (at fair value), calculation of technical provisions based on best estimate (provision for risks and uncertainty), and solvency margins likely to be estimated in accordance with a Risk Based Capital (RBC) approach.

The major implication of Solvency II to the insurance industry is the adoption of a three-pillar approach to supervision (illustrated in the Figure below), similar to Basel II in banking:

- Pillar 1 - Financial Resources defines the rules for technical provisions, assets and capital requirements.

In the past, firms were required to measure their exposure to credit and market risk only; in the future, they will have to measure operational risk as well.
- Pillar 2 – Supervisory Review assesses the strength and effectiveness of risk management systems and internal controls. Firms will be required to have a process for assessing their overall capital adequacy in relation to their risk profile, and a strategy for maintaining the appropriate capital levels.
- Pillar 3 - Market Discipline focuses on transparency and risk information disclosure. Firms will have to publish certain details of their risks, capital and risk management. The aim here is for firms to make information available that will strengthen market discipline.

Figure 13.1: Solvency II – three pillars

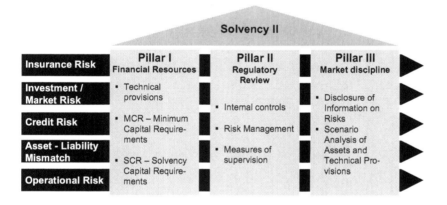

In order to account for a company-specific risk profile, the calculation of capital requirements (solvency margin) will be based on a two-tier approach:

♦ A standard approach will be applied to all European Union (EU) insurers, by introducing a target level and a minimum capital level. The target level should reflect the economic capital that a company would need to operate with low probability of failure. The minimum capital level, estimated for example as a percentage of technical provisions, would act as a trigger for ultimate supervisory action.

♦ Insurers using approved internal risk models might benefit from an optimal estimation of their target capital requirements on insurance undertakings.

Data Integration and the Insurance Information Warehouse

Due to risk management and Compliance challenges, insurance research shows that insurers' future reporting capabilities will be driven by:

- Increased scrutiny of financial reporting by regulators.
- Increased transparency of financial data required by C-level executives.
- Need for an enterprise-wide view of financial data to assess risk.
- Dynamic access to financial data demanded by CEOs and CFOs.
- Use of Internet-based technology to deliver financial data to key executives.

In order to be compliant, there are four important steps for insurers to take today:

- Review risk management processes.
- Develop internal risk models (or extend coverage of existing risk models).
- Quantify and manage assets and liabilities in a more rigorous manner.
- Gather reliable and complete data on company's risk exposures.

Moreover, the new requirements associated with fair value disclosures, the valuation of embedded derivatives and the liability adequacy tests will force insurers to:

- Review current financial models.
- Develop sophisticated stochastic models and options-pricing models to measure insurance liabilities and embedded derivatives at fair value.
- Enhance forecasting capabilities to project future cash flows on insurance products.

The biggest implementation issue for the new regulatory Compliance systems is the access to reliable risk, financial and customer data.

The typical insurer's data sourcing environment is characterized by data originated from a variety of sources:

- Detailed customer data, required to support product selection and pricing in addition to other relationship management decisions, from a Customer Information File.
- Premiums, Claims and Expenses information from the main policy processing systems.
- Balance Sheet and P&L information from General Ledger or similar accounting system.
- Standing data (e.g. exchange rates) via a download procedure or input directly into the Reporting system.
- Details on the corporate assets and the funds to which they may be allocated from a central corporate Asset Register, for example.
- Investment Management information (e.g., the structure of each fund in terms of the stocks, shares, land, buildings, cash) is extracted from different fund management systems on a daily basis.

- Actuarial Valuation information is fed from the core Actuarial System once a year as part of the annual accounting process.
- High-level history for as far back as nine years, probably residing on the Reporting system from the previous year's return.

Adding to this complexity is the time-consuming and error-prone tasks that have to be performed by the actuaries when producing the regulatory business reports. It could well involve performing the following tasks:

- Inclusion of other information from small, obsolete or other products and services not included in the mainframe processing.
- Fixing of known errors in the mainframe processing.
- Adjusting asset allocations to report 'admissible' assets as and when required by the regulator's rules.
- Manipulating data to comply with recent changes, which have not yet been implemented on the source systems.
- Allocating assets to individual funds in ways, which may not be required for day-to-day processing.
- Allocating management and operating expenses between funds, between products, and between new and existing business.
- Manually creating the new reports, which, under Solvency II, replace the 'Matching rectangle', a means of showing how well the business' assets are matched to its liabilities.

There are different ways to view insurance business data – and not all are well represented by either risk or financial systems. Executive management and regulators want coherent views. This approach requires an integrated data environment supporting the decision-

making and reporting requirements across the insurance company.
Given the connection between risk, finance and customer insight, insurers require an integrated data environment supporting the decision-making and reporting requirements across all aspects of the business and regulatory Compliance requirements.

The IBM Insurance Information Warehouse (IIW) is a design for an enterprise data integration environment. IIW has comprehensive support for SOX, IFRS / IAS and Solvency II, in addition to all other areas of insurance. Many insurers are now using IIW to support the integrated data requirements across all aspects of their business as represented below (see Figure below).

Figure 13.2: IIW integrated data across all business aspects

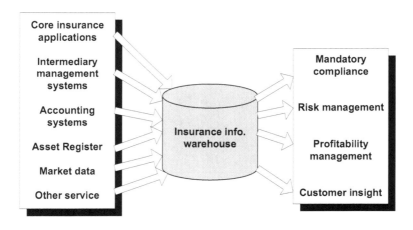

The benefits of using the IIW as the insurer's data integration hub with a single consolidated view of data include:

- Integrated risk and Compliance information
- Increased flexibility to address new requirements

- Faster response to new requirements
- Ability to better leverage data across lines of business
- Increased consistency in data usage
- IT cost savings due to a reuse of population, storage and reporting components.

Insurance Information Warehouse Components

The IBM Insurance Information Warehouse (IIW) enables insurers to build a platform to gather data across their IT solutions to suit their business intelligence, risk management and regulatory reporting needs.
IIW has the flexibility to enable the creation of a range of data gathering solutions, from departmental data marts to enterprise-wide data warehouses.

The IIW comprises a proven, flexible and scalable data warehouse infrastructure to address the following business reporting and analysis needs:

- Profitability and Business Performance Analysis
- Analytical Customer Relationship Management (CRM)
- Risk Management
- Financial Reporting and Regulatory Compliance

The IBM Insurance Information Warehouse content models are the cornerstone components of an insurer's customized development of a data warehouse and business intelligence environment, and can be integrated with the insurer's existing data mart or business information warehouse reporting environments.

IIW supports the data requirements of SOX, IFRS / IAS and Solvency II and it is currently being implemented to support these requirements on a number of projects.   IIW provides comprehensive data coverage for all lines of business in an insurance company. It can be integrated with other application solution providers who deliver a complete solution to both the regulatory Compliance data and analytical requirements.

The IIW content models and the benefits that they provide are detailed in the remainder of this document.

IIW Enterprise Data Warehouse Model

The IIW Enterprise Data Warehouse model is a customizable data model that provides the historical and atomic data needed for a data warehouse and business intelligence infrastructure supporting multiple lines of business and analytical functions within medium to large insurers.
The aim of this shared infrastructure is to provide a reusable platform and data structure environment that will reduce the development and operational costs in providing business intelligence functionality to the myriad of front and back office organization units.

This is made possible by creating a data integration environment and levering this information for business intelligence, risk management and regulatory reporting. In this way organizations can then focus on realistically managing the implementation of consistency of definition, transformation, and distribution of the data used for business intelligence across the lines of business.

IBM provides a default physical database design, generated from the logical entity relationship data model. This physical data model incorporates IBM's vast experience in implementing data warehouse databases for the financial services sector, and could be implemented as is, to show how a data warehouse database should work.
It is more likely though, that it will be customized further by a data warehouse design team of experts comprised of senior warehouse architects and database administrators,

so as to ensure optimal configuration for the financial institution's data distribution and performance characteristics.

The IIW Enterprise Data Warehouse model contains the data structures needed by an insurance company to support the SOX, IFRS / IAS and Solvency II requirements.

Business Solution Templates

The Insurance Information Warehouse contains over 200 Business Solution Templates (BSTs), reflecting the most common types of query and analysis for business performance measurement and reporting.

The IIW also supports other analytical functions such as ad hoc reporting, data mining and decision support.

The BSTs have three main components:

- 2000+ reusable business measures
- 30+ reusable financial dimensions of analysis
- 200+ assemblies of the above measures and dimensions into reporting templates that can be easily customized for local requirements.

Measures include, for example, the key performance indicators (KPIs) for an insurance company.

Each measure is fully defined and can be used either in its own right, or as a component contributing to another key performance indicator, which itself may contribute to other business performance measures. Where the measure is used in a formula, it is provided with a context sensitive calculation attribution (e.g. in one formula), the measure may be summed into the total, whereas in another, it may need to be subtracted from the total.

This reuse of measures ensures conformity of business measure use across the organization and is a key aid in the business metadata activities of a business intelligence environment within an organization.

Measures are used to drive value-based behaviour in an insurance company (e.g., operating income and operating expenses by function). The BST dimensions provide the headings under which measures can be broken down and compared and from which the organizations behaviour is monitored and tracked. Some 30 industry standard dimensions are supplied, with all members fully defined. As with the measures, calculation contribution attributions are provided to show how measures are aggregated along the dimension.

Dimensions are reused in several reporting and analysis templates, thereby enforcing conformity of dimensions used in different analysis areas.
This enables uniformity of reporting and the ability to cross reference measures from different areas of analysis (e.g., comparing profitability to risk measures across the same geographical and temporal breakdowns).
The BSTs provide an existing set of grouping of measures and dimensions taken from the available pools, that capture an analytical need in a given business area. The supplied set of templates can be fully customized and/or new templates created in order to exactly reflect the needs of a particular insurer. New measures and dimensions can also be added to their respective pools and incorporated into templates.

The IIW Regulatory Compliance BSTs

IIW embraces Sarbanes-Oxley Act (SOX) Compliance sections, such as 302, 404, 409, 802, 906 and 1001. For further details on these requirements refer to the information mentioned earlier in this Chapter.

IBM has been enhancing the IIW assets for support of the IFRS / IAS Bound Volume 2005 over a number of development phases. The main objective is to ensure that the IFRS / IAS specific enhancements are evolved into the IIW components.

This allows insurance companies to take advantage of the existing and proven data management architecture while addressing their specific IFRS / IAS Requirements.

IIW covers extensively the data requirements of IFRS 4, IAS 18, IAS 32, IAS 37, IAS 39, and IAS 40 – in relation to fair value, profit and loss, assets and liabilities, financial reporting and disclosure and so on.

IFRS connects to SOX through forms 10-K and 10-Q, on which companies report their annual and quarterly results. A Form 10-K is an annual report required by the U.S.

Securities and Exchange Commission (SEC) each year - that is a comprehensive summary of a company's performance, and 10-Q: a quarterly report filed pursuant to sections 13 or 15(d).
IIW includes content relating to emerging Solvency II requirements, based on interpretations of EU Commission Notes and Consultative Papers on the design of a future prudential supervisory system (refer to http://europa.eu.int/comm/internal_market/insurance/solvency/solvency2-workpapers_en.htm) and existing European regulations at national level, such as Solvency I, UK FSA's Prudential Rulebook and German Accounting standards GAS-5 for risk reporting.

The following Figure summarizes the list of BSTs currently available in IIW that support Financial Reporting and Regulatory Compliance:

- Profitability and business performance;
    - Business performance
    - Intermediary performance
    - Claims efficiency
- Analytical CRM;
    - Campaign analysis
    - Cross sell analysis
    - Customer analysis
- Risk management and regulatory Compliance
    - Solvency II
    - Sarbanes-Oxley
    - IAS/IFRS

Business Solution Templates in IIW - Project Views

The IIW Project Views are a series of business subject area views, which span across all IIW components.
The IIW Project Views give users a very clear understanding of the data coverage required for a specific business requirement, such as "SOX Consolidated Balance Sheet Analysis", and assist in focusing on only those data items in the IIW models that assist in solving the immediate business issue.
IIW includes an extensive set of Project Views specific to SOX and IAS.
Each project view is anchored on a particular reporting solution template, and only selects from that solution template the subset of measures and dimensions specifically needed to address the particular reporting requirement.
The scope of each IIW Project View can then be extended to include the relevant pre-defined mappings that exist between the BST and the IIW Enterprise Data Warehouse Model.

The following is a sample list of the specific IAS views in IIW:

- International Accounting Standard (IAS) 1
- International Accounting Standard (IAS) 2
- International Accounting Standard (IAS) 7
- International Accounting Standard (IAS) 11
- International Accounting Standard (IAS) 12
- International Accounting Standard (IAS) 16
- International Accounting Standard (IAS) 18
- International Accounting Standard (IAS) 19
- International Accounting Standard (IAS) 20
- International Accounting Standard (IAS) 21
- International Accounting Standard (IAS) 23
- International Accounting Standard (IAS) 27
- International Accounting Standard (IAS) 28
- International Accounting Standard (IAS) 30
- International Accounting Standard (IAS) 32
- International Accounting Standard (IAS) 33
- International Accounting Standard (IAS) 38
- International Accounting Standard (IAS) 39
- International Accounting Standard (IAS) 40

The project view Solvency II includes the following sample of BSTs:

- Admissible assets analysis
- Capital adequacy analysis for with-profits business
- Claims for Long Term (LT) insurance analysis
- Effect of financial engineering on solvency analysis
- Expenses for LT insurance analysis
- Financial analysis of claims
- Fixed and variable interest assets analysis for LT insurance
- Index-linked assets analysis for LT insurance
- Internal linked funds unit price analysis for LT insurance
- Liabilities analysis for P & C (non-life) insurance

- Liabilities and margins analysis for LT insurance
- Linked funds balance sheet analysis - LT insurance
- Loss adjustment expenses analysis
- Mathematical reserves analysis for LT insurance
- Net assets analysis
- New business for LT insurance analysis
- Non-linked assets analysis for LT insurance
- P & C claims and premiums by risk group - accident year basis analysis and underwriting year basis analysis
- P & C claims, expenses and technical provisions - accident year basis analysis
- P & C net claims and premiums - accident year basis analysis
- P & C premiums - accident year basis analysis
- P & C premiums, claims and expenses - underwriting year basis analysis
- P & C technical provisions - underwriting year basis analysis
- Premiums for LT insurance analysis
- Profit and loss (non-technical account) analysis
- Profit and loss analysis for P & C insurance - technical account
- Revenue account for internal linked funds - LT insurance
- Revenue account for LT insurance
- Solvency analysis for LT insurance
- Solvency analysis for P & C (non-life) insurance
- Solvency analysis for supplementary accident and sickness insurance
- Statement of solvency for all lines of business
- Summary of new business for LT insurance
- Summary of premiums and claims - P & C insurance
- Valuation analysis by contract and business for LT insurance
- Valuation analysis for financial instruments

- Valuation interest rate analysis for LT insurance
- With-profits funds - payouts on maturity analysis
- With-profits funds - payouts on surrender analysis
- With-profits funds - realistic balance sheet analysis

IIW Components and the Regulatory Compliance Architecture

The IIW components work together as a set of complementary content models that are aimed at solving distinct management information business requirement and data architectural issues.

The separate model components are delivered within an architectural structure, where elements of a model are mapped to corresponding elements in other models. For example, a data mart base measure may be mapped to an IIW Model attribute that is the source for the data to be loaded into the data mart report. This maps the information required by a business user (measure) to the data storage maintained by a technical user (database attribute).

By pre-solving problems such as these, the insurer is left free to concentrate on the real management information and business intelligence issues:

- Sourcing the data
- Defining how it should be transformed and aggregated
- Improving data quality management within the organization
- Reconciliation of transaction, risk and financial data.

This architecture outlines the six tiers of functionality needed to support Regulatory Compliance (see next Figure):

232

- Data Sources – the internal and external sources of all data required for Compliance reporting requirements
- Extraction – the processes and technology needed to extract the data from the potentially diverse sources in an efficient and timely manner
- Enterprise Data Store – the repository into which all the detailed data needed for Compliance reporting is gathered
- Transformation and Calculation – the area where the various calculations are performed
- Data Marts – the area where the aggregated data ready for reporting is stored
- Reporting – the actual creation and delivery of the reports to the various user groups including SOX, IFRS / IAS, Solvency II.

IIW supports these functional requirements in the following way:

- The IIW Model provides the design for the enterprise data store.
- The Business Solution Templates provide the foundation for the required data mart structures for SOX, IFRS / IAS and Solvency II.
- The IIW Project Views provide a filtered view across the data mart structures. Each view addresses specific reporting requirements defined in the latest SOX, IFRS / IAS and Solvency II documentation.

IIW Support for XBRL

What is XBRL?

eXtensible Business Reporting Language (XBRL), the financial and operational business reporting derivitative of the Extensible Markup Language (XML), is a freely licensable open technology standard which makes it possible to:

- Store / transfer data along with the complex hierarchies
- Data-processing rules
- Descriptions that enable analysis and distribution.

XBRL makes data "smart." It determines whether the information is segment information, part of an audited statement, or another type of business data. It supports the presentation, manipulation and allows the exchange of information using a set of standards and a family of taxonomies.

What is a Taxonomy?

A taxonomy is a description and classification system for the contents of financial statements and other business reporting documents.

XBRL Taxonomies represent:

- Individual business reporting concepts
- Mathematical and definitional relationships
- Text labels in multiple languages
- References to authoritative literature about how to display each concept to a user (Source: XBRL.org).

Why is the IASC Foundation Building a Taxonomy?

Under the IASC Foundation Constitution, the objectives of the IASB are to develop, in the public interest, a single set of high quality, understandable and enforceable global accounting standards that require high quality, transparent and comparable information in financial statements and other financial reporting to help participants in the world's capital markets and other users make economic decisions; to promote the use and rigorous application of those standards; to bring about convergence of national accounting standards and

International Accounting Standards to high quality solutions.

IASCF IFRS Taxonomy development is complimentary to these objectives. IFRS taxonomies assist the transfer of financial reporting information created pursuant to IFRS using the Internet - according to a single common protocol developed by the IASCF.

How does IIW support XBRL reporting?

XBRL may be integrated with reporting applications from other vendors. IIW supports XBRL explicitly by storing XBRL Instance or Mapping Documents as IIW Documents, as illustrated in the Figure below related to IFRS "Cash Flow Direct Analysis".

In addition IIW has the inbuilt capability to store historical versions of the XBRL Documents thus facilitating the production of previously generated reports.

The value of XBRL:

Financial institutions can use XBRL to save costs and streamline their procedures for reporting financial information.

Financial institution investors, analysts and regulators can receive, compare and analyse data much more rapidly and efficiently if it is in XBRL format.

ACKNOWLEDGEMENT AND THANKS:

The book's Author acknowledges and thanks IBM for contributing this White Paper to the book, as follows:

Financial Services Solution Centre
IBM Ireland Limited
Building 6
Dublin Technology Campus
Damastown Industrial Estate
Mulhuddart
Dublin 15
fssc@ie.ibm.com

Note:
The IBM home page can be found on the Internet at www.ibm.com
IBM is a registered trademark of International Business Machines Corporation.
References in this publication to IBM products, programs or services do not imply that IBM intends to make these available in all countries in which IBM operates.
Any reference to an IBM product, program or service is not intended to imply that only IBM 's product, program or service may be used. Any functionally equivalent product, program or service may be used instead. This publication is for general guidance only.

14.   Business Change and Compliance

Introduction

Business Transformation together with effective Compliance is an initiative to directly and interactively align IT infrastructure with organisation needs, business processes, work practices and operational procedures to fit well together, to adhere to compulsory legislative mandates.
It involves a full assessment and revitalisation of the business and IT systems together - both internal, customer and third party related interfaces.

So, how do we go about it?

Firstly;
Dig down under below the waterline of the iceberg tip of the business, to comprehend and evaluate existing IT infrastructure applications and systems, together with directly related business processes.

Secondly;
Formulate the best mix of projects or programmes to align IT spending with organisation goals and business objectives. Then, develop an implementation plan for these projects or programmes, and maximise exploitation of your existing company resources.

Fourthly;
Develop, build, modify and integrate the relevant IT infrastructure assets, applications and systems specified in the plan / Project Implementation & Quality Document (PIQD).

Fifthly;

Transport all your new assets, systems and applications into a suitable effective and efficient operational infrastructure of Web Service Architecture (WSA) – see below.

Subsequently, periodically revisit, review and revise your plans to reflect and activate changes according to your business needs, competitive environment, and Compliance requirements.

Enabling Web Service Architecture (WSA)

Evolution of distributed computing and component-based application development paradigm has led to WSA, which is critical for corporate ability to handle change expediently.

WSA provides companies with the chance and ability to standardise common business process and IT components and functions within a suitable of library of 'Lego-like bricks', used for numerous business processes and IT applications as reusable services.

It enables business-system analysts and developers to create unique processes within an application, because they can leverage common process functionality across systems simply by calling a WSA function, component or assembly of components, instead of starting from scratch each time a change is needed.

Forrester Research conducted a survey of 75 IT executives at large North American companies to find out what they are doing with WSA.
It found out among other things that:

- Internal deployment of WSA was at the top of the project list
- 83 percent of firms planned WSA inside their firewalls.

Corporate Ability to Handle Compliance Change Expediently

In the current business climate, the agility to make Compliance changes quickly is paramount to the business processes, IT infrastructure, and cognitive-psychological behaviour of managers and staff, if change is to be beneficial and introduced quickly with minimum pain.

This is not a one-off upheaval but a continuous travel into the future. Organisations must be prepared to handle mergers and acquisitions, downsizing, rightsizing, upgrading or downgrading - that require integrating heterogeneous applications.

Corporations therefore need:

♦ Better exploit business opportunities and maximise revenue
♦ Maximise reuse and return on existing assets
♦ Integrate well data, systems, and business processes
♦ Improve standards for development and integration
♦ Stay ahead of regulatory Compliance requirements

As companies grapple with these challenges, many are turning to software to help them comply with the law without adding staff.

Systems and applications designed for this purpose can help businesses identify common threads in their operating procedures, so each set of requirements can be implemented properly, and the mandated controls can become visible in the operational structure.

However, even if the above-mentioned business process and IT infrastructure changes are executed well – without

a profound psychological / behavioural paradigm shift –
such enterprise transformation initiatives are doomed.
Only a Cognitive-Synergetic™ transformation of mindsets
would enable a corporate turnaround successfully – see
next.

Compliance and Business Change – a Moving Target

According to Celent, between 2003 and 2005, financial
institutions will have spent an estimated $632 million on
anti-money-laundering software and related hardware and
services.
AMR Research predicts that publicly traded Fortune 1000
companies will spend as much as $2.5 billion on
Compliance-related projects.
31 of 60 companies surveyed by AMR stated that they
intended to make moderate to major changes to their IT
systems and application infrastructure in support of
Sarbanes-Oxley.

Large European banks are expected to spend an
estimated $124 million over the next five years to comply
with Basel II, updated legislation based on the Basel
Capital Accord established in 1998.
Due to the complexity and number of mandates, many
firms have appointed executives and teams to manage
their Compliance efforts.
Such efforts cost lots of cash, therefore, the pressure to
increase revenue becomes greater, and stress levels
within organisations reach epidemic proportions.

Many companies wonder how they can define the scope
of work necessary to become compliant, yet still manage
all their other day-to-day business operations, projects
and delivery deadlines.
Think of it as having to assemble a dishwasher or a
motorcycle with no set of instructions on how to do it!

In addition, US Federal and EU immutable directives are not the only requirements that financial organisations must comply with State and local regulations.
No wonder, company executives and accountants have sleepless nights and bags under their eyes!

Compliance Audit - a Holistic Approach

Auditors and bookkeepers need to look at almost everything, due to the new stringent Compliance rules and regulations, for example:

- Customer orders
- Shipments to customers
- Electronic and paper transactions
- Customer information verification
- Purchase orders
- Supplier details
- Goods received notes
- Quality inspection records
- Material records
- Sale records
- Financial reports
- Other reports
- And much more...

Holistic Compliance philosophy and execution is therefore a MUST!

Having to continuously validate Compliance together with the organisation's ability to handle change projects, business-as-usual operations and budget controls etc. etc. - is a significant challenge.
The current environment of stringent regulations is forcing companies to rethink the way they manage business processes, data and information across the enterprise.

Forward-thinking holistic companies are exploiting the opportunity to create systems and applications that improve real-time business process efficiency, effectiveness and control - beyond the scope of any specific regulatory Compliance requirements.

Today's strict regulations (at times conflicting) are like a trip through a jungle that demands that all transactions must be documented and tracked.
All records and documents must be traceable and retrievable throughout business systems and applications, so that the rigid controls specified by the regulations can be evidently met.

Therefore, IT and business task force teams must gather and analyse business and system requirements, map them against one another, and cross-refer them against Compliance requirements.
This is necessary to conduct a gap analysis, identify solutions and remedy the situation and consequently conduct meaningful tests to confirm Compliance (or otherwise), and subsequently repeat this cycle, as deemed necessary.

The right processes, tools and information must be right and fit-for-purpose, at the right time and the right place and the right format – a multi-dimensional approach.
While it is essential that IT comply with Compliance requirements, it is also necessary that the new processes themselves are made secure and safe.
Otherwise, unwarranted changes to these processes, applications, assets, services and systems could lead to a breakdown in checkpoints and controls, and resultant Compliance violations.
A number of vendors offer suitable tools for managing changes to information, hardware and software under development or changes. These include a complete Asset Lifecycle Management (ALM), project configuration

management and change control information, modelling ('what-if' scenarios), asset construction / modification and testing.

IT and Compliance Mandates

The following IT assets are being affected by the regulatory requirements listed below:

- Information storage / archive management
- Data / Business information warehousing
- Document / Records Management
- Content / knowledge management
- Business intelligence
- Process management
- Compliance software
- Accounting software
- International Accounting Standards (IAS) Compliance / consolidation Software
- E-mail storage / management
- Asset security / management
- IT infrastructure
- Databases
- Mobile services
- Communications, broadband etc.

The principles and prime movers to attain a profound and successful business turnaround, coupled with Sarbanes-Oxley and related Compliance mandates, it is necessary to embrace the following:

- Joining together separate IT systems via Enterprise Applications Integration (EAI) – containing all relevant portfolios in a relational / hierarchical structure
- Keeping up with ongoing Compliance legislation and IT staying ahead of this game
- Educating and motivating staff to stay on and reduce turnover and loss of essential skills

- Analysing the options to outsource development, maintenance and testing of systems and applications
- Reducing the cost and effort of application maintenance and modification by maximising a modular development approach
- Understanding the organisation not only technically but also psychologically, socially and organic-evolutionally.

Most businesses have their business departments and IT infrastructure units working in isolation — developing departmental applications, duplicating if not contradicting information storage databases that lead to erroneous reporting and mistaken business decisions.

According to Forrester, disparate / missing) portfolio sub-structures within most companies have a negative influence an their value.
For example:

- About 10-15 percent of organisations cascade their substructures into a summary reporting to facilitate better decision-making.
- Consequently, companies could be wasting 5-8 percent or more of their overall budgets due to duplicated, misaligned and ineffective spending. (The Author of this book can verify these figures from personal experience with a number of companies.)
- For example, a business spending $100 million per annum on IT budget, this means about $5-8 million per year of pure wasted money.
- IT complexity now demands that the haphazard ways of the past are no longer useful and relevant.

Business Governance Issues

The business governance should address issues such as:

- Measurement of cognitive-behavioural and psychological preparedness of staff and managers for the dawning of a new era, where every thing is changing fast, it's unsettling but a must to remain in business and retain one's employment
- Measurement of satisfying or exceeding requirements for the effectiveness, efficiency, confidentiality, integrity, availability, Compliance and reliability of IT and related information-based services
- Measuring execution of effective standards and controls for the design, development, implementation, maintenance, use, acquisition and management of services and assets to support new ways of working
- Measuring execution of optimised best practice for allocation and management of IT and human resources
- Measuring effective parsing and sharing of organisational responsibilities and tasks for managing change, including relevant decision-making processes and escalation of issues and risks identified
- Measuring delivery from newly established strategies, policies, procedures and practices implemented to ensure that the business derives maximum business benefit from its investments in business change
- Measuring as to how and who makes decisions about defining strategy, establishing objectives, prioritising developments, allocating resources, and monitoring results in relation to service delivery coherently with the wider governance of the organisation and its business activities as a whole.
- Measuring external variables outside the organisation's direct control, for example, legal, commercial and technological environments within which the organisation operates
- Measuring sector-specific variables, for example, local government, and new targets for electronic delivery of services.

- Measuring deviant results, actions and transactions.

IT Infrastructure Alignment with Business Change

Brenda Cammarano of IBM Rational, writes in her 13 April 2004 article, 'Facing the challenges of Enterprise Transformation[23]':

"A strong and successful enterprise requires a solid IT system and application infrastructure, providing a clear linkage between IT and corporate goals and strategies. This infrastructure should support the intricacies of your business while providing an integrated and flexible architecture to support the endless business challenges of tomorrow.

With an integrated and aligned IT system, you can be confident that your enterprise will run at top efficiency, enabling you to take advantage of every opportunity to strengthen your business and remain ahead of all competition.
Unfortunately, this integrated architecture does not exist at most corporations.
Instead, organisations maintain a disjointed IT landscape, with applications and systems all working independently, and developed vertically to address the needs of each department rather than horizontally, across departments, to address the needs of the business.
To help organisations effectively establish a more cohesive yet cost-efficient approach to IT in this economic environment, we encourage them to evaluate existing resources that can help them address alignment and integration needs.
As they go through this evaluation process and consider how to allocate budget dollars, companies need to keep

---

[23] Ref. **http://www-128.ibm.com/developerworks/rational/library**

the IT challenges driving today's business decisions uppermost in their minds."

Change 'Do or Die' Factors - Remember the Dinosaurs?

Business change, enterprise transformation, corporate turnaround, business re-engineering (NOT just processes), organisation re-design etc. embrace among other things, 'do-or-die':

- Profound Compliance-related, operational, strategic, project, and education-related programme re-structuring activities
- Re-defining, embedding, measuring and reaping the rewards of transformation into new beneficial values, attitudes, norms, and modes of behaviour that facilitate and enable a new culture, improved ways of working, including Compliance-related procedures etc.
- Building an organisation-wide consensus among staff, managers, customers and stakeholders about positive changes and re-engineered enterprise, designed to better meet their dynamically changing needs
- Above all, demonstrating that the changes are necessary and beneficial, even if not completely tangible and/or for short term gains
- Distinguishing between, and prioritisation of unclear, wishful changes on one hand, and solid business case benefits, on the other – working through 'traffic lights' in terms of importance, namely – green (fine, leave alone for now), amber (some work needed, second priority), red (for urgent action)
- Most importantly; ensure that change vision objectives and gaps are correctly identified and analysed, between as-of-now scenario, and wished-for changes, and that fit-gap solutions are fit for purpose
- Last but not least, re-training, re-education, and acquiring new philosophy, innovative thinking and

accordingly necessary skills are paramount for success, and treated as such.

The enterprise transformation, three-step PIE™[24] (Prepare, Introduce, Embed) approach outlined below, is the Author's change techniques and practices, developed and implemented during the past 3 decades.

The key for success is being proactive and communicating regularly and effectively what's happening and how the change is progressing.

---

[24] Abe Abrahami's Copyrights methodology: PIE™

Figure14.1: Three-step PIE™ approach to business change

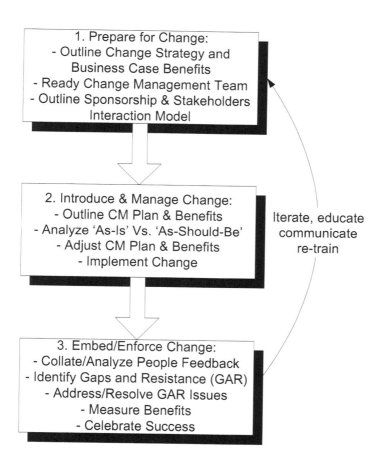

1. Prepare for Change:
- Outline Change Strategy and Business Case Benefits
- Ready Change Management Team
- Outline Sponsorship & Stakeholders Interaction Model

2. Introduce & Manage Change:
- Outline CM Plan & Benefits
- Analyze 'As-Is' Vs. 'As-Should-Be'
- Adjust CM Plan & Benefits
- Implement Change

Iterate, educate communicate re-train

3. Embed/Enforce Change:
- Collate/Analyze People Feedback
- Identify Gaps and Resistance (GAR)
- Address/Resolve GAR Issues
- Measure Benefits
- Celebrate Success

Change is dynamic and constantly evolving, so make sure your business does not freeze within any particular pattern for too long...it's a new challenging model of an ever-changing matrix.

Figure 14.2: Business matrix patterns change with time

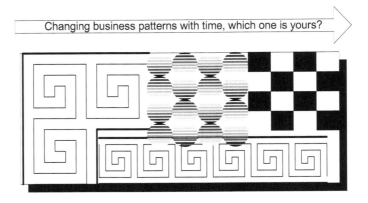

Changing business patterns with time, which one is yours?

Change and Personal Issues

Meaning of change - what it means to the organisation as a whole, its operational modes, and above all, its individuals, and how each person will fit into and be part of it, and make it happen successfully, adopting and exercising personal commitment and accountability.

Personal uncertainties – New/Modified roles and responsibilities, fear of change, how/what will we do next? Will the enabling technology work? Who do we contact when things go wrong? Have our procedures been suitably modified to correspond with the change? And what about education and training, will some of it be available on line, in addition to face to face? Will we increase our workload as a result? Will there be more admin involved? Do we have to re-apply for our jobs and/or relocate?
Assessments – survey tools, questionnaires etc. for analysing, and evaluating change and the organisation's readiness to embrace, embed and propagate business transformation.

250

Documentation - Critical documents and templates for planning and executing change management, including procedures, roles and responsibilities, new business process, Figures and guidelines, and checklists for the entire change management process, including communications, education, training and coaching. Customization guidelines - change management should reflect your unique change and the organisation that is changing - learn how to adapt to the specifics of your project.

Approach – Mundane approaches to organisational culture transformation and business change have been inadequate, partly because they have been based on outdated concepts and models of organisational dynamics, or the lack of it.
A multi-layered approach, considering both horizontal and vertical interactions, as opposed to a silo philosophy, offers a new paradigm, which leads to a radically different kind of practice for change management.
Simplification - Reduce the number of IT units, components or elements in your network. Drastically reduce or eliminate customization, automate business process re-engineering and associated change. Simplify everything and you are prepared for anything.
Standardisation - Use standard technology components and open-system interfaces. Create/Purchase reusable robust components, introduce consistent processes that well match and interact with any system, anywhere, any time.

Modularisation – Design, build, purchase and install architectures modularly, like bricks. Break down vertically stacked IT systems and assemblies. Create Virtual systems and assemblies, enabling to change one element without impacting the entire network.

Integration – Construct dynamic links between business processes and IT applications, inside and outside. Create and observe everything working together, map interactions, see and prepare for a change coming a mile away.

Understand and take advantage of change - Change is a natural process that can prompt revitalization in individuals and systems, although it can and has been unsettling and stressful. Maturity and full potential can only be realized through a process of personal, professional and cultural development, growth, adjustment, and renewal.

Learn to better understand the role and opportunities of change for making it a positive experience.

Winners and losers – Differences and variations of perception among people and organisational departments mean that change has winners and losers - beneficial effects and destructive results.

While frequently frustrating and off putting, change can facilitate long-term viability, quality and productivity. Learn how to identify and react to the organisational, emotional and physical influences of change.

People's reaction to change - During a period of a fast-paced or imposed change or both, people can be classified according to their willingness to try something new. Enthusiasm, cynicism, resistance etc. – are all part of the reaction.

Learn to identify personal feelings about the pending change and develop a change strategy and plan for working with all affected individuals.

Organisation and Culture Change

As we live and die, nature and our environment are constantly changing - nothing stays the same.

A moment, hour, day, week, month, year, century from right now, things will be different to what they are now; this is the very nature of our existence, universe, organisation, work place, home etc.

At this subconscious level, change is an integral part of our lives and we think little of it, except perhaps, when, for example, an old building near us is demolished and a new one is built, or when things directly or profoundly affect us. Organisational, business, work practice or culture change is one of these things that we pay more than a little attention to; in fact, some of us get paranoid about it.

Change is an emergent result of the continuing negotiations, contacts and interactions concerning values, meanings and proprieties between the members of that organisation and with its environment.

In other words, change is the result of our daily conversations, contacts or negotiations between members of our organisation, and third party individuals we do business with or come across.

Change is also the result of new IT systems and applications forced upon us or introduced with consultation and consensus, in part or full.

Most change programmes concentrate on the circumference; they try to introduce change by looking at structures, systems and processes, peripheral to the core issues and heart of the matter.

Individual human beings, their expectations, concerns, worries, wishes and aspirations are usually left out of the equation.

Experience shows us that these initiatives usually have a limited and short-lived success. A lot of time, energy and money are invested in the change programme, with all the usual communication exercises, consultations, workshops, hype and so on.

In the first few months, things seem to be changing but gradually the novelty and motivation and impetus for change wear off and the organisation settles back into something like its previous configuration and ways of doing things.

The reason for this is simple and often overlooked - unless the change paradigm at the heart of the culture is shifted, there will be no lasting successful change.

Paradigm Shift

According to Wikipedia - the free Encyclopaedia:
"The best known use of the word in the context of a scientific discipline was by philosopher Thomas Kuhn who used it to describe a set of practices in science.
It was and is widely abused. Kuhn himself came to prefer the terms exemplar and normal science, which have more exact philosophical meaning. However, in his book The Structure of Scientific Revolutions Kuhn defines a scientific paradigm as:
'What is to be observed and scrutinized, the kind of questions that are supposed to be asked and probed for answers in relation to this subject,
How these questions are to be put, how the results of scientific investigations should be interpreted'."

Therefore, a paradigm is a self-consistent set of ideas, attitudes and beliefs which interact as a cognitive filter, colouring and influencing as to how we perceive and how we make sense of things and people we come across.

In short, a paradigm is an assembly of concepts, values, perceptions and resultant practices adopted and shared by people in an organisation or a community, forming is the basis of the people's reality and conduct and reactions.

A paradigm can be a self-fulfilling prophecy or expectation; there is almost a boomerang intuition or a logic loop associated with its initiation and feedback result, which makes it hard to break.

When we promote and sell successfully the idea of "what's in it for me", and convince others and ourselves that being positive and understanding is not a one-off, but a constant, continuous paradigm in our lives, we know that change will be an asset and not a hindrance.

Practical Issues and Implications

Most change consultants or agents seem to think - how can I be a good professional, how can I re-engineer or fix an organisation, if I do not possess a tool kit, a silver-bullet technique or a golden methodology, or all of them? This attitude implies that the change agent may stand outside the organisation or system, diagnose and understand its working parts and then intervene to fix or re-design it to work better in a more effective and efficient manner.
In truth, however, a successful change may begin to work as described above, but to make it successful long term, you need to get inside the engine (so to speak) and get your hands dirty with muck and grease and oil, otherwise, no silver bullet will do the job for you and your organisation.
The chief reasons for the high failure rate of change initiatives, facilitated by highly complex systems and applications such as Enterprise Resource Planning (ERP), Client Relationship Management (CRM), and others, is too much reliance on technology, hype, unrealistic assumptions, poor adaptation and management of expectations.

These have been compounded and aggravated by lack of impact analysis, inadequate education and training, insufficient direct and personal contact between the business user community and IT and so on and so forth.

By building a greater and more cohesive connectivity and understanding between people and by encouraging them to make an individual use and derive a personal meaning concerning their day-to-day working lives and practices we help the organisation to demolish silo and compartmental barriers.

By doing these things, we open up channels of free energy flow and synergy so that people become self-reliant and more self-organised to deal successfully with their critical new positions and become much more able and willing to change.

Organisational and Compliance-related change - to be successful - must be not simply top down but horizontal, combined with vertical, for everyone who is involved, from the centre outward to the periphery, and in reverse, meeting in the middle, to ensure that all is covered.

Such a change to be successful - must be NOT 3-d, but 6-dimensional, like a cube-face.

Things are rarely simple in organisations, and once the true degree of change 'infection' is realised, the 'immune system' of resistance to change kicks into action, and tries its best to halt the progress of change.

Therefore, a suitable immune system 'suppression drug' is needed to overcome the adverse reaction to change or 'side effect', or better still, a holistic solution of reversing the immune system action, could be administered to save the organisation.

The following Table outlines some types of resistance to change (immune system adverse reaction to invasion of the change virus) and offers possible medicinal drugs or holistic remedies (we have a choice).

It outlines the three major phases of introducing change into corporations and organisations, via three part change actions.

Table 14.1: Working with corporations – three parts

Part One	Involve senior stakeholders, to gain a clear, mutual picture of critical success factors, benefits and barriers to these. Examine the current change-ability of the workforce. Develop a strategy and plan for success by outlining the steps involved and measurements of effectiveness and efficiency. Tell them about the pill they are about to swallow and be honest about side effects! Adjust these strategy parameters or benchmarks as necessary and gain sign-off and continuous support.
Part Two	Test the strategy, monitor feedback results and refine the plan as necessary. Prepare staff and managers for launching the change strategy. Launch the change strategy, combining the most suitable resources, internal and external, and that ensure people swallow the bittersweet pill.
Part Three	Monitor on-going implementation, and side effects from the pill, and administer remedies as required. Track efficiency and effectiveness; communicate and build on success upon success. Support continuing integration of success factors into the workplace culture and business practices, procedures and processes. Develop internal / external strategies for on-going success and adaptability and reflect it in ongoing communications.

Business change relationships

The following diagrams illustrate culture and business change and transformation activities and parameters etc.

Figure 14.3a: Culture and change engagement scale

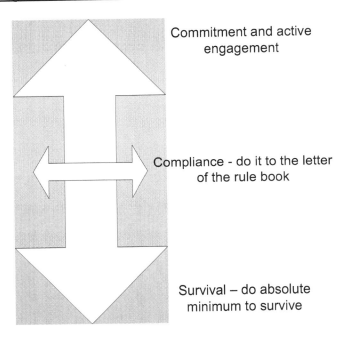

Commitment and active engagement

Compliance - do it to the letter of the rule book

Survival – do absolute minimum to survive

Figure 14.3b Change forces

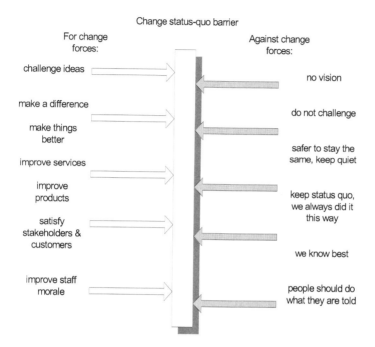

Change status-quo barrier

For change
forces:

Against change
forces:

challenge ideas

no vision

make a difference

do not challenge

make things
better

safer to stay the
same, keep quiet

improve services

improve
products

keep status quo,
we always did it
this way

satisfy
stakeholders &
customers

we know best

improve staff
morale

people should do
what they are told

Figure 14.4: Change power and acceptance

Exercising management change power

Coercive power, threat of punishment	Expert knowledge power, knowing better	Position / Role power in the company's hierarchy
Reward power, enticement and recognition	Connective power, social network power, knowing others	External consultant power, third party authority

Change acceptance lifecycle

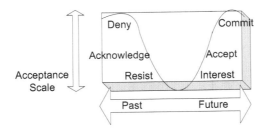

Figure 14.5: Change state of mind

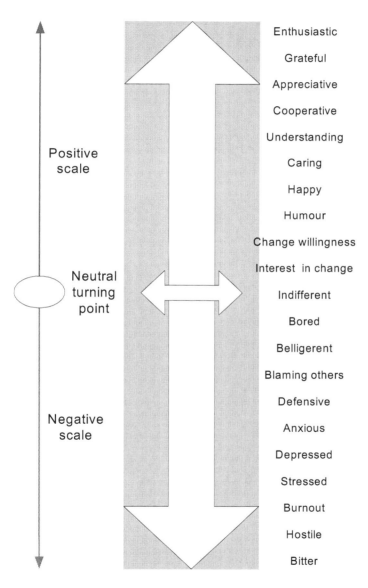

Figure 14.6: Business reengineering and culture change

Business re-engineering as a subset of culture change & business
transformation driving force

Alignment of old & new strategy, culture & structure changes,
business transformation re-engineering

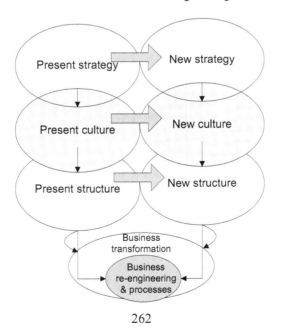

Business Re-engineering and Culture Change

The meanings of enterprise transformation and culture change to managers should be, if they are not already:

- Managers become more like mentors, less like supervisors
- Managers exercise more facilitation, less command-like orders
- Managers encourage reward based on added value not on years in the company or position
- Managers encourage continuing education to match dynamically changing environment
- Managers exercise fewer checks, audits and controls and rely more on staff, who are better trained, more independent and motivated
- The organisation has a flatter layer of management, more taskforce oriented, less hierarchical
- Fewer functional / hierarchical departments exist in the organisation, more process / taskforce oriented horizontal teams
- Team-oriented incentives as opposing to individual
- Any frameworks and work procedures must serve and help enable the above
- Any IT systems and applications must service and help enable the above

Change Implications

The following implications are involved within enterprise transformation:

- Clearly establish and agree the change objectives and communicate them well and often
- Ensure a suitable change plan is created and it is both holistic and cognitive of all major issues and challenges

- Some people fear the unknown and having to learn new things
- Some people are concerned about their job security
- People are rightly concerned about the need for change and expected benefits
- If the need for change is poorly communicated with no concerted education it fails
- Do not go for hype but for a level-headed management of expectation and education
- People ask "what's in it for me?" management must be able to answer this question
- If you cannot beat the resistors, bypass instead of fighting them
- Address honestly and openly all concerns raised
- Work together with HR and unions as applicable

Change Success and Failure Factors

One should follow as much as possible the following guidelines to ensure success via useful measurements:

- Establish baseline measurements as a reference point, if you do not have them be honest and say so, and instead state the perceived baseline
- Clearly establish and agree measurements where the business should be over a specific time period
- Clearly establish the change plan and milestone stages to reach the desired objectives
- Regularly report to the organisation, stakeholders in particular, progress, issues and challenges
- Request for change (RFC) should be aptly used to initiate, evaluate, introduce and manage variances to the change project delivery plan - together with all relevant controls, including but not limited to project implementation & quality document (PIQD)
- Recognise that behaviour changes are the most difficult ones to measure and satisfaction

questionnaires should be correctly used to obtain and analyse feedback
- Beware of shock / rapid changes because they usually crash spectacularly or fade away
- ABOVE ALL, COMMUNICATE AND ENSURE THAT CHANGES ARE BENEFICIAL AND NOT INTRODUCED FOR THE SAKE OF CHANGING ONLY.

Typical reactions to culture change and business transformation and re-engineering initiatives:

- "Working together across business functions and departments has enriched my experience and helped me to see other people's points of view; our teams know they work toward the same goals to get the customers what they want. Our cross-function teams greatly respect one another."
- "For the past few months we heard we do not deliver, that we are losing competitiveness and there is a lot of 'dead wood' but he have no picture of the future and roadmap how to get there."
- "Staff morale is low and people lie low, being inconspicuous, as no one wishes to take an initiative, and be shot at."
- "Oh' we remember the last initiative.... this one will also hit the dust in no time..."
- "It will be management hype probably but soon it will be forgotten and we go back to business as usual."
- "I do not have time to run my day time job, never mind taking on any new initiatives."
- "We have too many new things and changes on the go, insufficient time to get on with my job."
- "Too much paperwork and reports, a sledgehammer to crack a nut, I wish management knew what they are doing."
- "As I do not get a bonus for any extra effort or time spent, why should I care?"

- "Last time I made a suggestion I did not even get a reply, so why bother?"

The Ten Commandments for Change Success

One should take note of enterprise transformation belief and behaviour system 10 Commandments of behavioural changes (see Tables below).

Table 14.2: Ten Commandments of change belief transformation

From – failure behaviour	To – success behaviour	Why
1. Wait to do what I am told, lack of initiative	Take initiative, be more proactive	Opportunity for better, more satisfying self-expression and career development
2. Do not admit mistakes, blame others / circumstances	Take responsibility, be honest and open	Learn valuable lessons, being part of useful experience to help others
3. To do a job well I do it myself	Coach, mentor, train and delegate	Cannot do it all by myself, need help
4. This is my job, do not deviate / get involved	Narrow focus	Danger of working in a silo and missing out interfaces and overall picture
5. It's the quality or legal department jobs to deal with non-Compliance and risks	It's part of my job to deliver fit-for-purpose safe products with Compliance and minimal	Quality, safety and risk mitigation are an integral part of every person's responsibility, integrity and

	risk exposure	accountability, re-work and correcting errors are time and effort consuming
6. It's Finance / HR job to deal with expenses and other financial matters	It's part of my job to ensure that the financial aspects of my job are discharged responsibly and correctly	Correction of mistakes is time and effort consuming
7. Do not give others constructive feedback, it will not be appreciated, they might think I am showing off	Be positive and help others to save time, tell them it happened to you before, express peer sympathy	For the overall good and benefits of others in the organisation, your effort will be appreciated
8. If I offer a good word to an under-performing person, it will be a sign of weakness and endorsing 'slacking off'	Become a better coach and mentor, move from an autocratic to a persuasive mode of behaviour	Help to turn people from mediocre or under-achieving to a success and reap rewards
9. Afraid to take risks because the pain of failure is greater than the success reward	Become more adventurous and overcome fear, look at things more positively	We like success and praise to be appreciated some times you have to take calculated risks
10. Always say no to change, it's unsettling	Examine change positively	Opportunity to shine

The Table below depicts the second set of 10 Commandments of how to succeed with enterprise re-engineering and transformation, and avoid failure with enabling paradigms and winning techniques.

Table 14.3: Ten Commandments of business reengineering success

Business [process] re-engineering paradigm	Business culture transformation & change management paradigm	Enabling success approach or techniques
1. Establish driving force, needs and benefits	1. Establish driving force, needs and benefits	Discussions and survey questionnaire
2. Clearly/Regularly communicate needs, drivers, objectives and benefits	2. Clearly/Regularly communicate needs, drivers, objectives and benefits	Short-sharp workshops and communication briefs
3. Understand and outline current business process and work practices	3. Understand and outline culture characteristics and strategy	Discussions and diagrams and descriptive text
4. Determine how we want processes to be after re-engineering	4. Determine how we want the culture to be after change transformation	Discussions and 'how-to' method and roadmap
5. Identify the gap between current and future business processes and establish means to measure the differences	5. Identify the gap between current and future business culture and establish means to measure the	Discussions, quantitative and qualitative analysis

		differences
6. Agree major stakeholders and sponsors, initiate a project and create a PID – project implementation document, including quality and communication plans	6. Agree major stakeholders and sponsors, initiate a project and create a PID – project implementation document, including quality and communication plans	Discussions followed by relevant documentation
7. Implement re-engineering	7. Implement culture change	Task force approach, cross departments
8. PIR – post/in-between implementation review and lessons learnt, regular-interval assessments	8. PIR – post/in-between implementation review and lessons learnt, regular-interval assessments	Informal and formal assessments
9. After a predetermined period, measure differences and benefits	9. After a predetermined period, measure differences and benefits	Informal and formal measurements
10. Continuous improvement, back to 1	10. Continuous improvement, back to 1	Informal and formal discussions and active engagement of top management

The Table below outlines the third set of 10 Commandments of organisation structure change to avoid business transformation failure.

Table 14.4: Organisation redesign Ten Commandments to avoid failure

Hierarchical-functional old-fashion organisation - failure	Taskforce, business process oriented organisation - success
1. Vertical silo structure	Flat, multi-tasking structure
2. Departmental specialities	Business process broad specialities
3. Rigid organisation	Flexible organisation
4. Difficult to change structure	Dynamic, easily configured structure
5. People entrenched into old ways	People happy and willing to change
6. Non-adaptive people	Adaptive people
7. Procedure oriented focus	Customer focus
8. Information in closed buckets	Free-flowing information
9. Closed management style	Open management style
10. One-off project improvement	Continuous TQM improvement

Change Management and Leadership

Says Fred Musone of Federal Mogul:

"You cannot make a business better by looking at a balance sheet and you cannot run a business focusing on earnings. Earnings do not cause anything…. they are a result of excellence.
If you want to make business better, you would better focus on what causes earnings. Earnings are the ultimate judge of how well you have created excellence.
Sitting in interminable meetings talking about earnings, will not make your business better. The only thing that will make your business better is to exceed the expectations of your customers. And that comes from the value-creating processes.

270

Re-engineering an accounts payable process may create a cost saving, but it's not the same thing as re-engineering a value creating process".

Leadership and management is not the same thing:

The difference between leadership and management was once summed up as follows[25]:

"Imagine there's a sudden power failure on the underground train system.
The system halts and all the lights go out.
In the central control room someone is marshalling resources, implementing the standby facilities, rescheduling the trains, calling the emergency services. That's management.
Someone else is walking along the darkened platform with a torch bringing a trainload of people to safety. That's leadership."

Engineering-Science Model Approach to Change

Roger Dickout, writes in: 'All I ever needed to know about change management I learned at engineering school[26]:

"I am a mechanical engineer. We mechanical engineers tease our civil engineering colleagues that they only have to figure out how to make things stand up or fall down. Mechanical engineers have to figure out how to make things go round and round - a skill of a higher order. Making change always seemed to me like mechanical engineering, but a lot of the literature reads as if civil engineers wrote it.

---

[25] Yeates, D. & Cadle, J. (1996) - Project Management for Information Systems, Pitman Publishing: p249)
[26] The McKinsey Quarterly, 1997 Number 2

Nature consists of ecosystems in balance - structures in which different species live interdependently.
When an ecosystem is knocked out of balance for whatever reason, a period of often-violent flux follows, during which scarce resources are dynamically redistributed and the system arrives at a new balance that better reflects the new environment.
Similarly, when constituent interests are out of balance in a large corporation, a power struggle erupts."

The Author of this book, who is also an ex-mechanical engineer, brings from the laws of classic engineering science, several universal laws re-applied to successful business change and Compliance.

The 1st and 3rd laws of Isaac Newton's classic physics, as related to business change and Compliance:

1/ Unless acted upon by an unbalanced force (change), an object (business) will maintain a constant velocity (business inertia).

3/ All forces occur in pairs, and these two forces are equal in magnitude and opposite in direction (i.e. change and resistance to change).

The law of quantum mechanics, as related to business change and Compliance:

In quantum mechanics (QM), wave-particle duality maintains that light and matter can exhibit properties of both waves and flux of particles (as in a straight line). The idea is rooted in a debate over the nature of light and matter dating back to the 1600s, when Christiaan Huygens and Isaac Newton proposed competing theories of light.
Through the work of Albert Einstein, Louis de Broglie and other scientists, it is now established that minute

components, such as atoms, have both wave and particle properties, and that QM provides the bridging theory and empirical hypothesis to resolve this apparent paradox. Likewise, business change and Compliance may act in a straight line, and/or as a wave - impacting a multitude of business functions, internal and external entities that are linked to the company.

It is the combination of these factors that makes change management and Compliance implementation complex and difficult to achieve and measure. It is ESSENTIAL to assess how your forthcoming business change and Compliance initiatives will impact your enterprise in one way or another, and how to measure their results.
The 80-20 empirical rule is most useful here, and once you identify the 20% that critically influence the remaining 80% of your business, you begin with this portion.
Use 'traffic lights' – they are most effective – green (leave alone for now), amber/blue (non-immediate action), and red (immediate attention required).

The law of optics, concerning the human retina (a thin layer of cells at the back of the eyeball) of the human eye contains three-four different types of colour receptor cells, called 'cones':

Type 1 is relatively distinct from the other two, is most responsive to light that we perceive as *violet-blue*, with wavelengths around 420 nm (nanometre: a thousand-millionth of a metre) - *sometimes called a short-wavelength 'S-cone'.*
The other two types, 2 and 3, are closely related genetically, chemically and in response.
Type 2 (*sometimes called a long-wavelength 'L-cone'*) is most sensitive to light we perceive as *yellowish-green*, with wavelengths around 564 nm.
It is known as the "red cone" because this type is also associated with perception of the colour red.

273

Type 3 (*sometimes called a middle-wavelength 'M-cone'*) is most sensitive to light perceived as *green*, with wavelengths around 534 nm.

In short, the human eye essentially works with red, green, yellow and blue.
Likewise – in business – there are 3 or 4 primary change modes – each of a unique characteristic and wavelength.

The human brain and eye cognitively respond to light and stimuli of electromagnetic waves and reactions have been documented for centuries.
Our reactions to change use language; 'I can see it happening', or 'I cannot see it happening' – it's not a metaphoric response but a physical response – as to how we cognitively visualise business transformation in our mind eyes!
Just as we have short, medium and long wavelength of the cognitive light spectrum, so we have short-term, medium-term, medium-long, and long-term changes within our business change and Compliance programmes and projects; 3-6 months, 7-12 months, 13-24 months, and 24-36 months.
Human engineering TOGETHER WITH business process reengineering and culture transformation ARE THE KEY FOR SUCCESS. What's the point of introducing a highly complex and sophisticated system, if only a fraction of users is able to use about 20% of its functionality?
Is it not better to introduce a simpler IT system that will do less, but users will be able to embrace it happily and use 80% of its functionality?
WHAT MATTERS IS THE END RESULT, NOT HOW EFFICIENT IS THE SYSTEM! This simple but devastating and costly truth is often forgotten in the excitement to buy the latest technology!

Cybernetics re-applied:

It is the combination of person-machine interfaces, which makes or breaks the business. I call this - the BUSINESS TRANSFORMATION AND COMPLIANCE CYBERNETICS.

According to Wikipedia, the free encyclopaedia -
Cybernetics is the study of communication and control, typically involving regulatory feedback, in living beings and machines, and in combinations of the two (e.g. socio-technical systems).

The term *Cybernetics* stems from the Greek *Κυβερνήτης* (*kybernetes* - meaning steersman, governor, pilot, or rudder; the same root as government). It became a powerful vogue idea from 1948 to the 1960s; but since the 1970s use of the term has decreased because it covers such a broad field now. Current near-synonyms are: - complexity theory, control theory, and dynamic systems theory.

A more philosophical definition, suggested in 1958 by Louis Couffignal, one of the pioneers of Cybernetics in the 1930s, considers cybernetics as "the art of assuring efficiency of action".

This is the most appropriate and relevant definition in the context of change management and Compliance.

Too many managers are still getting it wrong. It's now high time to radically re-think our approach to change, particularly in light of very costly failures caused by repeated mistakes of reliance on IT solutions exclusively to produce a 'magic potion'.

It's the Cybernetics of business change and Compliance that defines success or failure, NOT the IT system we deploy!

The law of Statistics re-applied:

You do not have to be an expert in statistics to notice the remarkable similarity of the above light wavelength curves to statistical probability 'normal' distribution curves (see below).
The vertical Y-axis is the percentage of probability in fractions from 0 to 1 (0 to 100%), and the horizontal X-axis is the group of variables under observation or the population range being measured.

You can clearly see that the smallest the change/impact on the entity's population, the highest the probability of success, and the smallest the risk (tallest/middle curve). But the widest the change/impact on the entity's population, the lowest is the probability of success (shortest/most flat curve), and the highest the risk.

Therefore, a relatively small change, well contained with minimal side effects on a small entity's population size, is much more likely to succeed as it less risky and easier to implement with less impact on the whole entity, and the opposite is also true. A wide-ranging change across a very widespread range of the entity's population is far less likely to succeed, and its success probability is much lower.
The trick is, in large organisations, is to introduce and manage business transformation or turnaround in relatively small chunks, and join them together wisely and cohesively to achieve an optimal success.

See next Figure.

Figure 14.7: Common statistical curve distributions

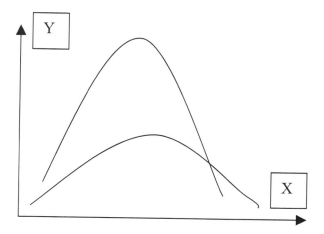

The change-success relationship is NON-LINEAR in terms of population size, granularity, and ability to change, and overall change impact and success. Implementing a system Compliance transformation, coupled with another change programme for say, 10,000 staff worldwide IS NOT 10 TIMES MORE COMPLEX OR DIFFICULT than doing the same for 1,000 staff, but probably somewhere between 20 and 80 times more complex or difficult.

CHANGE FATIGUE SETS IN – COMPANIES AND INDIVIDUALS HAVE NOT YET RECOVERED FROM THE LAST STRING OF CHANGES, AND NOW THEV ARE CONFRONTED WITH NEW ONES – FORE\ MOVING THE GOAL POSTS.
Many individuals therefore behave as zombies.

They are no longer able to cope or care but simply go through the motions, opt for another job, early retirement or sick-leave.

Many people suffer from stress-related illness; depression etc. brought about by poorly introduced changes.

The 1st law of thermodynamics, in relation to business change and Compliance, is re-applied as follows:

The increase in the internal energy (change momentum) of a system (company) is equal to the amount of energy added by heating (change impact on) the system, minus the amount (of change effort) lost as a result of the work done by the system on its surroundings (business departments, clients, contractors, suppliers etc.).

The trade-off clearly is that to gain something you have to sacrifice something, and as long as you can measure both and monitor them, and comprehend their impact, you are in control of the situation and should be successful in implementing change and Compliance initiatives.

Many companies spend millions on change initiatives that disrupt so much their business-as-usual operations that additional millions are lost BUT THE IT AND BUSINESS MANAGERS, AND COST ACCOUNTANTS SIMPLY IGNORE THIS SITUATION, OR FEEL UNABLE TO COUNTER-ACT!
The end result is over-extended losses, not only in the profit figures, but also a loss of goodwill and customers moving away from the supplier they have loyal to.
You surely know how difficult and costly it is to get new customers as opposing to keeping existing ones!
An innovative branch of psychology (developed by the Author) - called Cognitive-Synergy ™[27] *- provides new insights to understand the psychology of change, business transformation, turnaround and Compliance.*

---

[27] This is a Copyrights name of Abe Abrahami, invented and used to describe an innovative branch of psychology he has developed to deal with change successfully.

15. Business Performance and Change Management

Key Issues

Business performance and change management are closely related to Compliance, as one impacts the other two, and vice versa.

To plan, facilitate and execute change projects successfully, the right infrastructure and organisation must be in place, but above all, PEOPLE, the right mix of listeners, doers and thinkers, all suitably trained and motivated.
People make it happen, NOT processes, NOT fancy theories or wishful thinking, NOT computer systems and automation alone – these are tools and crutches, NOT prime movers!
Processes and infrastructure merely support and underpin what people need to do, and do it right, right from the start according to TQM (Total Quality Management) principles. These are the enablers to deliver performance improvements and benefits, using the appropriate tools, techniques, methods and software applications.

Whether projects are large or small, the tasks of planning, scheduling, managing and reporting on the relevant activities are critical to the project success and delivery of benefits.
The project timeline and schedule help to establish the critical path for completing the project or programme on time, to budget, and within resource capacity allocation. Key Performance Indicators are time, cost, and resource to complete, versus actually completed and invoiced/paid for work.

Therefore, a transparency of change across the organisation is a must in order to view and anticipate early or remedial actions concerning potential or existing problems.

For example, long-lead times or services need to be flagged very early in the project.

The daily responsibility of planning, initiation and managing multiple projects across diverse business areas, or regions is not easy, and the impact on human resources, finance, and procurement must be recognised and catered for.

Issues of quality, productivity, resources, cost and schedule overruns and clashes, and managing changes across numerous projects are complex and involve people from different parts of the organisation.

The silo approach will and does not work here, it is a new world that requires a different and better way to manage project portfolios to reduce risk exposure, overruns, budget under / over-spend, and deliver on time and fit for purpose products and benefits.

A modus operandi of a proactive Business Performance & Project Management (BP&PM), requiring not only a new set of skills – but also a demanding a new mindset, are a critical factor and key for success.

People can and should be trained to acquire the new BP&CM skills necessary to carry out their work, and convey this to their contractors.

However, to acquire a new mindset is not a simple question of training but requiring the ability and will to change one's behaviour – such a new type of personality of individuals will have to be reflected by new roles and responsibility and new job descriptions.

It will involve HR and unions, and this part of the jigsaw puzzle should not be underestimated.

On the dashboard of common Key Performance Indicators (KPIs), one should be able to view, analyse and take decisions concerning projects and programmes and quickly identify projects at risk, in order to take anticipative or corrective actions.

Because managers, technical and admin staff, sales and procurement officers make critical decisions daily to resolve business issues and changes, knowing the whole picture across projects and programmes is critical.

With a suitable, fit-for-purpose BP&PM tool and common reporting, all organisation project and procurement teams can better understand project status with a wide-range of real-time, interactive options, including 'what if' scenario simulation and impact analysis.

Benefits that such a tool and its successful implementation and wide acceptance and usage will bring along to organisation cannot be overstated.

A senior purchasing executive and a change management officer of a large logistics organisation stated that early visibility of projects to procurement to get involved at the right time is essential to reap benefits such as:

- Better plan procurement dept. workload
- Develop best procurement strategy at project level
- Develop pan-organisation 'procurement clans' as a single strategy for procurement for categories of expenditure, for example, information management software procurement. Such management of suppliers will involve developing relationships, for example, providing advanced warning of forward loading, and developing strategic procurement plans at organisation level, determine framework agreements etc.

- Gain visibility of future projects and factor them into overall change programmes
- Report on category of procurement required for each project
- Enable integration of functions i.e. shopping baskets and procurement events passed back to suppliers for delivery with overall commitments and dates.

As a CULTURAL CHANGE, the procurement agent and change management representative will become active integral members of the project team, not just an external service, as it used to be in the old days.

Please consider the following Business Performance & Project Management Press Release extracts[28]:

First press release:
Project managers lack confidence in Government's ability to successfully deliver major projects, 24 Jan. 2005

"78% of project managers do not have confidence in the Government to deliver a large project, like biometric identity cards, on time and to budget.
That's according to the latest research from the Business Performance and Project Management (BP&PM) event, 2 – 3 March 2005, Olympia, London.

61% said that their organisation's projects generally overrun, and a further 11% said that projects generally failed to deliver the expected results.
This compares to 6% running on time and to budget and 22% delivering the expected benefits.
When asked what areas of project management were most important to improve to combat this, respondents said: increasing support from senior management (50%);

---

[28] According to Business Performance & Project Management web site: **http://www.bppm.com**

improving stakeholder management (44%); and improving communication skills (39%)."

About 56% of respondents stated that the factor affecting the success or otherwise of a project mostly – was clearly stated objectives and benefits.

Second press release:
Organisational change – conventional thinking challenged and new approaches explored at Business Performance & Project Management
21 Feb. 2005

"80% of all corporate change-initiatives fail."

Change Management Experience

The most challenging corporate transformation changes recently experienced and recorded by selected interviewees in a major transport organisation are listed as follows:

- Rollout of Framework for project management methodology was inconsistent
- Disconnect between senior management, user and business change agent
- Culture / psychological change trauma experienced
- Disagreement / uncertainty between top management cascading down
- Introduction of new management / business processes inconsistent
- Burden of reporting increased, too many KPIs (Key Performance Indicators) driven
- New skill sets required for redesigned Roles & Responsibility (R & R) lacking
- Get a lot of change productivity increase by talking nicely to people, not necessarily following procedures

- People do not have a clue what's going on during / after re-organisation
- No clear vision, more personal / interactive education and business preparedness needed, including more consultations, workshops, to make people feel involved
- Lack of documented unified business process, unclear process definition as a reference point
- IT initially unable to manage business as usual problems after change is introduced
- After 3-4 recent organisation changes, starting to develop a new structure
- Business practice change to be delivered consistently throughout the organisation
- Reorganisation issues: reason for transition poorly explained, change timing / speed, communication plan – not well conveyed
- Inadequate consultation, people ordered to do things, fate complete
- Electronic time capture, poorly introduced / imposed, not explained, fizzled out
- Need more help with skills' development
- Human Resources (HR) – the way it is now working is a big change compared to the past, now using call centre automated telephony, which is unsatisfactory, having to deal with juniors before being able to speak to an HR professional
- Changes are rushed through, poor handover from project team to operational team; people left wondering as to who does what and how it all works
- Making transformation from a silo-style to a proactive organisation needed - a culture shock, new skills and mindsets are required
- Enterprise Resource Planning (ERP) system is not meeting expectations, a major cause for concern and unhappiness
- Poor / Non-business focused training in ERP system, helpers disappeared after a short period, leaving

organisation without suitable support, except hefty training manuals.

Significant Change Areas to Improve

The same people surveyed in 2.2 expressed the following concerns about corporate transformation changes as follows:

- Effective communications before / during / after change implementation - Communication needs to be constant even if nothing is happening, this prevents paranoia, rumour wildfire and a fall in morale
- Effective education sessions before / during / after the change
- Effective management of expectations
- Effective new work practices / procedures
- Proactive help from change ambassadors
- Greater involvement of HR / line manager
- Greater clarity of roles and responsibilities
- Effective change impact analysis
- Proactive help from IT support
- Better training in new skills
- More system testing before going live
- Higher quality / reliability of system being delivered
- Clear vision; demonstrate why are we doing this
- If the system involve more [down] time / effort, the overall workload must either go down or quality will reduce
- Accident life cycle / study reporting / processing should take no more than 3 days, but due to cumbersome paperwork, the task becomes more difficult and time consuming – business process to be improved to match requirement
- General business restructuring / re-organisation poorly / sparsely communicated, whereas at times – the opposite, perhaps too much information
- Greater information integrity / completeness

- Greater local support, ongoing and proactive
- Solid scope and business-case, freeze of scope
- Senior management buy-in, effective business process
- Better resource planning and matching of skills
- Sponsorship strength and vigour
- Computer Based Training (CBT) for new starters
- SIMPLICITY of change is a MUST
- What is the objective and bottom line benefits for the complexity introduced?
- More effective skill re-training of managers and staff
- Limit change scope
- Reporting - what the business actually requires, who are the key users?

Strength and Benefits of Change

The same people surveyed in 2.2 also listed the following strengths and benefits of enterprise transformation changes:

- Review how we do things now / in future
- Providing a better and more valuable service
- Invigorate / Motivate / Energise people, allow them to increase efficiency and effectiveness
- Becoming a first class / best of breed organisation
- Opportunity to improve efficiency / value for money
- Ability to innovate/anticipate market driven change
- Necessary to improve capacity planning
- Consistent practices across the organisation
- Result in better product delivery
- Develop / Evolve best work practices
- Address items usually low on priority list
- Enhanced information and control, single source of data
- Help re-evaluate business needs / question them
- Good understanding of benefits / business case
- Change is healthy and essential for growth

Weaknesses and Disadvantages of Change

The same people surveyed in 2.2 outlined the following weaknesses and disadvantages of change:

- Insufficient time to do daily tasks, simple tasks become complex
- Throwing the baby out with the bath water
- Split organisation, disruptions, disruption to business
- Benefits unclear plus business as usual required
- Does not improve delivery of projects
- Potential impact on staff morale / confidence
- Stifles opportunity for staff to grow / development
- Extent of change hinders delivery deadlines
- Management and staff ownership
- Reflect / Pre-empts changes in environment, including external legal requirements, new initiatives / ideas
- Instability, short-term impact on productivity
- Affect of change are unknown in advance
- Disruption, loss of control and additional (duplication) of effort during transition, validation of data
- Often too much change, ill thought out - causes further change later (chain reaction)
- Manage stakeholders' and users' expectations, - winners and losers
- To be effective - change must be embraced by a critical mass / majority.

Developing a Business Change Training Plan

A business transformation training scheme should be evolved and delivered in five major stages:

1. Goal-Setting
2. Assessment
3. Planning & Preparation
4. Implementation
5. Post-Delivery

The enterprise training / education plan should be driven by the needs of the business, the problems it faces and the goals it has set itself.

The more the training function can anticipate these needs and realise their implications for training activity, the more robust and effective its contribution to business performance will be.

I - Goal Setting: Objectives of the Education Programme

- What will success translate to, at the end of this programme?
- What outcomes do we contract to deliver over the next 6 months?
- How many people will we train, and in what subjects?
- What design work will be conducted?
- How many needs analysis and evaluations will be done?
- What other client facing activity do we need to conduct?
- The objectives should also include the internal development of the training function:
  - What non-client facing work will we be doing? How will this contribute to the long-term development of the business?
  - What activities do we need to undertake to develop the internal capability and expertise of the training function?

II - Assessment 1: Change Learning Organisation Assessment

- What performance goals is the business trying to achieve over the next 6-12 months? What are the critical success factors?
- How well is training / education currently performing?

- What changes and initiatives are on the horizon for the next 6-12 months?
  These could include:
  - Recruitment
  - New product launches
  - Organisational initiatives e.g. total quality, customer service, cost reduction plans, better information analysis / reporting, Investors in People
  - New software application and/or hardware from IT
  - New regulatory requirements
  - Organisational changes: e.g. restructuring, mergers, acquisitions, and takeover

- What problems is the business facing? Example - staff turnover, customer complaints, rework, accidents etc.
- What are the obstacles and constraints to achieving the desired level of performance?
- What are the priorities for the next 6-12 months? Do they involve a training solution either partially or fully?
- What remedial or refresher training activity would make a difference to performance, e.g. end user systems refresher training
- How much training typically cost, and pays for it?

II - Assessment 2: Change Education Impact Analysis

- Which business issues have a training solution or partial solution?
- What training activity would make a real difference to the business?
- Which training needs are urgent and important? And which are just urgent?
- What are the important training needs that may be neglected because they can happen at any time e.g. management training or personal development?
- What mandatory training is required e.g. health and safety, regulatory driven training?

- What are the key success factors / benchmarks of the intended training?

III - Planning & Preparation: Facilitating the Change Education Programme

- How many people will require training, and over what time scale?
- How long is the training likely to last e.g. 1 day, 5 days, or two weeks?
- What resources are likely to be required, i.e. trainer time, expertise, specialist classrooms and equipment, external help?
- What help and resources will we need from the client or other parts of the organisation e.g. subject matter experts, IT support, administration, communication and follow up coaching?
- Which of these is likely to prove a constraint or a showstopper?
- What options do we have around meeting these needs and success benchmarks?
- How much will it cost, and who will pay?

IV - Implementation: Delivery of Training Activities

Training programme delivery (see next Table) should be implemented along the following schedule, with example text inserted, based on a real business case:

Table 15.1: Change training delivery schedule (example)

Training Activity	Training Delivery Method	People to Train	Training Schedule	Goal Success Factor
Introduction to ERP-CRM to process new orders	Face to face, also CBT (computer based training) refresher	100, 20 people per group in 5 separate sessions / groups	5 Sept.-28 Sept. 2007, one-day separate sessions	Ability to execute order processing using ERP-CM within predefined parameters

V - Post Delivery Stage: Post Training Review – Lessons Learnt

- Were the objectives met?
- What was best implemented?
- What was least well implemented?
- What should improve next time?
- What should be cascaded throughout the organisation, as best practice?
- Who should do it, when, how, when?
- How did it actually cost?

Training needs analysis and delivery should take into account the parameters and factors outlined below.

Figure 15.1: Cost, Time, Resource in relation to change magnitude

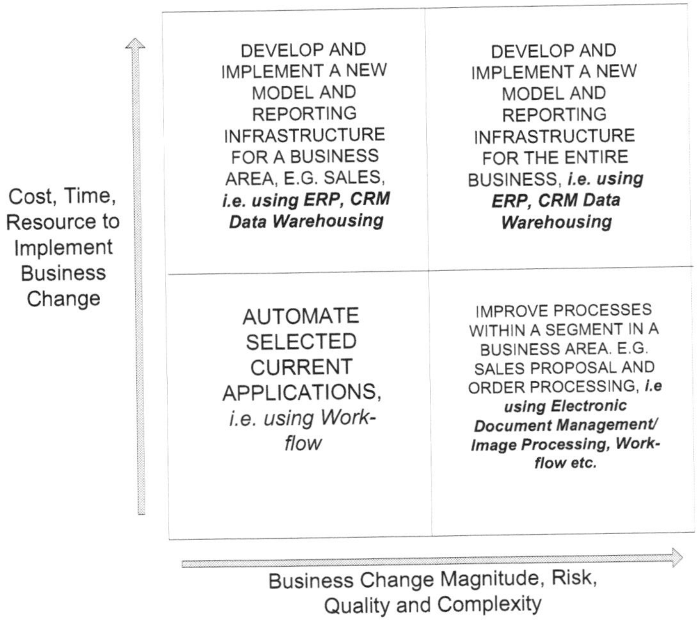

Cost, Time, Resource to Implement Business Change

DEVELOP AND IMPLEMENT A NEW MODEL AND REPORTING INFRASTRUCTURE FOR A BUSINESS AREA, E.G. SALES, *i.e. using ERP, CRM Data Warehousing*	DEVELOP AND IMPLEMENT A NEW MODEL AND REPORTING INFRASTRUCTURE FOR THE ENTIRE BUSINESS, *i.e. using ERP, CRM Data Warehousing*
AUTOMATE SELECTED CURRENT APPLICATIONS, *i.e. using Work-flow*	IMPROVE PROCESSES WITHIN A SEGMENT IN A BUSINESS AREA. E.G. SALES PROPOSAL AND ORDER PROCESSING, *i.e using Electronic Document Management/ Image Processing, Work-flow etc.*

Business Change Magnitude, Risk, Quality and Complexity

292

Questionnaire Survey

The following questionnaire was devised for a major logistics enterprise, and based on the feedback from a population of about 250 individuals, the statistic analytical Figures that follow were produced.

BUSINESS & IT CHANGES - A SURVEY QUESTIONNAIRE

Part One – Recent Experience

1. What is the most challenging <u>business change</u> that you have experienced in the past 3 years? (Please write below the name and nature of the business change programme.

2. How was this <u>business change</u> introduced in terms of change management process? (Please tick <u>one</u> option only)

1=Poorly	2=Average	3=Well	4=Exempla ry

3. Did the <u>business change</u> ultimately meet your expectation? (Please tick <u>one</u> option only)

1=Somewhat	2=Half way	3=Mostly	4=Fully

4. What was the impact of the <u>business change</u> on your work practices/procedures? (Please tick <u>one</u> option only)

1=Small	2=Medium	3=Significant	4=Extensi ve

5. What is the most challenging <u>IT system change</u> that you have experienced in the past 1-4 years? (Please write below the name and nature of the IT system).

6. How was this <u>IT system change</u> introduced in terms of change management process? (Please tick <u>one option</u> only)

1=Poorly	2=Average	3=Well	4=Exempla ry

7. Did the <u>IT system change</u> ultimately meet your expectation? (Please tick <u>one option </u>only)

1=Somewhat	2=Half way	3=Mostly	4=Fully

8. What was the impact of the <u>IT system change</u> on your work practices/procedures? (Please tick <u>one option</u> only)

1=Small	2=Medium	3=Significa nt	4=Extensiv e

Part Two – Future Aspirations & Concerns

9. If you were in charge of a major business/IT system change, what specific areas would you <u>improve/concentrate on</u>? (Please tick as <u>many options</u> as you wish)

	Area	Please Tick
1	Effective communications before/during/after change implementation	
2	Effective education sessions before/during/after the change	

		Please Tick
3	Effective management of expectations	
4	Effective new work practices/procedures	
5	Proactive help from change ambassadors	
6	Greater involvement of HR/line manager	
7	Greater clarity of roles & responsibilities	
8	Effective change impact analysis	
9	Proactive help from IT support	
10	Better/More training in new skills	
11	More system testing before going live	
12	Higher quality/reliability of system being delivered	
13	Other – please specify below	

10. What are your <u>greatest concerns</u> in connection with a new IT system? (Please tick as <u>many options</u> as you wish)

	Area	Please Tick
1	Forced to use an application not considered suitable	
2	Changing the way of working for the worse	
3	Having to spend more time to plan and produce reports	
4	Insufficient training to acquire new skills	
5	Insufficient support from line manager/HR	
6	Insufficient change impact assessment	
7	Insufficient change impact education	
8	Incompatible interface to	

		electronically communicate with outside contractors	
9		Incompatible interface to electronically communicate with ERP/CRM applications internally	
10		Insufficient business preparedness for change	
11		Insufficient testing before going live	
12		Poor quality/reliability of system being delivered	
13		Other – please specify below	

11. How would you describe your organisation's management style concerning change management? (Please tick as many options as you wish)

	Current Change Management Style	Please Tick
1	Coercive/Forceful	
2	Collaborative/Democratic	
3	Anticipative	
4	Proactive	
5	Sympathetic	
6	Don't care much	
7	Visionary	
8	Other – please specify below	

12. What do you feel about pending changes? (Please tick as many options as you wish)

	Feeling	Please Tick
1	Enthusiastic	
2	Challenging/Stimulating	
3	Fearful/Anxious	
4	Prefer not to think about it	
5	Don't care	
6	Hoping for the best	
7	Against them/keep status quo	

8	Other – please specify below	

13. In your experience, what does <u>change mean to you</u> in terms of?

♦ Strength/Benefit of change:

♦ Weakness/Disadvantage of change:

♦ Opportunity that change presents (spin off):

♦ Threat to business as usual/on going initiatives:

14. Do you enter the same information more than once to generate business/project plans, estimates, reports etc., and if Yes, which, and why?

15. What is the single major change/improvement you wish and expect from a new IT system/business change to deliver to make your work easier and more effective?

End of Questionnaire

The respondents' feedback indicated that the impact of business transformation on work practices was significant.

Business change met expectations much better than IT system changes, and people on the whole, despite frustration and setbacks, were positive about future change.

Disenchantment and frustration with complex ERP applications, coupled with poor training and change delivery, were strongly evident.

16.   Change Management and E-Learning[29]

To Successfully Implement E-Learning, Forget What You Know About Change

Introduction by this book's Author:

E-Learning is more and more exploited today in the modern electronic age, saving time and money for learners. CBT – Computer Based Training – has become the norm in many instances and industries. Due to the growing importance and relevance of self-learning in relation to this book, it is inserted herein.

Actual article:

Implementing E-Learning means a lot of change. The good news for trainers is that we are involved in it. The bad news is that much of what we know about change is wrong.

We believe in getting management support, large-scale implementations, long-term efforts, roll-outs, kick-offs, being change agents, overcoming resistance, accountability, and the four levels of evaluation.
These beliefs are part of our training culture. They are mostly wrong. We need to forget them and adopt new ideas about change and implementation.

E-Learning is a chance to reinvent the role of training in the organisation. Training can be at the big Table now —

[29] This Article by Tom Werner, was reprinted with kind permission of the Author. Its content is extremely useful and fascinating, as E-Learning is an essential part of business transformation, and for change education managers - see Acknowledgement at the end of this Chapter.

nowadays E-Learning is discussed in the same breath with e-business and e-commerce. We've always wanted to be strategic partners — this is our chance. But we won't be with our traditional mindsets about change.

We should approach E-Learning implementations from a stronger position. Instead of being staff people looking for vision, hoping for support, and working to please, we need to be business people — forming our own visions, initiating new conversations, and focusing on results. To have your plan for E-Learning accepted across the enterprise, here are nine ideas about change to consider.

Forget about Seeking Management Support! Instead, Build the Business Case

Joel P. Henning, in *The Future of Staff Groups,* indicts the subservient thinking of traditional staff people: "The only important question at the end of the day is 'How did it go?' It is code for 'Did we please them?'"
Henning notes that traditional staff groups spend most of their time soothing, selling, and seeking sponsorship instead of focusing on what they offer the business. His solutions? Stop trying to please in exchange for approval. Be a business rather than a function.

Don't look at senior management as the customer; the operating units should be your customers. Think of senior management as your banker.
Don't look for support; look for capital, like everyone else in the organisation. Discover your clients' business problems.
Request capital from senior management to solve those business problems and be prepared to show a return on that capital. Don't expect a place at the Table unless you can make a positive impact.

Make the business case for E-Learning. What can E-Learning do for the business? Where is the most likely business impact, the best relevance and fit? Have a vision. Develop a point of view. Write a position paper. Don't ask your clients for a business case.
Don't instruct them to "Link E-Learning to the business." Link it to the business yourself. Understand their needs well enough that you can build the case for E-Learning.

Learn the facts. How much is spent on training in your organisation? What are the best measures of success for training?? How many people take which courses? How do managers see that training has helped their business? Explore some hypotheticals. What if travel for training were cut in half? What if training was accomplished in one-half the time?
What if salespeople were to make their first big sale of a new product 20% faster? What if the workforce learned your new software and was productive 15% faster? You may not know if E-Learning can deliver these results, but these are right kinds of questions.

Actions:

- Look at the numbers for traditional training in your organisation and develop a snapshot of what's working and not working.
- Study benchmark information to identify how other organisations are focusing on business results, developing business cases, and calculating returns.
- Develop a point of view about how and where E-Learning could help the business and write a white paper.
- Resolve to approach senior management with "why we need to" propositions, not "do they want to" questions.

Forget about Reaction and Learning! Instead, Focus on Business Results

Kirkpatrick's four levels of evaluation (reaction, learning, behaviour, results) are engrained in the training culture. Forget about them for a while. Assume that there is <u>one</u> level of evaluation: business results.

How might E-Learning help your clients' business? How could E-Learning be a success factor?

Managers of a business care about results of the business: money, time, and impact. (They don't care about our course evaluations!) They want to do things better, faster, cheaper, easier.

Which of E-Learning's potential strengths could help your clients' business? Is it global consistency of content? Is it learners being able to learn at the most convenient time and place? Is it learners being able to learn just the chunks they need? Is it easier identification of who has what competency?

Is it the opportunity to test and require mastery? Is it the use of simulation? Is it having access to a wide range of outside content? Is it some other capability or feature of E-Learning?

Don't let measuring business results become a paralyzing activity. You don't have to build a balanced scorecard or measure fuzzy intangibles. Just ask your client what's important.

The client's answer will probably point to people creating a business result faster or better, or obtaining the same learning faster, more cheaply, or conveniently.

Surprise your clients by not playing into the stereotypes about trainers. Don't act like your biggest concern is whether people like E-Learning. Don't act like E-Learning would be a staff project that they should support. Propose E-Learning as a business strategy, not a training project.

Actions:

- Only start E-Learning where a business result is clearly targeted.

- Focus on business results (Level 4) evaluation. Only look at behavior, learning, and reaction in the context of ensuring business results.

Forget About Rollouts! Instead, Create "Pull"

The 1980s and 1990s were the golden age of organisational improvement rollouts. (Insert your list of rolled-out initiatives here!).
In a roll-out, we typically form a plan for broad (simultaneous or staggered) implementation, make or buy content, set goals and timelines, conduct training and other events, track progress, and have follow-up reviews.

The rollouts of the 1980s and 1990s sometimes produced benefits (you be the judge), but they also produced resistance and "program fatigue." "Flavour of the month" became a universal expression. Cynicism was raised to an art form (I still smart from a Dilbert cartoon about "qualicide").
Rollouts are based on two highly questionable mindsets: rationality and directiveness. The rational mindset assumes that if we can just define the right steps clearly and persuasively enough, people will do them. The rational mindset misses soft, squishy things like fear, loss, and uncertainty — the emotions that fuel resistance.

The directive mindset assumes that we can actually roll things onto people. In the directive mode, we decide what should happen to other people and how to do it to them. The directive mindset misses the precariousness of line-management accountability (see number 4 below).
Instead of rolling E-Learning onto people, think about pulling them in.
Nancy J. Lewis and Peter Orton have written about the power of Everett Rogers' research on the diffusion of innovation (*Training and Development,* June 2000).

Everett Rogers spent decades studying the adoption of innovations, from hybrid corn in Iowa to modern math in Pittsburgh and snowmobiles among the Lapps in Finland.

Rogers identified five factors that pull adopters toward innovations:

1. Advantage.
The new thing has to be better than other alternatives.

2. Compatibility.
The new thing has to feel familiar and fit my beliefs.

3. Simplicity.
The new thing has to be simple to use.

4. Trialability.
The new thing has to be easy to try.

5. Observability.
I have to be able to see other people's positive results from it.

Lewis and Orton describe how IBM has applied Rogers' concepts to its Management Development E-Learning effort. Notice how the effort differs from a traditional roll-out:

1. Advantage.
IBM Management Development offers Quick-Views — instant on-line briefings on 40-plus leadership and people-management topics. They are easy-to-access, available as needed, and allow classroom sessions to focus on discussion rather than presenting information.

2. Compatibility.
IBM Management Development sites replicate the look and feel of Lotus Notes, the standard IBM interface.

3. Simplicity.
IBM Management Development sites require no plug-ins. Ease of use is the top priority in design.

4. Trialability.
IBM Management Development allows free access to all sites without passwords or personal tracking so that learners feel safe and comfortable.

5. Observability.
IBM Management Development implemented Quick-Views first so that learners would experience immediate solutions to practical problems.
Instead of pushing E-Learning onto people in a roll-out, consider how to "pull" them to it by making E-Learning easy to adopt.

Action:

Apply Rogers' model to your E-Learning initiative. How could you "pull" adopters?

Forget about Accountability! Instead, focus on Engagement

Line-management accountability has always been the Holy Grail for trainers. We want senior managers to make training matter through a combination of direction, reward, and pressure.
Relying on line accountability as a way to drive change is iffy. We fantasize that senior managers can "make" people embrace new approaches to learning. But it's a shaky approach.

First, it's unlikely that senior managers will wield significant consequences on behalf of our latest initiative. There are so many other meat-and-potatoes issues that they need to use their influence on.

Second, people know so well how to resist accountability — articulate excuses, vicious Compliance, "checking off the boxes," criticism of the initiative, and cries that "we're different," to name a few.

Third, accountability mechanisms paper over what really needs to happen — people have to decide they are going to make real changes.

We need dialogue more than consequences. Don't try to *make* people embrace E-Learning. Talk about reality — the situation, gaps, opportunities, and possible solutions. Engagement means real conversations. Peter Block in his recently updated classic *Flawless Consulting* states that engagement means high-intensity participation, not just briefing people on what they're supposed to do.

Engagement means:
Focusing on the problem more than the prescription.
Allowing real choice instead of "slam-dunking" an initiative on people.
Admitting doubt about the potential solution rather than promising perfection.
Structuring ways for people to have conversations, not just hear speeches.

Action:

Have real dialogues with your clients about the business and how E-Learning might help.

Forget about Large Scale! Instead, Implement where the Need is Greatest

When we think about change, we tend to think about broad, universal application - let's start at the top, cascade this out, get everyone walking the talk, and make this a way of life.

We want to do something big. We imagine sweep, momentum, and ubiquity. We're afraid that small efforts will be piece-meal and disjointed.

The problem with big scope is that we're not conscious enough of risk.

We're too ready to spend other people's time, money, and effort when need and readiness may not be there. We're not afraid enough of failure and not concerned enough about true fit.

Cultures don't change when everyone is forced to do something at the same time. Cultures change when pockets of people find success and the word spreads. We should look for where the need for E-Learning is greatest. Who has a capability problem that traditional training has trouble addressing? Look for the fit. Where are measurable business results most likely to come? Where is skill development most related to business success?

Where is traditional training most inconvenient, most expensive, and least effective? Where are resources available? Who's ready?

Action:

Identify where the need is greatest for new ways of learning.

Forget about being a Change Agent! Instead, Build a Change Agency

Counselling theory heavily influences organisational development. So we tend to envision the lone change agent gradually persuading the client organisation.

One-on-one skills are important, but don't think of yourself as a priest or therapist.

Don't be a loner; be in cahoots with others. Build a coalition. Set up a network. Form alliances. Be the underground railroad! Don't look upward to senior management. Look sideways for the oddballs, the experimenters, and the discontented. Think insurgency, syndicate, and community! Break down silos and build bridges to other groups. Be an ambassador, dealmaker, and networker.

Who's got a business problem that E-Learning could help? Who can benefit from your skills? Whom do you need? Who has parallel interests? Who has passion for change, for learning, for technology? Who is working on knowledge management, quality, teamwork, speed, service, or global consistency? What enterprise-wide projects are underway? Who's tired of traditional training? Who would fund an experiment? Who wants to be a pioneer? Who might be better off with imperfect E-Learning instead of "perfect" traditional training?

Actions:

- Contact interested clients and colleagues and stay connected electronically and in-person.
Initiate conversations with your IT department and form a partnership.
- Connect with E-Learning people in other organisations as well.

Forget about kick-offs! Instead, Communicate with Frequent, Specific Messages

Was there a kick-off for fax machines? For using cell phones? For using palm computers? Who knows and who cares? It wasn't the kick-off that mattered.

Kick-offs meet the emotional needs of the kickers (to feel special), not the needs of the receivers. People don't get excited at initial events. People get excited when they sense a movement in progress. Kick-offs just give people a reason to say, "That doesn't apply to me," "That won't work," or "This looks like another flavour of the month."

Skip the kick-off. People don't need excitement; they need to be educated. Just start telling people what's available in E-Learning. Show peoples a demo. Tell people what successes others have had, including competitors. Explain how E-Learning can solve a problem for them. Send frequent, targeted messages to specific groups about specific E-Learning solutions.

Action:

Send regular, specific communications about E-Learning.

Forget about Taking Years to Change! Instead, Focus on Speed and Quick Wins

We know the phrases — it takes a long time to change a culture, we have to be in it for the long term, it's a journey. While those ideas may be true, they're not very helpful. In the 1980s it was common for people (including me) to say that it takes years to change a culture. It was meant to be comforting. Traditional organisations seemed so intractable and opposed to new ideas, it seemed necessary to say, "There's no magic bullet; change takes a long time."
The problem with the slow-change concept is that removes our sense of urgency. We end up working slowly and our audience doesn't see anything happening.
Cycle time has to matter to us just like it does to our constituents. We have to live on Internet time too. There was a time when we took a year to plan a new course, get

it approved, build it or buy it, pilot it, revise it, certify the trainers, announce it, and implement it.

Trainers lived on organisational time, not business time. That has changed. We have to think about "time-to-market" just like everyone else. Speed counts. Change needs momentum. Figure out how to win early and win often, even if it means winning small, with E-Learning.

Actions:

- Plan for quick wins with E-Learning.
- Slash cycle time in the development of E-Learning courses.

Forget about Overcoming Resistance! Incorporate Resistance

What if we encounter resistance to E-Learning? What if enrolment rates or completion rates are low? What if people are put off by E-Learning technology? What if people miss the classroom?

We will instinctively want to overcome the resistance. "Overcoming resistance" is usually code for one of two things: selling the idea harder or telling senior management. In the face of resistance, we're tempted to pitch the concept better or put down the rebellion. Overcoming resistance usually really means silencing the resistance.

But we can't just ignore or put down resistance. As Peter Block has famously said, "Resistance means something important is going on." We need to note the resistance, talk about it out loud, and listen to what the resisters are saying.

People usually resist if their senses of competence, control, credit, or comfort are being "pinched." Be conscious of how E-Learning might offend someone's sense of competence. How might it take away their sense of control? How might it make them feel robbed of credit? How might it make them uncomfortable?

Empathize by realizing your own resistance. Remember that feeling when you refused to use a new piece of software because you didn't want to have to learn it. Remember the feeling when you first thought your job as a trainer might go away. Remember when you thought no one realized how hard training really is. Remember that feeling when someone tried to tell you how you should run your training class.

Incorporating resistance into the dialogue means talking out loud about objections, feelings, and opinions.

It also means remembering to give credit, share information, and involve others in planning and implementation.

Actions:

- Use resistance as something important to talk about, not something to be overcome.
- Expect resistance when E-Learning pinches people's senses of competence, control, credit, or comfort.

Summary

- We need to forget those old ideas about change that never worked that well anyway, such as:
- Seeing senior management as the customer and seeking management support as the driver for initiatives.
- Treating the four levels of evaluation as being of equal importance.
- Using rollouts as the vehicle for implementation.
- Relying on accountability to motivate people to accept change.
- Planning large-scale, blanket change efforts.
- Thinking of change agents as lone individuals.
- Using kick-offs as a way to create excitement.

- Taking years to implement change.
- Letting "overcoming" be our natural response to resistance.

Instead, we need to:

- Build the business case for E-Learning.
- Document business results (Level 4) as the way to evaluate E-Learning.
- Create "pull" by making E-Learning easy to adopt.
- Have real dialogue with people about their business and learning needs.
- Build a change agency by building a coalition among likely clients and colleagues.
- Communicate frequently and specifically to inform and educate about E-Learning.
- Move fast and get quick wins with E-Learning.
- Talk openly about resistance, and the reasons behind it, instead of trying to conquer it.
- Let's use E-Learning to change training's typical role, image, and modus operandi. Let's change ourselves and the traditional culture - Let's stay at the big Table by focusing on the business.

ACKNOWLWDGEMENT AND THANKS:
The Author of this book wish to express deep gratitude and appreciation to Tom Werner is a researcher and consultant with Brandon Hall Research, who kindly gave his permission to reprint his paper, as follows:

Brandon Hall Research
690 W. Fremont Ave. Suite 15
Sunnyvale, CA 94087
Phone: (408) 736-2335
E-mail: tom@brandon-hall.com
Web: www.brandon-hall.com

17. Changing the IT Department – A Case History[30]

Introduction

At the heart of any business today, particularly large multi-regional companies and organisations, is Information Technology (IT).
Without a robust, efficient and effective, customer-delivery-focused IT department, well aligned with business objectives, policy and strategy, the business is doomed. Therefore IT is not about IT alone but primarily and foremost about the business.

IT related change programmes and projects can consume a hungry chunk of the overall business budget cake (at times up to 80%), and therefore, changes and improvements in the IT dept. have far reaching consequences.

This Chapter is about a case history of restructuring and enhancing the value of the processes within the Information Technology (IT) department of a major London based Insurance PLC in the insurance business.

Before embarking on this project, the Managing Director of this PLC spoke to the Author of this book, who was responsible to introduce this change, and told him:

- If I could only get my products to market 3-6 before the competition...
- If I could only get the IT dept. to deliver what I want when I want...
- If I could only get my projects to deliver on time and budget...

---

[30] From a personal experience of the Author at Trade Indemnity plc

- If only...

This Insurance PLC tried unsuccessfully for a period of about 2-3 years to introduce Total Quality and improved processes, to increase productivity, quality, and value for money for the company. Based on a personal recommendation, the Author was called in to assess the situation, propose and implement a remedial solution within 6 months.

He found that the processes were inefficient, patchy, and left a lot of room for uncertainty. Important things were missed out, while development effort duplication, cost, time and resource wasting were evident.

System developers and operations support staff were not quite sure about their responsibilities, which does exactly what and when, and their interfaces were unclear and poorly defined.
For example, it happened on a number of occasions that the IT Support/Help Desk was confronted by users who called to ask about a new application, which the Development team had released without informing the Help Desk.

Moreover, there was no framework or formal structure to envelope distinct life cycles for product development and customisation.
The company management realised that with increasing commercial pressures and squeezed margins the company could not continue like this for much longer. Something had to be done, and fast.

Accordingly, after a short discussion with management, it was agreed to set up and implement a Value Enhancement project with the following objectives:

Save 5% of the $7 million IT/IS budget of the company ($350,000) in the first year, which will grow to 10% in the following year.
Cut product development and customisation total life cycle time on average by 20% (faster time to market to gain a competitive edge over the competition).

Cut product development and customisation errors and re-work on average by 20%.
Formalise and make more efficient the individual stages and their interfaces within the development and customisation life cycle.

Remove uncertainties and ambiguities among staff members caused through lack of a formal development and customisation life cycle.
Enable the smooth hand-over from development and customisation to operations and support, by defining clearly what work had to be completed before progressing to the next stage.
The methodology, which was chosen and successfully implemented, in this case was the Author's <u>Process Value Enhancement</u>™ (PVE™[31]); see below.

1. Request for change (RFC)
2. Terms of reference (TOR) and feasibility
3. Project implementation document (PID)
4. Quality plan (QP)
5. Functional requirements
6. Technical specification
7. Design specification
8. Programming and unit testing
9. Code and system testing
10. Training
11. Going live
12. Bedding in

---

[31] Copyrights of Abe Abrahami

Project Implementation Results

The following results were attained as an outcome of the Value Enhancement project:

- 10% ($700,000) saving in the $7 million IT budget in the first year, thus exceeding the target by 100%.
- Product development and customisation life cycle time, errors and re-work were cut by 20% on average for the large and medium size projects.
- IT staff professionalism, morale and job satisfaction increased, while staff turnover decreased.
- Customers of the IT department reduced their complaints by 50% during the first year a result of a more responsive service provided to them.
- Total number, nature and priority of product development and customisation projects within the IT department were audited. It was subsequently reduced from 220 to 70 essential projects.
- Before project implementation, developers and IT Support staff did not have a complete set of deliverable document templates (e.g. Functional Requirements, Technical Specification, Test plans etc.) plus quality procedures and standards to work from.
- Post project implementation, a consistent flow of work steps was followed to achieve higher productivity and quality. The relevant templates, procedures and standards - all available electronically on line - not on the shelf in some bulky ring binders, enabled this.

Product Development Life Cycles

Three major types of product development and customisation life cycles were identified, analysed (after conducting a series of interviews), and subsequently drawn and discussed.

315

Then they were amended, further discussed, finalised, agreed, and implemented. Before the launch of the newly structured life cycles, the Author trained the 90 staff of the IT department, and also held separate briefing sessions for the Business Users.

This was necessary to make them aware of the pending improvement to the service provided to them by the IT department. All met the introduction of the formalised life cycles outlined below with great enthusiasm and commitment.
The Author ensured that communication with the IT/IS managers and staff and with Business users was kept going on a regular basis to keep them up to date and keep the momentum going. This was an essential ingredient for the success of the project.

The 3 standardised modular life cycles, which were successfully constructed and implemented, are as follows:

- Major Projects: major e-Business applications; in house developments, and developments with suppliers, software houses or partners
- Office Systems and Communications: mostly bought in, slightly customised and installed Off the Shelf Commercial (OSC) applications
- Minor Projects: short duration jobs, mostly minor system enhancements

Of the 3 life cycles mentioned above, the first one (Major Projects) is described in some detail, including the various stages, deliverables and associated processes.

Major Projects Life Cycle and Deliverables

The basis for the formalised and restructured development life cycle were 4 major components introduced to add value for money, namely:
Request For Change (RFC) to initiate and assess the development benefits and costs; being the basis for deciding to continue or not.

Product Implementation Document (PID) to plan the project time scale and resource requirements, on which basis the project cost was estimated.
Quality Plan (QP) to assure quality and value for money. Formal Quality Reviews (QR) and Walk-through sessions to enforce quality and minimal rework.
All the necessary procedures, templates and forms were designed, created and placed on an easily accessible directory.

They were subject to Configuration Management and Document Version Control. The Quality Management System (QMS) to contain and manage the relevant procedures, templates and forms was Quality Workbench.

The client already decided on it before the Author's arrival. Another QMS type used by the Author elsewhere for similar purposes is Paradigm Quality. Word, Excel and Visio were used to create the necessary documentation.

'Create' and 'Amend' permissions were in the hands of the Quality Value Manager, the Project support Office Manager and his deputy.

Only they could create new procedures, forms and templates, and change them. The rest of the IT staff and managers could read these documents but not change the originals.

They could also copy and paste the necessary text and diagrams into their working/deliverable documents (e.g. System Design Specification, Test Plans etc.). Individual Team Leaders controlled the deliverable documents produced in their domain.

All the working documents and life cycle deliverables of the product development and customisation project were placed in a separate repository under QMS' control.

A.   INITIATION PHASE

1/   Request for Change (RFC)

IT/IS Business analyst discusses new initiatives and requirements with the Business.

Where an IT solution appears initially to be viable then the Business Analyst would assist the Business User to complete an RFC.

The RFC is then approved by senior Business personnel and submitted to the IT Project Office.
Where an initial assessment of the RFC indicates the work necessary to fulfil the requirement is not 'minor' the RFC is then forwarded for Feasibility.

2/   *Define TOR[32], Conduct Feasibility Study (FS)*

The scope of the Feasibility Study is documented and agreed by means of a Terms of Reference.

A feasibility study would then be undertaken in accordance with the TOR to investigate the following:

- Problems in the current system (computer or manual)

---

[32] Terms of Reference

- Business requirements
- Any constraints
- Each feasible solution would be documented stating:
- The impact on the Business
- The problems that are being addressed
- The perceived benefits
- Initial estimates of cost
- Associated risks

Only one solution would be recommended to take *further (or not at all; in which case the subsequent steps will not apply, and the development is shelved)*.

Customer Sign Off.
The Recommended solution is formally endorsed by the Business and an agreement to continue given.

3/   *Project Planning & Implementation Document (PID)*

The scope of the Project has to be documented and it must state:

- Specific problems to be addressed
- Specific requirements to be met
- Benefits to be achieved

Major project activities would be identified, enabling a high level plan to be produced showing:

- Resources required from IT
- Resources required from the Business.
- Major milestones and delivery time scales
- Detailed project plan for first stage
- "Running in warranty" period, and PIR - Post Implementation Review

The PID should also identify the controls to be exercised within the project stating:

- Composition of the Project Board
- Those responsible for reviewing project deliverables
- The significance and frequency of project meetings and progress reports
- *Quality Review, Customer Sign Off*

The scope of the project and commitment of resources should be formally agreed between IT and the Business.

4/ Produce Quality Plan (QP)

Immediately after the PID has been drafted, or if possible - in parallel - the Quality Plan should be prepared stating:

- All project deliverables
- The main criterion and methods for quality reviewing

B. ANALYSIS AND PROCESS IMPROVEMENT PHASE

5/ Functional Requirements (FR).

IT/IS Analysts and Business staff fully investigates the current and as newly required business processes within the scope of the project to define the functionality required of the new system.

They add value by proposing better ways to do the job. This is followed by initial screen and report designs created and used to identify information input and output.

The analyst documenting would produce a Functional Requirements specification:

- Information (data) flows, definitions and structure, and system interface links
- Computer and manual processes with their inputs and outputs, including the reports required
- Audit and security requirements
- System availability, performance and recovery requirements
- The success criteria of the project
- Security requirements and procedures
- Sarbanes Oxley Act (SOX) COMPLIANCE / similar REQUIREMENTS
- Business continuity and disaster recovery requirements

Project estimates stated in the PID would be reviewed as a result of the increased understanding of the requirements, including revised and extended details of the subsequent stages.
Walk-through (Quality Review), Customer Sign Off.

Corrective action necessary must be taken and the review process repeated as necessary.
Finally the Functional Requirements should be formally agreed between the Customer and IT together with any Project Plan revisions.

C.   DESIGN PHASE

6/   *Technical Specification (TS).*

The Functional Requirements should be translated into a high level System Design showing how the individual elements of the system fit together as a whole. Duplicated processing is identified and resolved into common modules.

This high level design would be documented as the Technical Specification and state:

- Hardware and software requirements
- System LAN design, including software links between systems
- Operating systems and conversion routines and protocols.
- Physical Database design
- Report design
- On-line processes
- Batch processes.
- Common Processes
- Interfaces with other systems
- Data conversion and load processes.
- Data archiving processes
- Privacy, security and audit controls
- Sarbanes Oxley Act (SOX) / other COMPLIANCE REQUIREMENTS
- Business continuity and disaster recovery plans.
- Data Protection Act considerations

Completing the Technical Specification may identify areas where the agreed functionality is too costly to implement. In such cases the Functional Requirements specification must be reviewed and revised.
Quality Review, IT Sign Off

7a. Parallel Activities

In parallel to production of the Technical Specification the following deliverables should be produced:

- Detailed Build Implementation Plan (BIP)
- Data Base Administrator (DBA) Operation Guide
- User Guide
- Business Practice Procedure
- IT Support Operation Guide
- Customer acceptance criteria and SLA (Service Level Agreement)

- System and Customer Test specs
- Business work procedures
- Training material and courses

7b.   *System Design Specification (SDS)*

Each computer process within the Technical Specification would be expanded in detail identifying and documenting the business rules that apply to validation of input, displayed output and internal processing.

Access and privacy restrictions would also be documented.
The BIP must be completed at this stage.
Quality Review, Customer Sign Off

System Design Specifications will be formally walked through with the Customer and any corrective action agreed.
Customer sign off SDS prior to Program Specification being started

D.   COMPUTER PROGRAMMING PHASE

8.   *Program Specification (PRS)*

Each System Design Specification should be translated into one or more program specification defining the technical rules and logic.

Program Specification has to be reviewed against the SDS to ensure all business rules have been applied.
IT Sign Off

8a.   *Programming and Unit Testing*

Programs are written to specification, unit tested, errors and fixes are reported, in accordance with the relevant standards.
IT Sign Off.

E.   SYSTEM INTEGRATION TESTING PHASE

9.   *Complete System Test Plan (STP)*

System Test plans should be written using the System Design Specification and Technical Specification as input.

9a.   *System Test and Performance Test*

Testing at this point verifies that all Business Rules have been incorporated within the developed processing and that all elements are integrated as per the Technical Specification.

This should include network performance and volume testing. Detected errors should be resolved and re-tested prior to Customer Acceptance Test.
IT Sign off

9b.   *Complete Customer Acceptance Test (CAT) Specification*

Customer Acceptance Test plans should be written using the Functional Requirements as input. Agreement to proceed is obtained.

9c.   *Pre-Customer Acceptance Test Deliverables Review*

The deliverables initiated or planned at an earlier stage should now be completed and Quality Reviewed in preparation for inspection and Customer Acceptance Testing.

10. Training and Customer Acceptance Testing

Users involved in the CAT (Customer acceptance Testing) are trained on the new system to enable efficient testing. Testing at this point is to verify that the required functionality agreed to in the Functional Requirements has been delivered.

Manual procedures should also be tested alongside the system processes to ensure that no gaps exist between the two.
Problems are listed and fixed, and testing repeated where necessary.
Final Product Quality Review and Sign off.

The status of all deliverables within the Quality Plan should be checked. Outstanding documentation would be completed and signed off.

Any outstanding reports from Customer Acceptance Test that do not prevent the project going live should be documented with an agreement on when they will be completed.

Finally, the Customer and IT Support sign off the system and give a formal agreement to go live.

F. SYSTEM GOING LIVE PHASE

11. Hand Over and Installation

All training necessary prior to installing the system is undertaken including the training of Service Desk and Support areas.
All project deliverables should be formally handed over from the Development team to IT Operations Support and moved to a 'live' status and secured.

This phase has to include database reorganisation, loading and conversion processing from the Development environment to the live Operations environment. *UNDER NO CIRCUMSTANCES SHOULD THE DEVELOPMENT TEAM RELEASE A NEW PRODUCT OR AN ENHANCED APPLICATION TO THE USERS. ONLY AFTER A FORMAL HAND OVER FROM DEVELOPMENT TO IT OPERATIONS SUPPORT, THE PRODUCT MAY BE RELEASED TO USERS BY IT OPERATIONS SUPPORT.*

12. Warranty Run-In period

The development team would support the system during agreed bedding in period.

All reported problems should be recorded and resolved. System and network performance should also be monitored.

12a. Post Implementation Review (PIR)

Following an agreed period of usage (stated in the PID), the developed system would be reviewed from both a Business and IT viewpoint.

The success of the project should be determined by measuring the delivered benefits against those stated in the RFC / Business Case and Functional Requirements.

The problems experienced by the IT department, which the Value Enhancement project successfully identified and resolved, are neither new nor unique. They are common today to many companies.

Although there are no wonder cures or magic pills, it is clear that only a consistent Total Quality/Value

Engineering (TQ/VE) approach, which aims at zero faults and profound attitude change, has a serious chance to succeed.

The Japanese have successfully proved it time and again in the last few years, based on philosophies and methodologies which were developed in the USA (Crosby, Deming, and others).

18. Successful Change Delivery with PrMS™[33]

Introduction

A quote from:
'Is poor project management a crime? (EVMS[34] and the Sarbanes-Oxley Act)
A White Paper By: Ruthanne Schulte, PMP
www.welcom.com - published on Mar 25, 2004, states:
"Is poor project management a crime? The answer could be yes?

Consider the many stories in the press about large projects with huge cost overruns. If this kind of cost overrun is not foreseen and anticipated in the financial forecasts of the company, the effects could seriously impact the projected profit for a given period.

To be compliant with Section 404 of the SOX - Management Assessment of Internal Controls - CEOs must establish and maintain an adequate internal control structure and procedures for financial reporting.

Section 409 - Real Time Disclosure mandates that companies must disclose on a rapid and current basis material changes in the financial condition or operations of the [company], ...which may include trend and qualitative information.

As a result, companies undertaking large projects will need a process that provides detailed cost/schedule metrics for all projects with time-phased cost reporting and continually updated completion estimates. Senior management will need visibility into this project performance data at all times along with the confidence that the underlying process is sound."

---

[33] Project/Programme Management Structure - Copyrights of Abe Abrahami
[34] Earned Value Management System

Companies create and manage changes by projects individually. They also manage a collection of related projects, called a *Stream*.

A collection of streams is called a *Programme*. The success of the whole business depends on achieving the benefits of projects, streams and programmes in a cost effective and efficient manner.

Whether the manager uses one tool or another, the result should be that the PROJECT/STREAM deliverables are produced to the required quality, budget and time-scale – fit and timely for purpose.

The Project/Stream Manager (P/SM) requires know-how skills and experience in a number of key areas, including, but not limited to:

- Request For Change (RFC) analysis, scope of work determination
- Cost Time Resource (CTR), planning, estimation, analysis and control
- Risk Evaluation & Management, what can go wrong and what to do about it
- Change Control & Management (CCM), Impact Assessment (IA) of change
- Total Quality (TQ) &Value for Money (VFM)
- Reviewing, Monitoring & Communication
- Resource Management
- Client Relations
- Third Party & Vendor Relations
- Work in Progress (WIP)
- Time & Cost to Complete.

This methodology is proven and is endorsed and recommended by The Institute of Management Specialists in the UK to achieve better value for money and greater control on spending.

Request For Change (RFC) and Scope of Work PID[35]

Typically, in most companies, the business would identify a new need in response to customer changing requirements, competition-imposed changes, or new Compliance rules.
Alternatively, as is the case with corporate growth, turn-round in the business fortunes, mergers or acquisitions, there is a need to combine, optimise or rationalise competing or inefficient systems.

Understandably, the IT dept. would be faced with an RFC from the business for analysing the RFC in more depth, and responding with an outline scope of work for a feasibility, or going directly ahead with a full-scale project scope of work and a PID document.

An outline PID – Project Planning & Implementation Document - would be initially prepared, followed by detailed Cost Time Resource estimating, and a detailed PID to be updated as the project progresses. This PID should include CTR sheets, Work Packages (WPs), Work Breakdown Structures (WBSs) etc.

Cost Time Resource (CTR)

Planning, Estimation and Control is the process of determining and controlling time-scales and milestones, scheduling resources, and calculating their costs to the Project/Stream, using CTR Sheets.
It is carried out once the Stream and Project scopes of work have been defined and the Work Breakdown Structure (WBS) has been established.

---

[35] Project Planning & Implementation Document

This is a dynamic iterative process, reflecting the development and implementation processes.
A Work-Package (WP) is a collection of related CTR Sheets - the tasks, activities and assignments necessary to complete a specific job, which is broken down to component parts on the plan bar chart.

A change in any of these, e.g. Task duration, resource allocation or cost, will necessarily require a review of the other levels for Impact Assessment, either upwards or downwards, and possibly side ways.
Any subsequent change to a plan baseline will involve Change Control & Management (CCM).

This reinforces the hierarchy and working relationships between the Programme, streams and projects, and the relationships between the Task and associated elements below.
The CTR Sheets should cover each Project/Stream team member Assignments in relation to the WP, Task, Scope of Work, Earned Value, Start Date, Finish Date, Cost Code, Schedule Reference, Quality & Inspection Checks, and other associated parameters.

Figure 18.1: Project, work packages and CTR sheets

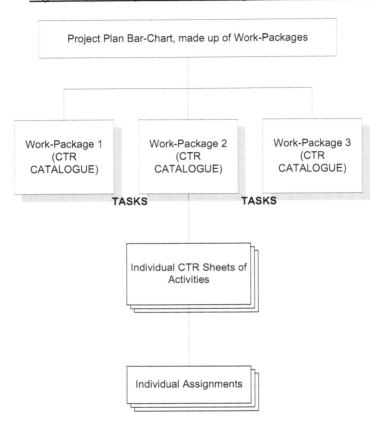

The CTR Sheet is the cornerstone and basis for activity and task planning and estimation and overall project control, top down and bottom upwards. Usually it is an iterative process and a combination of both.

Any change associated with information on a CTR Sheet must be recorded under Change Control & Management (CCM).
Any consequent change to the relevant Task(s) on the bar chart(s) must be made and recorded appropriately.

332

The RFC form - plays a major role within CCM. Any Request for Change form should be completed under this procedure, and any impact on the Project/Stream must be examined by the PS/M and given the go ahead or rejected.

No Change Request should be left hanging without a decision for longer than specified in the CC&M procedure. Many projects fall behind when a decision concerning a Change Request has been outstanding for too long - forgotten or ignored.

Total Quality/Value for Money (TQ/VFM)

The purpose of TQ/VFM is not to create an unwelcome burden on the P/SM and the team members, but instil the discipline, awareness and framework conditions under which the PROJECT/STREAM outputs are delivered.

TQ/VFM is everyone's responsibility, not just the TQ/VFM Coordinator.

TQ/VFM is necessary to ensure that the PROJECT/STREAM deliverables are:

- Fit and Timely for Purpose
- Complete
- Clear
- Consistent
- Auditable
- Compliant.

Informal and formal walk-through (TQ/VFM Review) sessions for the PROJECT/STREAM deliverables - as part of the Quality Plan - should be undertaken for all significant deliverables.

Not every Project/Stream deliverable requires a formal TQ/VFM Review, but it is the responsibility of the P/SM, TQ/VFM coordinator, and Team Leaders to discuss and agree at the outset what will require formal Review and what will require Informal Review.

This means among other things that the outline and purpose of the TQ/VFM Review has to be prepared in advance, and the actual Review has to follow accordingly. In addition to the document Author or person responsible for the deliverable, an independent Moderator has to be appointed to run the Review.
The document Author or person responsible for the deliverable must record the Review results and agreed actions, and ensure they are subsequently carried out.
The informal Review is normally followed by a formal Review, at which time hopefully all previous actions, including correction of errors, should have been completed.

Monitoring and Communication

Monitoring is the process used at all management levels within the Project/Stream to measure actual progress against the base-line project plan.
Data on usage of key indicators must be collected and analysed on a regular basis.
Metrics covering time-scales, Slack Time, Earned Values, CTR Variances, Accruals, WIP, Resource Usage, Cost To Complete, Cost To Date etc. must be defined and then used to provide analysis, control, and remedial action information.

A planned and agreed schedule of progress monitoring reviews is the principal means by which the P/SM ensures that the base-line deliverables are produced in each life-cycle phase and meet their specification in a timely, cost effective and quality fashion.
The P/SM must therefore ensure that these reviews are conducted properly, and that Team Leaders and team

members are adequately familiar with the relevant
reporting and review contents and procedures.

Communication between all the layers of the Programme,
Stream and Project is of critical importance, and it is
usually not done enough. It is not just progress reporting
which is important but also general status information
reporting to the rest of the organisation.
A Newsletter and brief presentations are good channels to
convey the required information to the target audience.

Resource-Matrix Management

Effective Resource Management is one of the key factors
in the Project/Stream Management success.
It is found at times that a conflict exists between vertical
function lines of responsibility and horizontal function lines
of responsibility (see next Figure).

The Project/Stream is structured like a Taskforce,
horizontally crossing vertical department lines of authority
in the organisation.
A team member or a Team Leader may have 2
managers; one is a vertical function (departmental)
manager, the other is the P/SM.

It is necessary therefore to establish at the outset an
arbitration procedure, should a conflict of interest or
priorities arise between the PROJECT/STREAM and any
other piece of work, which has to be undertaken by a
team member.

Figure 18.2: Horizontal vs. vertical matrix management

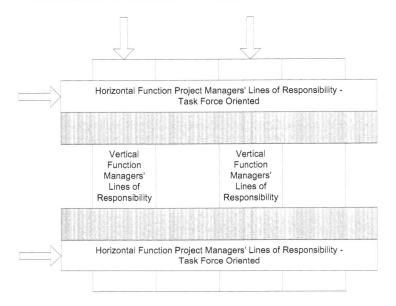

Horizontal Function Project Managers' Lines of Responsibility - Task Force Oriented

Vertical Function Managers' Lines of Responsibility

Vertical Function Managers' Lines of Responsibility

Horizontal Function Project Managers' Lines of Responsibility - Task Force Oriented

This will ensure that the consultation and resolution process is speedy, effective and satisfies all concerned.

Client Relations

The relationship with the customer is an important aspect of the Programme, Stream and Project, which should not be overlooked.
The Programme Manager/Director (PM/D) and (Projects/Stream Manager) P/SM should aim for a friendly but above all professional relationship.
Formal lines of communication should be set up at the outset, with both parties understanding the associated authority limits.

A firm undertaking from the customer to respond within an agreed time-scale to requests for information or to carry out Tasks impacting the Programme should be obtained.

Particular attention should be given to those instances where customer team members are involved directly with the Project/Stream teams. Procedures and requirements for managing this situation should be agreed between the PM/D, P/SM and the customer.

Properly managed, the customer can help the Project/Stream in a number of ways. The customer should assist in the definition of the scope of work, which is probably *the most important document* that is produced by the Programme.
This is the basis for the Project/Stream scope of work and subsequently defined Tasks, Planning, Estimation and Control. It is very important that the customer agrees to this document as early as possible.

Any delay in producing the scope, should be subject to CCM, and should be discussed and agreed with the PM/D and the P/SM.

Third-Party and Vendor Relations

The Vendor Manager within the Project/Stream has the prime responsibility to ensure that all third parties and vendors perform to the required standards and time-scales.
In case of serious problems, which have to be escalated, a clear escalation procedure must determine the steps should be encountered all the way to/from the P/SM and if necessary, the PM/D, and the Steering Group.

It is incumbent upon this process that any problem which may arise in any phase of the Programme, will be resolved by the necessary authority to warn about and impose the necessary actions.
Within the Terms of Reference (TOR) of Vendor Management and Risk Evaluation/Management, there

should be a contingency plan to resolve a problem caused by a third party's inability to deliver as required.

Cost Time Resource Efficiency Indicator

The CTR Efficiency Indicator for a specific WP, Project or Stream is defined as: PBC – AST - ECC

Where:
PBC = Planned-Budgeted Cost
AST = Actual Spend To-date
ECC = Estimated Cost to Complete

A positive balance is favourable, and a negative or zero balance is unfavourable, as illustrated below.
Example:

Planned-Budgeted Cost for a group of tasks and activities in a Work Package (WP) = $10,000
Actual Spend To-date = $7,000
Estimated Cost to Complete the WP = $5,000

In this case;
CTR Efficiency Indicator = 10,000 – 7,000 – 5,000 = - 2,000, which is an over-spend by $2,000

In reality the picture is not so simple, because an over spend (negative balance, see next Figure) could mean we underestimated the job and conversely, an under spend could mean we over budgeted. Therefore, the CTR efficiency indicator is a rough trend, although valuable guide – see next Figure.

The same indicator may be calculated for Time and/or Resource availability vs. spend.

Figure 18.3: CTR delta, actual vs. planned spend

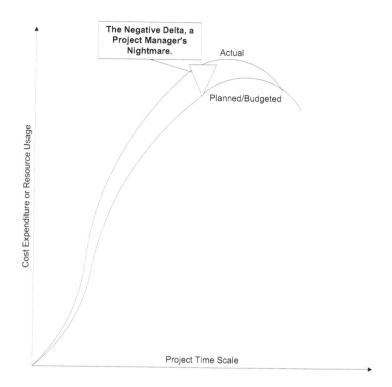

Typical reasons for overspend by project team members' Time and Cost are:

* Original estimates are too low, or do not cover the full work-scope
* Time/Cost/Resource is booked to another Task/Activity
* Team members are not properly trained or experienced
* Original estimates are reasonable but some team members are not up to it

- Unplanned changes in team members and tasks
- Too many interruptions prevent the team members having a good run at the work. This occurs due to diversion or lack of resources
- Excess overtime or poor working conditions has fatigued members to below their effective productivity level
- Excessive working time, travelling time and accommodation costs
- There is possibly a lack of Project/Stream Office (PSO) support
- Inadequate/Unsuitable tools and applications to do the job
- Deficient/Ineffective contractor[s].

The remedial actions recommended include but are not be limited to:

- Reassess the team members, the original criteria for the estimate recorded in the project plan, and the amount of interruptions
- Obtain a correct level and competence and experience of Resource
- Reduce rework
- Improve PSO support
- Improve quality checkpoints
- Improve tools and applications
- Re-assess contractors and seek remedial actions.

If the assumptions in the original estimate no longer hold then they need revising and other Task Assignments may need re-estimating; A CTR Sheet Impact Analysis and action are required under CCM.

Discuss the problem with the team members. Are they finding it difficult? Locate Tasks to which they are booking time, but which lack of resources hinders their progress.

Examine team members' training, past experience, and familiarity with the relevant system applications.
Invest in more short-term training and agree funding with the Steering Group and the client.
Ensure that the Project/Stream Support Office services are more proactive.

Work In Progress (WIP) Indicator

WIP Indicator is an Open Task pointer for a specific Task or a group of tasks' Resource deployment and utilisation. It is calculated as:
WIP Indicator = Planned Cost or Time - Cost or Time of Started but not yet Completed tasks.

The greater the value of the WIP Indicator, the greater is the potential problem, because there may be too many Open Tasks in this case.
For example, a team member has been diverted to other assignments away from his main Task. Or, he is engaged on Task Activities that encounter delay, e.g. a Compliance gap analysis or due diligence takes twice the time than estimated.
When the Task is completed the WIP Indicator should be zero.
To counteract the delay, he/she may work on one or two other Assignments at the same time period to compensate for the delay.
While the newly started Assignment(s) may be advanced, the original delayed Assignment is indicated as being behind schedule.

It is also possible that Tasks, which had been started, were later abandoned due to lack of resources, or it is possible that too large time gaps exist between Tasks. Team members should as far as practical be active on one Task at a time and complete all the relevant Assignments under the Task.

Also, the P/SM should encourage the Team Leaders and team members to include low level Assignment segments which are usually hidden and can take substantial time, for example, word-processing, drawing diagrams, waiting for Review comments etc.

It is possible that team members have been taken off their current Assignments to begin other Tasks, which have not been authorized formally.
There are other reasons for a high WIP Indicator, e.g., under-estimation of the time it should take to complete a Task.

Tighter control on Start and End Dates for Task Assignments, swapping Resources or Tasks in a given period, and effective CC/M would greatly reduce the problem.

The situation could affect the Project/Stream plans, schedules and critical path, which need to be examined carefully and remedial action taken. Formal changes may be necessary.
Formal changes to a plan are always negotiated with the P/SM first, who decides if they should be negotiated with the customer.

Changes to the plan usually occur when:

- There is an increase/decrease in the cost to the customer
- There is a longer/shorter delivery date imposed or perceived
- Tasks which require customer input are rescheduled or altered
- The customer has changed the scope of work and/or requirements

- External changes in legislation, Compliance or some other political factors.

At regular intervals the Team Leaders review future plan key dates in the light of the current Project/Stream status and experience gained to date.
For example, have we been using excessive time to test a contingency plan?
How then we may have underestimated the test periods for all the relevant Tasks in the project? How can we recover the position? And so on and so forth...

Project Performance Indicators (PFIs) and Earned Value

Chief among PFIs is Earned Value (EV).
EV, together with indicators discussed previously in this Chapter, plus the ones outlined below, enable to report real-time progress of Compliance, business transformation, and other types of project or programme.
Any or all of these PFIs may be used by the company's CEO, CFO, CIO, or COO[36] to report current status and projections.
In some cases the PFIs are weighted, qualified or factored d by risk analysis statistical simulations of likely and less likely probabilities of occurrence.

Actual Cost (AC)
Actual Cost of work performed during a given time period; money spent up to the current date

Budget-At-Completion (BAC)
Planned costs across a specified time period; the project's overall approved budget

---

[36] Chief Executive Officer, Chief Financial Officer, Chief Information Officer, or Chief Operations Officer

Earned Value (EV)

Budgeted cost for work performed, or "Earned." This is the fiscal (dollar/euro/sterling) amount of work that has actually been completed as of the current date. *EV=BAC x Percent Complete*

Cost Performance Index (CPI)

Earned Value over Cost Variance is a ratio instead of a dollar amount. A ratio less than 1 indicates that the value of the work that has been accomplished is less than expected for the amount of money spent.
CPI = EV / AC

Cost Variance (CV)

The value of what you have accomplished to date, versus what you have spent to date*; CV = EV - AC*

Planned Value (PV)

Planned cost for work scheduled to be completed within a given time period; *PV = BAC x Percent of Duration to the Current Date*

Schedule Performance Index (SPI)

Schedule variance related as a ratio instead of a dollar amount. A ratio less than 1 indicates that work is being completed slower than planned. *SPI = EV / PV*

Schedule Variance (SV)

The value of what you have accomplished to date, versus what you planned to have accomplished to date; *SV = EV - PV*

PrMS™ Building Blocks Summary

PrMS™ methodology and its pivotal CTR instruments are usefully and practically applied to create, manage and deliver change projects, streams and programmes.

PrMS™ methodology is a powerful and proven technique, which is based on sound practices in the early days in the oil, gas, and petrochemical industries for over 40 years. The IT industry has been catching up, but has still a long way to go.

From the Author's extensive experience of more than 32 years, it has been evident that the IT industry in particular, despite adopting and adapting structured methodologies, is still not very good in delivering complex projects and programmes successfully on time and to budget.

Other project delivery methods, do not appear to offer the depth, breadth and detail to estimate, plan, and control projects the lowest level, which is a very strong feature of the PrMS™ methodology (see next Figure).

No other methodology, known to the Author, is as comprehensive, successful and effective as the PrMS™ technique, which helped a blue chip financial services company in the UK – Lombard - save about £10 millions per annum (14 million euros, or 17 million US dollars).

What makes PrMS™ uniquely successful and cost-effective is above all, pinpointing and obliging individuals to undertake personal responsibilities to deliver their scope of work in a quality and timely fashion.

Figure 18.4: PrMS™ - brick by brick modules

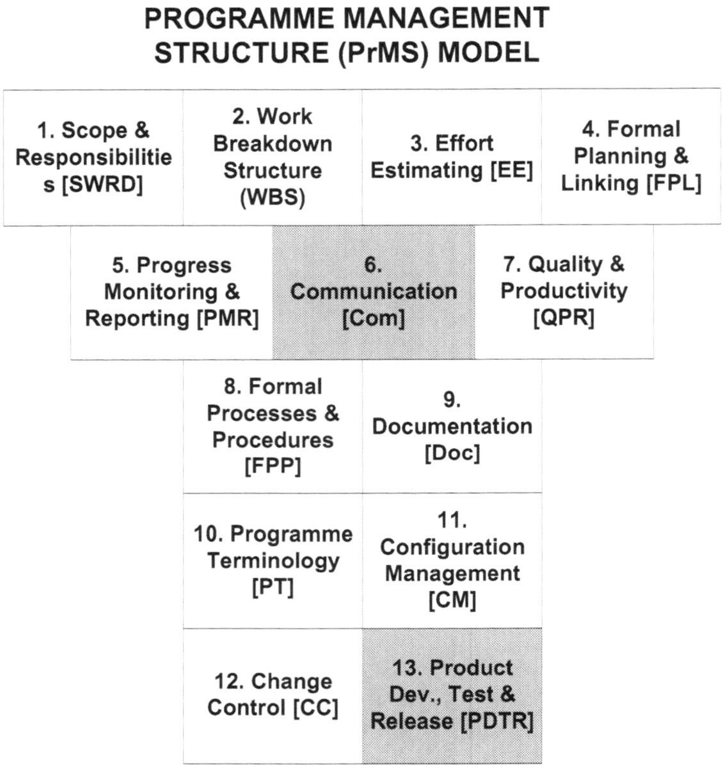

PROGRAMME MANAGEMENT
STRUCTURE (PrMS) MODEL

1. Scope & Responsibilities [SWRD]	2. Work Breakdown Structure (WBS)	3. Effort Estimating [EE]	4. Formal Planning & Linking [FPL]
5. Progress Monitoring & Reporting [PMR]	6. Communication [Com]	7. Quality & Productivity [QPR]	
8. Formal Processes & Procedures [FPP]	9. Documentation [Doc]		
10. Programme Terminology [PT]	11. Configuration Management [CM]		
12. Change Control [CC]	13. Product Dev., Test & Release [PDTR]		

346

19.   Risk Management and Costs

Introduction

Risk and risk assessment and mitigation features highly in Compliance and change management.

Risk is a major consideration, to be planned and mitigated for, as an integral and critical component of enterprise transformation planning, project management and product delivery.
The risk cause and impact, mitigation, liability and remedial actions are major risk management factors.

"Risk management[37] is the process of measuring, or assessing risk and then developing strategies to manage the risk.
In ideal risk management, a prioritization process is followed whereby the risks with the greatest loss and the greatest probability of occurring are handled first, and risks with lower probability of occurrence and lower loss are handled later.
In practice, the process can be very difficult, and balancing between risks with a high probability of occurrence but lower loss vs. a risk with high loss but lower probability of occurrence can often be mishandled.
Risk management also faces a difficulty in allocating resources properly. This is the idea of opportunity cost. Resources spent on risk management could be instead spent on more profitable activities.

In project management, risk management includes the following activities:

- Planning how risk management will be held in the particular project. Plan should include risk

---

[37] Ref. http://www.indopedia.org/Risk_management

management tasks, responsibilities, activities and budget.
- Assigning risk officer - a team member other than a project manager who is responsible for foreseeing potential project problems. Typical characteristic of risk officer is a healthy scepticism.
- Maintaining live project risk database. Each risk should have the following attributes: opening date, title, short description, probability and importance. Optionally risk can have assigned person responsible for its resolution and date till then risk still can be resolved.
- Creating anonymous risk reporting channel. Each team member should have possibility to report risk that he foresees in the project.
- Preparing mitigation plans for risks that are chosen for mitigation. The purpose of the mitigation plan is to describe how this particular risk will be handled – what, when, by who and how will be done to avoid it or minimize consequences if it becomes a liability.
- Summarizing planned and faced risks, effectiveness of mitigation activities and effort spend for the risk management."

Possible risk-mitigation actions are:

1. Avoidance - Not performing an activity that could carry risk.
2. Reduction – Example: sprinklers to put out a fire to reduce the risk of loss by fire.
3. Acceptance - War is an example, since most property is not insured against war.
4. Transfer - Another party taking on the risk, i.e. an insurance contract.

Investment always carries a risk, and project resource-time and materials, involves cost – as input – in order to obtain the desired profit from the investment.

Return on Investment

Consider the following alarming statistics so far as investments in IT related business change related projects are concerned:

- 9% of projects are delivered on time or within budget
- 90% of projects fail upon delivery
- 15% of actual time is spent on miscellaneous work
- Re-work constitutes up to 10% of overall work effort
- 20% of overall work effort is spent on Compliance to testing standards.

(Source: Standish Group)

The main reasons for the poor return on investment track record are:

- Shaky business case and unproven, wishful benefits
- Lack of understanding what the risks and tangible benefits are
- Not knowing how to quantify and qualify risks and benefits
- Not knowing how to mitigate and manage risks
- Not knowing how to avoid risks; prevention is more cost effective
- Lack of understanding of risk trade off with costs and investment returns
- Inadequate project, risk/impact analysis and change management skills
- Inadequate or lack of integrated IT and business contingency plans.

Most IT expenditure involves risk. The level of risk can vary from a low level risk to a high level risk. For example, a non-critical project being 3 months late will not make a significant impact on the business.

However, a critical project, which will add a new product to the business in a very competitive market; if it fails, it could make a big hole in the company's balance sheet. Such a high-risk project could have catastrophic consequences if it were to fail.

This is particularly true if this high-risk project is linked to other critical initiatives - the domino effect comes into play here.

Risks may be miscalculated or not accounted for at all. For example, some companies take an enormous risk without even being aware of it by their failure to have in place adequate risk/impact assessment, business continuity and disaster recovery plan.

Good IT and business management should be aware of all the risks inherent not only in IT, but the associated business snow-ball effects, and affect on customers' good-will plus profit figures.

Most IT returns on investment risks are related to cost/risk trade-offs and good decision-making requires information about, and understanding of this. In addition, a sound process and method to assess and mitigate risks are essential.

These imply:

- Understanding exactly what are the risks in a given course of action.
- Knowing the strategies available for managing these risks.
- Knowing the cost and effectiveness of each strategy.

With this information, management can decide on what level of risk it wants to accept and the implicit cost of that level of risk.

Alternatively, management can decide how much it wants to spend and determine the implied risk that will be taken on. RiskLess™[38] methodology puts this in the right perspective with a consistent approach.

Let's consider a simple example.
Du-Du Corporation (a fictitious name) operated a telephony response system staffed by 12 operators, who handled between 2,000 and 2,500 calls per day, to supply mail order items.

Customers who rang in were answered by an answering machine and put into an automatic telephone queuing system.
The average waiting time for an answer was 140 seconds and the average transaction time to process an order was 2.25 minutes, some of which was due to a relatively slow response by the computer system.
The company's IT management estimated that an upgrade to the computer system might reduce the transaction time by at least 25 seconds, but would cost $25,000, with an additional continuing annual maintenance cost of $3,000.
To evaluate this potential investment, the company installed a sophisticated monitor on the telephone system to estimate how many customers per day hung up before they were answered and decided that, if they could reduce the waiting time to 25 seconds, they would gain approximately 100 additional sales per day.

The average profit margin on a sale was $1.25, which would yield $125 per day, approximately $43,750 per year or a net $40,750 after allowing for the additional maintenance costs of $3,000.

The management computations, rounded for simplicity, were as follows:

Cost of new system upgrade	$25,000
Training	$2,000
Implementation costs	$5,000
Total up-front upgrade cost (expense)	$32,000
Additional orders per day	100
Average gross profit per order	$1.25
Additional gross profit per year	$43,750
(=1.25 x 100 x 350)	
Less additional maintenance costs	$3,000
Net contribution of upgrade (income p.a.)	$40,750

Thus, the system had a potential payback time of about 9.5 months (= 32,000 / 40,750 x 12).

But in reality, computing the impact of the new system upgrade was not so straightforward.
The additional orders were based on the assumption that there would always be a customer waiting and that there would be no 'idle time'.

It was estimated that the new system upgrade could reduce the average time to process an order by 25 seconds to 2 minutes.
It took detailed business analysis and several assumptions about customer demand levels and patterns to estimate that additional 100 orders per day could be achieved.

In reality however, the additional orders turned out to be of the order of 60 per day, enough to justify the investment but not achieve such a spectacular return as the initial calculations had projected.

Accordingly, the annual monetary benefit turned out to be:

60 / 100 x $40,750 = $24,450, which means an investment return in about (32,000 / 24,450 x 12 =) 16 months.

So far so good, but one very important factor was forgotten by management and the business analysis. Downtime was dramatically improved by the new system upgrade - from 15% (with the old system) to a mere 5% (with the new system).

A net 10% reduction in system downtime, is equivalent to:

0.10 x 2000 calls/day x 0.8 business conversion factor [80% probability] x 350 working days per annum x $1.25 profit per call on average = $70,000 per annum EXTRA PROFIT.

THE ABOVE EXTRA BENEFIT OF $70,000 PER ANNUM MAKES A MUCH BIGGER TOTAL OF $94,450 COMPARED TO THE $24,450 BENEFIT CALCULATED ABOVE.

On the basis of the revised calculation, the system upgrade would pay for itself in a matter of 4 months (= 32,000 / 94,450 x 12), and not after 16 months! If management recognised this fact, they would have committed to the upgrade much sooner than they did (though in reality other reasons prevented an earlier system upgrade or replacement).

The positive impact of an improved and faster service could also help to leverage the company to add value to the business by using the extra system availability to tell customers about new products or services, which was not possible to do with the old system.

The business analysis was conducted by the IT dept., which perhaps explains why the downtime was not taken into account.

IT departments do not have a habit to objectively report fully on their problems and mistakes. If an independent consultant or another segment of the business conducted the business analysis, the system downtime would have probably been identified as a major issue at the outset.

Cost of Expected Risk

Expressing risks as probabilities is likely to be adequate for some decision processes. Talking in terms of probabilities can become abstract and difficult for management to interpret or understand, especially when there are many risk factors involved.
Probabilities in themselves do not provide a complete metric. However, a limited but effective use of probabilities can be usefully exploited, as illustrated below, in the assessment of risks and their likely costs.

To assess risk, probabilities need to be converted into something to which management can relate. The two commonest metrics are: time and money.
As time is nearly always convertible into money, it is therefore useful to express the risk being taken in financial terms. Risk can be converted to cost by using the concept of its expected cost.

Accordingly:

Expected Cost of Risk (ECR) = *Problem Occurrence Probability (POP) x Cost of Problem (CP)*

For example, suppose the probability that a central computer disk drive will fail in a year is 0.3% (POP), and the cost in lost business of such a failure is estimated as

$6,000,000 (CP), then the expected value of the risk (ECR) is:

Expected Cost of Risk (ECR) = $6,000,000 x 0.3/100 = $ 18,000
If the costs of mirroring the disk were, say, $17,000, then clearly the level and cost of risk exposure would justify of this expenditure.

However, in reality, there are other, more complex considerations and components that should be incorporated into the risk analysis and mitigation equation, for example:

- Business Goodwill
- Compliance Mandates
- Personal Safety
- Legislation
- Political
- Environmental
- Social etc.

Failure or non-Compliance of a physical system or a business-related component could trigger a far more detrimental failure, the cost of which may be much greater than cost of a single component or assembly. The wider coverage of failure probability and cost calculations, which involve IT and business systems, can be very complex and far-reaching.
Taking the Performance Reliability of say five physical system components arranged in series, for sake of simplicity, with individual Performance Reliability (PR) factors; PR1, PR2, PR3, PR4, PR5, it soon becomes apparent how prone to failure the overall system is.

A PR value of 0.99 (99.90%) of a computer application usually means that it functions correctly for 99.9% of the time on average.

So, for every 1000 working hours, the system is working fine for 999 hours on average. 1 hour in every 1000 is the average expected downtime (being out of action) on average.

During this time, if all works well, the backup system will kick into operation to compensate, and no data will be lost, at least in theory.

In reality of course, the application could function well for many thousands of hours and break down sporadically or rarely, or more frequently.

The 5-component system overall Performance Reliability [performance availability] is calculated as:

Overall System PR = PR1 x PR2 x PR3 x PR4 x PR5

Assuming PR1=0.99, PR2=0.95, PR3=096, PR4=0.98, PR5=0.97; then -

The Overall System PR = 0.99 x 0.98 x 0.97 x 0.96 x 0.95 = 0.858 (or 85.8% of the time)

Therefore, only during 858 hours in every 1000 on average will the total system assembly work correctly perfectly; this is a big difference compared to 999 hours in every 1000 for a single component application.

The figure of 0.858 Performance Reliability for the total system means that the system will be on average available and working for 85.8% of the time and 14.2% of the time it may be out of action. Therefore, 0.142 is the risk factor, or failure probability.

If the cost of a system failure is say $250,000, with a 14.2% chance, then:

Expected Cost of Risk (ECR) = $250,000 x 0.142 = $35,500

Accordingly, the risk avoidance or risk mitigation cost should not in theory exceed $35,500.
In reality however, there are many more factors and risk considerations involved, not just IT related. Some of these are difficult to quantify (e.g. the loss of customers' goodwill and other considerations outlined on the previous page).
If such risks are quantified and qualified, the above ECR figure of $35,300 could jump to say $250,000, and this would make the risk trade off much different and more complex. In principle, risk management and mitigation is analogous to insurance.

The expected cost of each risk is weighed against the cost of possible preventative or recovery actions, and probability, using a number of risk analysis and simulation models, including Monte Carlo simulation (see footnote at the end of this Chapter).
Risk is not only financial; today directors may be held personally and legally liable in case of system failure which could effect the environment, the employees or public at large. Take the case of an international oil company, which is based in the UK or USA.
The parent company headquarters are fully aware of year non-Compliance risks and penalties and take every reasonable step to protect its assets, employees and the public.

However, the same company has lots of dealings with its subsidiaries in developing countries, which are not tackling the risks and problems as the parent company.
So, the weakest point in the chain of links and interfaces between the headquarters and the affiliates could bring down significant parts of the business with huge losses.

The same major oil company's subsidiary might encounter a serious oil spill could cause a multi-million dollar damage to the environment and involve extremely costly litigation. However, the oil company has to weigh carefully the risks and potential damages against the measures and costs to protect itself. Accordingly, a consistent qualitative as well as quantitative elimination and selection process has to be employed.

Similarly, a bank or a financial services company has to carefully weigh the risks and costs of a major non-Compliance error, which could adversely affect its corporate and individual customers. This in turn could bring as a consequence claims for damages and a huge cost expenditure plus the loss of goodwill and adverse publicity.

The 80-20 rule applies in most cases.
Discovering which 20% of the business significantly and probably presents the major risks to the remaining 80% of the business is the key issue which management has to tackle.
In every investment decision, there are costs and risks, which need to be quantified in fiscal terms.

Return on investment has to be calculated and analysed so that management can decide how much to spend. To appreciate the cost/benefit/risk scenario, let us consider the following example.

Allocating IT Infrastructure Costs

Many companies do not know how they spend there IT budget and how to charge the business for the IT infrastructure (shared costs) and therefore run a high risk of over spending.
Where it is decided to charge the business for IT infrastructure costs, the basis of charging should be usage and added value for money.
These shared costs should include usage such as:

- Processors
- Networks
- Disk storage
- Archive storage
- Disaster recovery
- System development
- Support, including third parties
- Added Value for Money

The simplest and fairest way to allocate infrastructure costs is to calculate a periodic standard charge according to the level of usage.

Level of usage may be measured in different ways, including:

- CPU usage
- Network traffic
- Staff hours of development and support time
- Third party contractors and service providers

The projected level of usage is the normally expected level of demand for the service.
Thus, for example, if the total network cost for the month is $2,000 and the average traffic is [expected to be] about 50,000MB, then the standard charge would be:

$2,000 / 50,000MB = $0.04 per MB.

Similarly, if the support centre employs three staff at a monthly total cost of $6,000 and the IT department expects them to spend a total of 500 hours during the month working on user problems, then the standard charge is:
$6,000 / 500 = $12 per hour.

Users are measured on, and charged at the standard rate. Obviously, it will only be in a rare month that the actual network traffic or hours come out at or even close to the projected usage.

In this case, there will be a *variance,* which may be positive if usage is greater, or negative if usage is lower than the projected level.

If the cost and projected usage figures are accurate, over a long period (say, a year), the cumulative variance should be small, providing variance analysis and trend plots are produced and monitored on a regular monthly basis.

Variance = *Actual System Usage MINUS Average Projected System Usage.*

There are several advantages to the standard costing approach (shown above):

- Users are charged pro-rata with their level of usage;
- Users cannot play 'beggar my neighbour', i.e. incur expense for which other users have to pay;
- Users totally control their own costs - they know the rate per unit usage (which should change only infrequently - say, once or twice a year);
- Services, which are very heavily or very lightly used are highlighted - this can; for example, show up services which are providing very poor value for money.

The only drawbacks are that this system requires the IT department to:

- Decide and implement a suitable basis of usage measurement
- Project usage on that basis
- Carefully and regularly monitor system usage rates.

IT Mandatory and Discretionary Expenditure

IT expenditure may be mandatory or discretionary. If it is mandatory, the benefits of (or at least the reasons for) the expenditure are, by definition, self-evident.

The following are mandatory reasons for IT expenditure:

(a)   Compliance / Regulation. Some IT expenditure is driven by regulation or external events. For example, a decision by the government to change the tax system will mean changes in every computer-based payroll in the country. Basel II and Sarbanes-Oxley Act, which has far reaching implications for businesses world wide, are costing many millions of dollars to implement and continuously monitor and audit.

(b)   The business could not run otherwise. Many businesses simply could not operate without extensive IT systems. It is impossible to imagine a modern company, a utility, bank or airport operating without its extensive IT systems. Even organisations which have not traditionally needed extensive IT systems (e.g. textile firms and fashion houses) may find that certain expenditure is essential if they are to continue to operate.

(c)   It is the cost of staying in business. Much of IT expenditure is driven by the need to stay competitive. If one's competitors use up to date IT applications in a particular area, then the company may have no choice but to follow - even in circumstances where the actual business benefits in other terms may not justify the expenditure.

Take this example: a major credit lending company called CFTLL plc had discovered that on average it spends nearly $10 to process a loan application, whilst the competition does the same for less then half on average.

As a matter of urgency CFTL Credit plc decided to look at its business practices and IT systems with the view to increasing efficiency and reducing costs over a period of 12 months. The driver for this initiative was the company's crippling overhead, which if allowed to continue for another 18-24 months, would force the company into liquidation.

With discretionary expenditure, benefits need to be identified more clearly and prioritised according to; "must have now", "should have soon", or "nice to have in future", using a 'what if' risk/impact analysis. Such analysis would include 3 main scenarios; "do nothing for now", "go all the way with best of breed, longer term solution", or "an interim shorter term, early win solution".

With discretionary expenditure, IT may be competing with other projects for scarce resources. Benefits may be any combination of the following. For instance, IT may:

- Improve efficiency. IT can improve efficiency in a number of ways, including:

    - Eliminating or replacing unproductive work
    - Improving ease of communication between staff
    - Reducing or eliminating paper processing.

- Provide new/improved products and services to customers. Examples include:

    - On-line quotations and price lists
    - 24-hour delivery
    - Direct monitoring of stock levels with automatic reordering
    - Provision of product or market information
    - On-line access to accounts.
    - Reduced ordering times
    - Faster response to enquiries
    - Reduced paperwork

- Better after-sales service
- Better communication.

- Reduce costs. IT can reduce costs in many ways - for example, by reducing:

    - Staffing levels
    - Required stockholding levels
    - Amount of paper flow.

- Restructure costs. This has a major significance in many organisations, brought about by:

    - Shifting costs from labour to capital
    - Altering the balance of production costs
    - Changing the allocation of overhead costs.

- Gain competitive advantage by differentiation. Much of the justification for IT today is in terms of greater competitiveness, for example:

    - Shorter delivery times and/or door-to-door delivery (convenience)
    - Adding value to the product at minimal cost
    - Giving customers on-line access to product information
    - Using IT to form mutually beneficial alliances, e.g. EDI.

- Provide more timely and accurate information, which leads to a better decision-making. This can be obtained by:

    - Identifying most profitable products/customers
    - Online analytical data processing and/or data warehouse/reporting systems
    - Expert/third party system access

- Risk/impact/benefit analysis and decision making models.

- Improve staff working conditions/reduce stress and frustration. Staff morale and productivity can be improved by better working conditions. IT can do this by:

  - Use of Graphical User Interfaces (GUIs) to replace text-based computing
  - Use of colour to replace monochrome screens
  - Pre-emptive multi-tasking (e.g. Workflow)
  - Better performance
  - Better ergonomic design in equipment.

- Making process local or easier:
- Providing more relevant and needed information
- Providing a better and more rewarding work environment
- Eliminating boring and repetitive tasks
- Enriching and empowering staff
- Helping to retain staff and reduce staff turnover
- Attracting creative and innovative staff, to use their skills
- Attracting staff that likes more responsibility.

- Improve the organisation's image. This can be effected by:

  - Higher public visibility (e.g. automatic point of sales/credit machines);
  - Personalised letters
  - Use of smart card technology
  - Loyalty schemes.

- Give better insight into performance and operations. Modern IT systems can carry out analyses that were hitherto impossible or only available to organisations with very large computer systems. For example:

- Faster/better performance analyses and reporting;
- Online access to external/affiliated information systems;
- Use of powerful financial and business models to explore and understand the business.

It is not sufficient that benefits are simply identified. They must also be measurable in some way if Value For Money (VFM) is to be assessed and attained.
This is one of the most difficult areas in change benefits analysis and IT finance.
Benefits should be qualified and quantified versus costs and associated risks, plus their relevant probabilities, which should be assigned as weighting factors.

To help attain VFM, RiskLess™[39] methodology helps to enhance product quality and profitability. It also helps to quantify and mitigate risks associated with change programmes and business transformation initiatives, organisation re-design, business and Compliance turnaround (see next Figure).

---

[39] Copyrights of Abe Abrahami

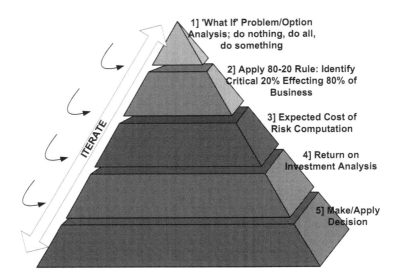

As integral and critical part of RiskLess™ technique, the next Figure illustrates the matrix components of risk, cost, probability and impact analysis.

According to the table below, one can qualify and quantify risk both objectively and subjectively and put a price tag on actions intended according to their extent and estimated cost.

There are trade-offs and statistical methods, for example, Monte Carlo simulation[40], and specific software

---

[40] This is a simulation that calculates multiple scenarios of a model by repeatedly sampling values from probability distributions for uncertain variables, using those values for the spreadsheet cell. Simulations can consist of as many trials (or scenarios) as you want - hundreds or even thousands - in just a few seconds or minutes. This type of spreadsheet simulation, called Monte Carlo simulation, randomly generates values for uncertain variables over and over to simulate a model, as though as you are playing a roulette in a casino, hence the name. The statistical analysis curve generates a number of

applications and tools may be used to help assess risk consequences and mitigation.

The next Figure helps to explain the risk quadrants.

Once you have classified your risks versus costs, plus mitigating actions, you will have a scenario you can qualify and quantify in priority order to tackle.

---

probable values and consequent options, and the curves may be Normal, Skewed, Triangular, Lognormal, and Uniform etc. Likely and less likely (high, medium, low) values and probabilities are generated as a result of the simulations, for consideration.

Figure 19.2: RiskLess™ matrix of risk, cost and probability-risk analysis

Highest

▲

LOWEST RISK, HIGHEST COST	MEDIUM RISK, HIGHEST COST	HIGHEST RISK, HIGHEST COST
LOWEST RISK, MEDIUM COST	MEDIUM RISK, MEDIUM COST	HIGHEST RISK, MEDIUM COST
LOWEST RISK, LOWEST COST	MEDIUM RISK, LOWEST COST	HIGHEST RISK, LOWEST COST

Mitigation Cost Scale

Lowest ————————— **Risk Probability Scale** ————————→ Highest

Appendix: COMPLIANCE, AUDIT AND TRIGGERS

What is Compliance?

Compliance is when people and objects (actors) obey an order, a law, a set of rules or a request, and execute and adhere to its explicit and implicit laid-down criteria and instructions.

What is a Compliance Audit Trigger?

This is a date or an event that manually or automatically causes an audit alert to be created and sent to pre-assigned individuals (e.g. process owners, chief/deputy chief Compliance auditor/officer) to take specific actions.

These will be mandated in order to initiate, conduct and complete a Compliance audit according to specific criteria, process/procedure and questionnaire checklists.

A date usually means, a predetermined time at which the audit should begin and end.
An event, could be, for instance; exceeding a preset tolerance level of deviation from a normal distribution range of business rules' execution, operational or risk parameters of a department, system or application. For example, customer loan acceptance/rejection rate exceeds or falls below certain percentage points. Or; human/system errors exceed a normal distribution range of a certain tolerance.

What is Audit?

According to ISO 9000, an audit is a systematic, independent, and documented process, used to obtain audit results and to evaluate these results objectively in order to determine to what extent the criteria of the audit have been fulfilled.

Audit is the action of verification of Compliance or otherwise, and producing a Compliance a report on Compliance conformance and/or deviation

Who Conduct an Audit?

An audit may be informal or formal and it may be carried out by the enterprise's own specially trained staff (using self-assessment checklists), qualified auditors, and also by an external firm of certified auditors.

What is an Audit Report?

An audit report is a document that contains all important information related to the audit, including comments, findings, and the corrective/preventive actions that have been concluded and recommended.

The audit report is an official document by the lead/chief auditor and the head of the audited area. Sub-audits by individual process owners may from parts of the overall audit report.

An audit report typically embraces:

♦ Introduction and objectives of the audit and its criteria
♦ A summary of the audit findings and proposed remedial actions
♦ The audit results, conclusions and recommendations
♦ A list of deviations, problems and potential causes
♦ Checklist questions and evaluation of replies
♦ A list of the persons involved

Audit Types

There are 4 main types of audit:

- ◆ Results based: checking that operations are being carried out economically, efficiently and effectively
- ◆ Transaction based: checking that operations have been carried out in accordance and comply with standards, frameworks and procedures
- ◆ Risk based: checking that company accounts have not been misstated as a result of errors or fraud because the auditor failed to detect errors or fraud
- ◆ System based: checking that internal controls are adequate to ensure that operations are being carried out properly and securely; that physical IT, financial and intellectual assets are safeguarded

The means to activate Compliance audit and subsequent remedial actions are typically:

- ◆ Checklist questionnaires
- ◆ Self-examination/assessment
- ◆ Frameworks, ITIL, COBIT, ISO
- ◆ Performance measurement
- ◆ Audit report
- ◆ Remedial actions
- ◆ Re-assessment

Extract from Checklist Questionnaires

This book is not about checklist questionnaires, although the Author developed very extensive templates for various clients.

If you are interested in questionnaire templates and checklists please contact the Author at:
info@peachqc.com

The extract below gives a basic idea about the type of questions asked of a provider of Software Asset

Management (SAM) and Information Security
Management System (ISMS).

Table A1: Checklist questionnaire extract

Do you formally document reviews of business performance (at least 6-monthly)?
Do you have policies and procedures for managing customer-side relationships?
Do you have definitions of responsibilities for managing customer-side business relationships?
Do you formally review the current and future software requirements of customers and the business as a whole (at least annually)?
Do you have formally documented reviews of service provider performance and customer satisfaction (at least annually)?
Do you have policies and procedures for managing contracts?
Do you record contractual details in an on-going contract management system as contracts are signed?
Do you hold copies of all signed contractual documentation securely with copies kept in a documents management system?
Do you have documented reviews (at least 6-monthly)?
Do you have documented reviews (at least 6-monthly) prior to contract expiry?
Do you have definitions of financial information relevant to the management of software and related assets?
Do you develop formal budgets for the acquisition of software assets?
Are actual expenditure on software assets and the related support and infrastructure costs accounted for against budget?

Do you have available clearly documented financial information about software asset values?
Do you have formally documented reviews of actual expenditure against budget (at least quarterly)?
Do you have Service level agreements and supporting agreements for services that are performed within the scope of Software Asset Management (SAM)?
Do you have definitions of services relating to software acquisition and installation of software assets?
Do you have definitions of services relating to moves and changes of software assets?
Do you have a definition of customer and user obligations and responsibilities?
Do you report (at least quarterly) actual workloads and service levels against targets for SAM?
Do you have regular reviews by the relevant parties to review performance against service levels for SAM?
Do you have an approved formal policy regarding security/access restrictions to all SAM resources?
Is there a document that describes unambiguously the scope and boundaries of the Information Security Management System (ISMS)?
Does the ISMS hold information/characteristics on business, organization, locations, assets and technology?
Are exclusions from the scope identified and the reasons for their exclusion clearly explained and justified?
Is there an ISMS policy in place, which covers the defined ISMS scope?
Does ISMS policy include a framework for establishing objectives, direction and principles?
Does the policy take account of business & legal/regulatory requirements & contractual security obligations?

Does the policy align with the organization's strategic risk management context in which the ISMS are enforced?

Does the company have a retention policy for electronic information and paper documents?
How does document retention lifecycle (DRL) work in the enterprise and is it visible?
Do you realise that if you do not have a formal DRL, it could be a 'material weakness'?
Are DRL control reviews incorporated into all system implementations / modifications?
How often do you back up your data and information and test it?
What control procedure is used to avoid tampering with the data / information?
What is the procedure to permanently delete documents and records?
Are IFRS, SOX / other regulatory data-retention requirements being met? Please elaborate
If DRL regulations are not fully met, do you realise it may be a 'material weakness'?
Are KPIs the financial drivers delivered to operational managers' desktops regularly?
How are KPIs produced and distributed?
Can KPIs be traced to/from the company's reports / statements?
Is there a formal procedure indicating how KPIs are produced / distributed?
Are there any manual adjustments in this process and/or to the figures (i.e. spreadsheets)?
Is there a segregation of authority among those involved in KPIs preparation / changes / approval?
Are non-financial drivers/KPIs measured (leadership, innovation etc.)?
Do you link SOX compliance with KPIs and/or Business-Balance Scorecard (BBS)?

Contrasting Traditional Assurance Strategies and ERAM - Enterprise Risk & Assurance Management[41]

From Traditional:
Assign Duties/Supervise Staff
Policy/Rule Driven
Limited Employee Participation and Training
Narrow Stakeholder Focus
Auditors and Other Specialists are the Primary Control Analysts/Reporters.

To New Vision:
Empowered/Accountable Employees
Continuous Improvement/learning Culture
Extensive Employee Participation and Training
Broad Stakeholder Focus
Staff at all levels, in all functions, is the Primary Control Analysts/Reporters.

From Traditional:
Individuals are responsible for complying with prescribed methods and procedures.
Receive limited training on control and quality assessment and design.
Often consider auditors, consultants, and other specialists to be the experts on control and quality systems and design.
Outside specialists are often called in to analyze areas where concerns and/or problems exist.
People are often not allowed or encouraged at lower levels to analyze and make decisions relating to risk acceptance or control design.

[41] Rearranged and Reprinted with kind permission of Tim J. Leech, FCA·CIA, CCSA, CFE, Principal Consultant, Chief Methodology Officer, Paisley Consulting. See acknowledgement at the end.

375

The personnel doing the work are often not directly responsible for selecting the controls used that help assure that their business/quality objectives are achieved. Candidness and full disclosure on the current state of control and risk is not encouraged and is often discouraged and punished.

Fear and blame are sometimes utilized as strategies when problems surface.

Internal control and total quality/continuous improvement are not integrated programs or concepts.

To New Vision:
Personnel are accountable for designing and maintaining control systems that provide the desired level of assurance regarding the achievement of business/quality objectives.

Are provided with adequate risk and control assessment and design skills to properly fulfil their responsibility to report to Officers, the Board, and others on the current status of control, quality and risk.

Consensus at all levels on relevant business/quality objectives and levels of acceptable risk is a primary goal.

Candid disclosure of the state of control and the risks being accepted by the unit/organization is encouraged and rewarded.

Accountability for business/quality objectives exists and is accepted by staff at all levels, in all functions.

Employees at all levels are responsible for finding new and better ways to improve and optimize control portfolios to better achieve key business/quality objectives.

Employees at all levels and in all functions continually reassess the adequacy and appropriateness of control choices and make adjustments when new information emerges regarding risk status, prioritization of objectives, and the control options available.

Control and quality management are considered to be synonymous terms and are fully integrated programs/concepts.
A primary objective is to perform audits and report findings to senior management, and/or external stakeholders.

From Traditional:
Relations with auditees are sometimes adversarial.
Auditors are viewed as the control "experts". Control assessment training is directed primarily to auditors and staff specialists.
A primary audit objective is to report on whether units are complying with prescribed controls, procedures and standards.
How auditors decide what constitutes "effective" or "adequate" control frameworks. How much risk is considered acceptable is often not explicitly disclosed.
Auditors are measured primarily on execution of prescribed audit and review processes.
Auditors receive limited training on risk and control design concepts and ways to "optimize" control frameworks.
Internal auditors rarely examine and report on control frameworks related to customer service, product/service quality, safety, environmental Compliance, and other "non-financial" areas.
Quality auditors rarely examine or report on regulatory Compliance, corporate ethics, fraud prevention and detection or the reliability of management representations to the Board and/or external stakeholders.

To New Vision:
Primary audit objectives are to:
Raise the risk and control assessment and design skills of all staff.
Provide accurate and complete information to the Officers, the Board and external stakeholders on the state of risk and control management systems;

Assist staff at all levels to design and maintain better, more optimal risk and control management frameworks. A key audit role is to foster more effective risk and control management through training, coaching, facilitation, and feedback to staff - unless quality assurance reviews suggest that representations by work units are misleading and the "good faith" assumption is not appropriate. Auditors help to ensure that the organization's business/quality objectives recognize a range of stakeholders, including customers and regulators, and that operative objectives are consistent with the corporate mission/vision.

Auditors are measured on, and accountable for, achievement of the primary objectives noted above, not on excellent execution of traditional audit processes (i.e. focus on results not activity execution).

Auditors should be skilled and knowledgeable risk and control design analysts and excellent technical auditors. These skills should extend to customer service, product quality, environmental Compliance, fraud prevention and detection, and safety, as well as traditional financial reporting objectives.

ACKNOWLEDGEMENT AND THANKS:
The book's Author acknowledges and thanks Tim Leech, Chief Methodology Officer of Paisley Consulting, for contributing his White Paper, as follows:

Paisley Consulting
Corporate Headquarters
400 Cokato Street East
P.O. Box 578
Cokato, MN 55321 USA
Toll free: 888.288.0283 (U.S. and Canada)
Phone: 320.286.5870 (All Other Countries)
Fax: 320.286.6196
E-mail: Tim.Leech@paisleyconsulting.com
Web: www.paisleyconsulting.com

Multi-Compliance & Change Delivery Training Course, leading to a CMCP[42] / MIMS[43] qualification

Introduction & Purpose

The following text describes the topics to study and qualify as a Certified Multi-Compliance Professional (CMCP) and/or a Member of the Institute of Management Specialists (MIMS). Our courses and methodologies to deliver compliance and business change are accredited by the IMS. Our course graduates may apply to the IMS for membership, and we will be happy to sponsor your application.

All course graduates automatically join our consultants' register and receive newsletters, press releases, special offers etc.

This is your unique opportunity to learn corporate change and compliance together to benefit your own career path and improve your company's compliance and performance together. While other courses specialise either in compliance or in performance measurement, our unique 5-day course combines both, for maximum benefit to you and your company.

What is so SPECIAL about this Course?

Most corporations spend a fortune on compliance and change programmes, well into 6-figure sums.

Imagine a corporation just smarting from implementation of Sarbanes-Oxley Act compliance, now it has to face Basel II, next year it has to comply with MiFID, not to

---

[42] Certified Compliance Professional – applicable to 5-day course only

[43] Member – Institute of Management Specialists – applicable to both 2-day and 5-day courses

mention other regulatory mandates – this is truly a nightmare.
Most companies work in silos, in different project teams; involving duplication, and triplication - even quadruplicating their efforts, delivery times and budgets. But there is an easier way – Abe Abrahami's unique way of mapping multi-compliance mandates to common reference points, identifying the overlaps and cutting budgets, delivery times and task forces by up to 50%!

Audience

Who should take this course?
Any person working within corporate change, compliance, audit, IT, finance, business operations, quality assurance, performance improvement etc. – should take this course, from the CEO, CFO, COO, CIO to any member of staff. If you are a recruiter, consultant or a vendor and wish to better understand compliance and change to improve your services or products, then a version of this course is for you.
If you are an MBA student, a graduate with a business degree or a lecturer – you will learn things you have not encountered in university or college, so please come along.

Course Duration

Our detailed course runs for 5 days, but for those who wish to learn and understand multi-compliance mandates at a high level, we deliver a 2-day cut-down version of the 5-day course, after which they will receive a certificate, and with our sponsorship, may apply to and become a Member of the IMS, to enhance their professional status and enjoy other membership benefits. Please contact us for more details about this course - info@peachqc.com

Course Modules & Topics - A 5-day crash-course leading to a Multi-Compliance Proficiency Certificate plus an MIMS qualification

Day 1 – module 1.1: Leading Compliance Mandates & Audit
- What is a regulatory compliance mandate?
- Why/Who needs to comply?
- What are the penalties of non-compliance?
- What are the differences between an auditor and compliance officer?
- What are the main types of compliance audit?
- What are the major views of compliance?
- What do we mean by climbing up and down the compliance ladder?
- What are the main compliance mandates in the EU, USA and worldwide?

Day 1 – module 1.2: Sarbanes-Oxley Act (SOA/SOX Act)
- What is SOX?
- Why/Who needs to comply?
- What are the penalties of non-compliance?
- What are the sections of SOX?
- What are the most important parts of SOX?
- Self-Assessment Questionnaire, how to use it?
- How does SOX affect/is affected by finance, business operations and IT?
- How does SOX affect/is affected by asset management?
- What are internal controls and material weakness and how to deal with them?

Day 2 – module 2.1: Basel II
- What is Basel II?
- Why/Who needs to comply?
- What are the penalties of non-compliance?
- What are the 3 pillars of Basel II?

- What are the most important parts of Basel II?
- Self-Assessment Questionnaire, how to use it?
- How does Basel II affect/is affected by finance, business operations and IT?
- How does Basel II affect/is affected by asset management?
- What are controls and weakness in relation to risk and how to deal with them?

Day 2 – module 2.2: MiFID
- What is MiFID?
- Why/Who needs to comply?
- What are the penalties of non-compliance?
- What are the 4 levels and 5 titles of MiFID?
- What are the most important parts of MiFID?
- Self-Assessment Questionnaire, how to use it?
- How does MiFID affect/is affected by finance, business operations and IT?
- How does MiFID affect/is affected by asset management?
- What are best execution and conduct of business and how to deal with them?

Day 3 – module 3.1: Solvency II
- What is Solvency II?
- Why/Who needs to comply?
- What are the penalties of non-compliance?
- What are the 3 pillars of Solvency II?
- What are the most important parts of Solvency II?
- Self-Assessment Questionnaire, how to use it?
- How does Solvency II affect/is affected by finance, business operations and IT?
- How does Solvency II affect/is affected by asset management?
- What are controls and weakness in relation to risk and how to deal with them?

Day 3 – module 3.2: Other Compliance Mandates, Standards and Frameworks

- HIPAA
- FDIC
- GLBA
- IFRS
- SAS 70
- Compliance analysis and paralysis

Day 4 – module 4: Quality Compliance-Cost-Reduction (QCR3000) and Change Delivery

- Questionnaire-template construction
- Information gathering, workshops, interviews
- Business process, data, system and application analysis
- Project planning, objective briefings, education and presentations
- PIQD (project implementation & quality document) preparation
- Project scope, work package/element definitions – Project Management Structure (PrMS)
- Agree roles & responsibilities; SPOC (single point of contact)
- Deliverable progress reporting and outline solution formulation
- Working with Finance & Accounting auditors, business people, IT dept., system application users, third party suppliers and outsource service providers
- Solution build and initial testing
- Quality assurance
- Re-testing and fixing
- Training & web info.
- Solution rollout
- *Evaluation, remedial actions.*

Day 5 – module 5: Benchmarking, KPIs and Change Delivery

- *Price and Delivery* - Select company products and services, plus key contractors and suppliers will be assessed for compliance.
- *Quality and Reliability* - Quantitative and qualitative measurement of Mean Time Between Failure (MTBF) of IT systems and the organisation itself will be conducted.
- *Performance to Cost Ratio* - PCR will be derived, including cost of quality and compliance from KPIs.
- *Service Level and Customer Satisfaction* - Service Level Agreement / Contract (SLA / SLC) will be studied.
- *Training and introduction of new Practices and new Technology* - The Company's training policy and practices, together with course sample material will be evaluated.
- *Measure of perceptions of the company and its culture* - Select people will be requested to discuss frankly issues, challenges and proposed remedies.
- *Workable contingency and recovery procedures being in place* - Evidence will be sought to illustrate that workable plans are in place, which are visible to the work force.
- *Management style and leadership by personal example* - Measure of employee perceptions of the company's management and its culture, and the reverse will be sought.
- *Interfaces between different parts of the company* - Assessment of linkages between company departments and how they interact will be conducted.
- *Linkage between personnel performance and reward* - HR, select management and staff performance will be assessed against financial and other rewards.

A SPECIAL MESSAGE FOR CLIENTS, PARTNERS AND AGENCIES

For partners and agencies:
After a successful introduction of one to three delegates to our course, you will receive an introduction fee, and if you introduce four or more delegates to our course, you will receive a higher introduction fee.

For clients and others:
If you offer a suitable place on your company's premises to run the course, you will benefit from the a discount, dependent on how many of your company's people attend.

If you wish to find out more and book a course, please contact:

Peach
35 Highview Avenue
Edgware, Middlesex
England HA8 9TX
Office Phone: +44 20 77 54 55 17
Mobile Phone: + 44 795 007 1830
E-mail: info@peachqc.com
Fax: + 44 208 905 3344

Bibliography

- Brand, Koen / Boonen, Harry IT Governance: A Pocket Guide Based on COBIT. van Haren Publishing,The Netherlands
- Brown, Kerry / Osborne P, Stephen. Managing Change and Innovation in Public Service Organisations (Routledge Masters in Public Management S.). An imprint of Taylor & Francis Books Ltd
- Cameron, Esther, Green, Mike. Making Sense of Change Management: A Complete Guide to the Models, Tools and Techniques of Organisational Change Management. Kogan Page
- Damelio, Robert. Basics of Process Mapping. Quality Resources
- Hamilton, Albert. Management By Projects. Thomas Telford publishers
- Hartle, Franklin. Re-engineering the Performance Management Process. Kogan Page
- Henning, Joel P. The Future of Staff Groups. San Francisco: Berrett-Koehler
- Haren Van. Foundations of IT Service Management, Based on ITIL.
  van Haren Publishing,The Netherlands
- Kirkpatrick, Donald L. Evaluating Training Programs: The Four Levels. San Francisco: Berrett-Koehler
- Rogers, Everett M. Diffusion of Innovations (Fourth Edition). New York: Free Press
- Patching, David. Business Process Re-engineering: Getting to the Heart of the Matter. Soft Systems Engineering & Training Service (SSETS)
- Tarantino, Anthony. Manager's Guide to Compliance, Wiley

Made in the USA
Charleston, SC
03 May 2014